You Mean I Have To Look At The Body?!

Stories of
Dying and Living

You
Mean
I Have
To Look
At The
Body?!

Stories of
Dying and Living

Marcia M. Cham

Book design by Ann Thompson Nemcosky

Cover art "Looking Up" © 2007 by Ann Thompson Nemcosky

Angel art by Marcia M. Cham

You
Mean
I Have
To Look
At The
Body?!

Stories of
Dying and Living

Contents

Acknowledgements

MY APPRECIATION AND THANKS for reading and critiquing my writes and re-writes to: the High Country Writers, Boone, North Carolina, the Fellowship of the Rose: Ingrid Kraus, Wendy Dingwall, Judith Banks, Chloe Coleman, Merle Guy. My first writers group: Eleanor Hughes, Janice Bacon, Rosemary Brennan, Carol Ertman, Virginia Pomeroy, and Catherine Royce. Friends and family: Sandy Sisson, Elizabeth O'Connor, Priscilla Popper, Mary Jo Grubbs, Kate Colclaser, Catherine Scantlin, Susan Geldmeier, Evelyn Asher, Lissa Brown, Judy Geary, Shelly Wilson, Charles Carter, Marian Baer, Betsy Jancaitis, Connie Beal, Adine Kretschmer, Rosemary Arthur, Jay and Mary Ann Crane, Lynne Hillegas, Barbara Wilson, Marge Leedom, Maureen DeLuca, Maggie Cham and my mother Evelyn Mitchell. Thanks to my husband Ken Cham for his critical eye and continual support. And special thanks to Sandy Horton for her editorial skills, her sensitivity, encouragement and patience as she pushed to me to dig deeper into my being until the depths of the story surfaced.

A Letter of Gratitude and Dedication

I WRITE THIS BOOK for you, the dying and your families, who trusted me with the sacred parts of your lives. As a pastor, I faced death with you. You carried me through my fears of death, my despair and my anxieties. Your strength encouraged me and your moments of joy sustained me. Through your dying, you taught me about living. By walking this path with you, I found deep within each of your stories, my story. I hope that a word or an image will touch and honor your life.

With my deepest gratitude, this book is dedicated to you and your families.

Prologue

An Observation

I lie here on the bed next to
Olive Adelaide Linscott Jermyn.
She's nearing 100 and ready to die.
I lie here on the bed next to her
not as a patient, but as her pastor
listening to her daughter's questions.

> Hazel asked,
> Marcia, why the struggle?
>> She's ready to go.
>> Why such a struggle?
> We've given her permission.
>> Why still the struggle?
>> She's ready to go.

> Why the waiting?
>> Is there something that needs to be settled?
>> Is there someone who needs to say goodbye?
>> Is there…?

We listened to Olive — to her deep, long, peaceful breathing.
We watched the nurses tend to her comfort.
The nurse spoke of a friend in the birthing center;
Birth and death linked themselves in my heart.

> Hazel, dying is like birth,
> Sometimes births are easy;
> sometimes difficult.
> Some births come after a long labor,
> others after one sharp pain.
> And yet for others, labor starts,
> then stops and begins again.

And so it is with death.
Our predictions, expectations,
timetables and guesses are just that:
    predictions,
    expectations,
        timetables,
        guesses.

Hazel, in death as in birth,
there is no pattern;
there is no A, B, C or 1, 2, 3.
There is only the assurance
that death will come
And God's promise of new life.

FOR YEARS I'VE FELT the persons in the book pushing, even urging me to write their stories to show the truth of *this observation* about living and dying. I am sure that they, along with me, hope others will find something of value in their stories. A speck of truth. A moment of comfort. A glimmer of hope. And maybe even affirmations of your own experiences, feelings, questions and wonderings about the mysteries of death and life.

A PASTOR'S WORK IS multi-faceted. This book focuses on one aspect: the calls concerning death. My life as a pastor was balanced with calls about death, along with calls about life, celebrations, and joys. Teaching, preaching, laughing and playing. Baptisms and marriages. Work camps and retreat work. Time with family and friends. Time for self. Study and prayer. So, as you read call after call, please know that in between these calls I enjoyed all the other aspects of ministry.

Accidental Death

God is silent, catching breath
Because our Creator
is crying,
hurting along with you.
Be silent.
Can you feel God's tears in your heart?[1]

The Blare of the Car Alarm

THE PHONE WAS RINGING as I came in from clipping flowers and weeding beds. I grabbed for the receiver on the fourth ring. "It's your friend Jan. They need you at the emergency room."

"What's happened?" With the phone under my chin, I wiped dirt from my hands.

"A gang of kids built a pipe bomb in Keeler's garage. It exploded in Dean's hands. Dean was pronounced dead a few minutes ago." I froze and my heart pounded.

"Marcia, I know this will be new for you, but a group of kids in the emergency room need you."

Jan repeated, "They need you."

I found my voice. "I'm on my way. Send along prayers, please."

"You know I will."

DEAN LIVED ON THE edge. He challenged the norms. He sought the thrill. Recently his parents had found renewed hope with a special doctor for high risk adolescents. Now this.

Scared, I drove to the emergency room. Thoughts tumbled through my mind. Dean. Dead. A teenager like my own kids. His parents. Shocked. Me straddling fear and Jan's words, "They need you." Then my father came to mind. Dad had died earlier in the year. I imagined Dad meeting Dean in heaven with his elbow hug, welcoming Dean to his new life. A needed calm settled my mind.

At the hospital stunned and frightened youths surrounded me. They knew me. I had taught science at the middle school. They knew I was working toward becoming a pastor, yet they knew me as a teacher. I sensed a bond of trust and relief that I was not a stranger invading their shock and grief. Their faces filled with guilt, fear, and questions. I hugged them. They clung to me.

THE NEXT DAY THE local headline read, "Teen, 17, Dead. A Pipe Bomb Accident." Below the headline in a box outlined with heavy black ink, the article supplied detailed illustrations and complete directions on how to make a pipe bomb. Newspaper reporting. Irresponsible. Shameful. Heartless.

At the church office the secretary, Betty Ann handed me a couple of messages.

9 a.m. From Pastor Jeff.
I'm shocked about Dean and
I'm sorry I will be away from
the office for your first funeral.

9:30 a.m. From Rev. Cliff Harden.
I had a call from Jeff.
I'll drop by to give you
some assistance.

I stared at my desk piled with books and samples of funeral rituals. I breathed in the words, "my first funeral." Questions raced through my heart. "Where to begin? What words and scriptures will help the family? The church will be filled with teenagers. What will they need?" The intercom interrupted my questions.

"Marcia, Cliff is here."

"Show him in." Cliff put his hat on the coat tree to the right of the door to my office. "Cliff. Thanks for coming. I'll join you in those chairs." I motioned to two chairs in the corner. I moved from my desk to the chair opposite him.

Cliff wasted no time. No condolences. No pleasantries. He took off his glasses and used them to gesture at me. "You need John 14:1-3 in this service."

"I do? Remind me of John 14:1-3."

"Let not your heart be troubled…" A raw chill ripped through my body. Not troubled? Dean's parents are devastated. How dare you?

"Believe in God and believe also in me. In my Father's house are many mansions; if it were not so, I would have told you; for I go to prepare a place for you." Cliff recited from memory.

"Cliff, I know that you are trying to assure the family that Dean is with God, but I hear a mandate with the words, 'Let not your heart be troubled.' If I were the devastated parents, I'd shout to God, what do you mean not troubled? We are troubled indeed."

15

Cliff adjusted his glasses and went on as if he didn't hear me. "This passage is appropriate for this death. We know he is in one of the lower rooms of the mansion. He will have to earn his way to other rooms."

I grasped the arms of my chair to hold my anger to a simmer. "How are you so sure about Dean's place in the afterlife? Who gave you the right to pass judgment? At the hospital the only thing that kept me going in the midst of all the terrified high school youth was the vision of Dean being met by my Dad at the Pearly Gates. I know my Dad is not in any lower room of God's house. I know my Dad and Dean are together in the loving presence of God."

I stood, my anger now reaching near boiling point. "Cliff, I can do the rest on my own." He stood and strode across my office. Jerked his hat off the rack. Without a word or a look back, he left. Together the family, friends and I created the funeral service.

ON THE MORNING OF the private graveside burial and the subsequent public funeral service, I rose early from a restless night. I paced the kitchen picking at my breakfast. I dressed and stood at the kitchen counter. I sorted my notes and clipped them in a binder. I ran my hands over the cover and prayed. "God, this is my first funeral. Be with me. I need your strength and your love more this day than usual. Let your presence fill the family. Hold us and our tears. Amen."

I checked the clock. Eddie, the funeral director, had encouraged me to arrive early. I drove to the cemetery. Eddie motioned to a place for me to park. He opened my car door. "You'll do fine." He smiled and with his hand on the center of my back guided me to the artificial green carpet at the head of the casket.

As the family arrived, I heard the quiet closing of the car doors. Their steps to graveside were soundless. The air was tense and tears flowed freely. The director nodded for me to begin. The words of comfort sliced through the air and landed I know not where.

Then a car horn blared. Dean's friend, Chuck, looked over at Dean's parents. "It's Dean saying he's okay." He laughed and we all laughed. The tension in the air relaxed. Smiles appeared through the tears. The remainder of the words of comfort landed more softly and hugged all, including me.

I have no idea if the car horn malfunctioned, but I do know that moment of laughter breaking in at the edge of death gifted us with the assurance that Dean was with God. That moment of laughter graced us with renewed energy to face the crowds at the funeral service.

The church overflowed with young people and parents and adults, relatives, friends and community supporters. Dean's doctor directed her message to Dean's friends and their parents. Her words painted the reality of the lives of teens that lived on the edge, teens that challenged the norms of safety. She gave them hope with the news of better medications and therapies to control the emotions that feed life-risking behavior. She spoke the truth we needed to hear, not the judgment that had been suggested by my colleague. The young people listened and, for a few brief moments, faced the possibility of their own mortality, before heading out at the end of the service and daring death once again.

AT HOME AFTER THE funeral and relaxing for the first time in days, it dawned on me how I coped with Dean's death. I'd launched fully into the funeral service, wanting it to be what the family needed. I had no idea of what I needed. I did know a wall had gone up between the professional me and my personal emotions. Not one of solid steel, but more like the privacy window in a limousine. The privacy window stood somewhere between my inner and outer self. It operated unconsciously. It allowed me to tend to the family and the details of the service but it left me wondering what I needed to do for myself.

Grace in the Depths of Sorrow

I SAT AT THE volunteer's desk in the office. Joanne, the morning volunteer, brought coffee for us from the kitchen off the gathering area. The secretary's high pitched voice called from her front office. "Call for you, Marcia, on line two." I picked up the receiver.

"It's Nancy Brooks." Her voice sounded strained.

"Hey, Nancy. Thanks for introducing me to your good friend Cathy. Have you recovered from the wedding?"

"Not exactly." Suspicion and concern rose in my body from the strange tone in Nancy's voice. "And I don't think I ever will." Her voice shook through the telephone. "A moped bike accident. Cathy's been injured and Steve's dead."

A cold shock surged through me. Images of Cathy and Steve standing in front of the fireplace in an old New England inn with purple and blue flowers cascading over the edge of the mantel filled my mind. The gorgeous bride filled with happiness, and the handsome groom brimming over with joy, repeating their wedding vows; "I, Cathy, I, Steve...till death do us part."

"No. It can't be." I yelled into the phone.

Betty Ann, the secretary, came running. "What's wrong?" Joanne now stood by the desk, the coffee cups shaking in her hands. My voice alarmed them both.

My hand over the receiver I whispered, "The bride from Saturday's wedding is hurt and the groom is dead." Joanne sat the coffee down, walked around behind me, and put her hands on my shoulder.

"Marcia," Nancy's voice brought me back to our conversation, "Cathy asked if you have any faith connections in the Bahamas."

I repeated. "A faith connection in the Bahamas?"

Joanne tapped my shoulder. "Bill, my cousin has a friend in a retreat house on the island. If someone has a need, I am sure she'll be there. Her name is Beth Evans."

"Nancy, Joanne, who is here in the office, is going to make a call. A woman named Beth Evans, will contact Cathy."

"Thanks, Marcia." I sensed Nancy's agony as she attempted more conversation.

"Nancy, I'll stop by later this afternoon."

I stared off, stunned by the news. Joanne made her phone call. Betty Anne tapped nervously on the desk looking pale and broken. "Why?" She'd met Cathy and Steve several times when they came to the office for pre-marital work.

I struggled to my feet. I felt Betty Anne and Joanne's love supporting me as I grabbed the railing and descended wearily down each step to my office.

I SAT FROZEN AT my desk trying to absorb the reality... Steve dead. Cathy seriously injured. The news...stark and blunt. No way to soften it. A moped bike accident. What about Jason, Cathy's five-year-old son? I searched through my desk for their file...their wedding file. I located the number for Cathy's mother and called. "Mrs. Leland. Marcia Cham. I'm so sorry."

Mrs. Leland hesitated and spoke between sobs. "It's terrible. I can't believe it. On Saturday they were so happy; now this. Why?"

"I don't know." I wished for, longed for, something concrete to say, but I knew there was nothing to say that didn't sound trite. I hung onto the telephone until Mrs. Leland spoke again.

"Jason doesn't understand."

"I'm sure he doesn't."

"What should I do?"

"How about if I come over and take Jason to the playground and for ice cream?" I heard muffled cries.

"I'll be there within the hour."

"Okay," she mumbled in a weak, parched voice.

JASON AND I SHARED AN ice cream at Peaceful Meadows. The clink of spoons on glasses and the soft yellow walls made it feel warm, cozy, and familiar. He licked the melted ice cream that had dripped over his fingers as he had done on our first meeting. "Grandma says that my mom will be away longer now."

"You're right, Jason."

"She's hurt, I think and Steve died."

"Yes." Pain jabbed my heart and I could hardly breathe. I looked into the innocent face of this five-year-old; his expression asked me to make it all better. "Let's go to the park," he said and jumped off the counter stool and grabbed my hand.

We walked to the park. Jason and I played on the swings and then on the slide.

"Come on the merry-go-round with me." Jason pulled me along as he ran.

"Jason, you know it makes me dizzy." He let go and flew on his way. I sat on a bench nearby amazed at his energy. Jason whirled and whirled, round and round, as some older kids pushed the merry-go-round faster and faster. He grinned and my heart sank. He loved Steve…a real dad he'd said.

I took Jason home to his grandmother. He ran into the house. I stood in a silent hug with Mrs. Leland on the porch. Jason came huffing and puffing back to the door. "Marcia, see my new Matchbox." I held the shiny new fire engine with bright yellow ladders and he grinned with pride.

BACK AT MY OFFICE I listened to a CD of mellow cello music while letting this reality sink in and remembered when I first had met Cathy Leland. Cathy had called and we arranged a meeting in my office. After the first moments of introduction, Steve and Cathy wasted no time.

"We've both been through several difficult relationships, but we think we have found the real thing in each other." Steve touched Cathy's sleeve as he spoke. "We hear that you require couples to do premarital work or you will not agree to officiate at their wedding."

"That's true. I ask that couples sit for an inventory assessment tool with those trusty No. 2 pencils." I held up an example of the yellow pencil. "You each mark your answer sheet with strongly agree, agree, undecided, disagree, or strongly disagree to over one hundred statements. I send your answer sheets to PREPARE-ENRICH *by Life Innovations, Inc.*. After your responses are collated, they send back the results. The results indicate your strengths and growth areas in communication, conflict resolution, family relationships, personality traits, spiritual values, money issues and leisure time."

Cathy and Steve sat for the assessment. We spent several evenings discussing their relationship strengths and growth areas. They were candid with me and each other. At our last session, Cathy held Steve's hand, "We trust each other. We treasure the new beginning we've been given." Steve put his arm around Cathy and they shared a long hug.

At their marriage ceremony friends, family, and a future filled with hope surrounded Cathy and Steve. As I led them through their vows I felt the strength of their commitment and the bond of love they embraced.

THE SHRILL RING OF THE office phone stole me away from that moment of love. I responded to a former student who wanted a recommendation for honor society. I moved papers around on my desk as I thought: from tragic death to honor society, life goes on.

I turned off my CD player and left the office. I breathed in fresh air as I climbed in my car for the drive home. My dog Ebony greeted me at the door. I poured coffee and sat at the kitchen table. Ebony nuzzled close sensing the grief that sat deep in my heart.

TWO WEEKS AFTER THE accident and jumping through the hoops of government red tape, Steve's body arrived by air and lay in the cold room of a local funeral home. Cathy, with emergency attendants accompanying her, flew to a hospital near home. She had a series of surgeries to face in the coming weeks and months. On my first visit to the hospital, the expression of pain and hurt on Cathy's face stopped me short.

She took my hand with her one functioning arm. "Jason can't even look at me. The doctors are making no guarantees for any further mobility in my arm and leg."

I listened to the depth of her darkness, her expressions of guilt. "If only we had not ridden the moped," and her frantic words, "Steve's family is questioning the validity of our marriage."

I offered the only verbal assurance I knew. "Cathy, the license was signed and sent to the Town Clerk the evening of your wedding. It's valid." She shut her eyes and sleep came. The frantic look melted from her face. I lingered by her bed.

That night in the warmth of my home office, I turned to my journal and wrote.

> *God, Cathy's life is dark. She's crying for moments of peace, for moments of hope. Fear for the future looms. Give her strength and hope. Give her glimpses of a brighter future. Heal her bones, renew her broken spirit. Amen.*

I STRUGGLED WITH THE service. The traditional scriptures and words of wisdom sounded hollow. The organist, Jean, stopped by the office. "I think this service for Steve may be one of the hardest I've ever played for and maybe the hardest you've had to plan."

"I believe it is," I said.

Jean adjusted a pile of sheet music she'd brought with her. "Maybe a balance of music, moments of quiet, and psalms of lament will be all we can offer."

"Psalms of lament." Startled by her suggestion, I stared at Jean. "When I first studied those psalms, I wondered when life would be so desperate, so unfair that I'd need to use them."

SIX WEEKS AFTER THE accident the funeral took place. Guests appeared wearing dark suits and dark glasses. Ushers greeted and seated them. The organist played deep sorrow-filled tones. Stillness filled the sanctuary. Stillness punctuated by pain and sorrow. Stillness layered with question upon question. Is this God's will…God's plan? If so, who wants anything to do with that God? Why? Why now when life held new possibilities for Steve and Cathy?

The once hope-filled bride sat in the front row. Bruised face. Useless arm taped across her chest. Blank eyes. Jason wiggled, squirmed, and craned his neck to see who was seated behind him. I caught a glimpse of the yellow ladders on his fire engine Matchbox car sticking out of his pocket.

Standing behind the lectern on the elevated pulpit, I read paraphrased excerpts from the psalms of lament.

> My God, my God, why have you forsaken
> me? The words of my groaning do nothing
> to save me. My God, I call by day but you
> do not answer, at night but I find no respite.
> My strength is trickling away, my bones are
> all disjointed. My heart has turned to wax,
> melting inside me. Psalm 22:1,2 and 14.
>
> Heal me, Yahweh, my bones are shaken, my
> spirit is shaken to its very depths. I am worn
> out from groaning, every night I drench my

pillow and soak my bed with tears. Psalm
6:3,6.

My eyes, too, are worn out waiting for your
promise, when will you have pity on me?
Psalm 119:82.

My heart is numb with fear I stretch out my
hands to you, my heart like a land thirsty for
you. Show me the road I must travel for you
to relieve my heart. Psalm 143:4b, 6, 8b.

You have turned my mourning into dancing,
you have stripped off my sackcloth and
clothes me with joy. So my heart will sing to
you unceasingly. Yahweh, my God, I shall
praise you for ever. Psalm 30:11-12.

Stepping down from the pulpit to the floor of the sanctuary, I stood close to Cathy. I rested my hand on her shoulder as I spoke words that I hoped would land somewhere
inside her. Some words for her to discover, when her pain
was not so raw.

The Psalms have been created by people like
you and me. Some of the Psalms have been
written by persons living through heartache,
agony, endless suffering, and desperate times
as we are experiencing with Cathy.

As you heard in the excerpts of biblical
laments, the singers of these psalms
addressed God boldly. No holds barred. No
censored version of feelings and questions.
They raged and engaged God, naming the
painful reality, the scary depths, and the
abyss, as we have since the day we learned of
Cathy and Steve's terrible accident.

How do we get through this? My suggestion
is to imitate the ancients…to repeat and
repeat, rave and rave, question and question,
until a tiny seed of hope, a glimmer of peace

and a sign of new life makes its way through
the darkness to the light.

We are literally walking through the "valley
of the shadow of death" as did those who
sang the twenty-third Psalm. They remind us
that through their experience of the darkest
of valleys they were not alone, God was with
them.

All those gathered here today in God's name
witness to you, Cathy, that you are not alone.
We walk with you as God's people. God, let
it be so.

The organist played a soulful lament as the guests filed out
of the sanctuary into the sunshine. The grief-stricken bride
stood and whispered to me, "One day something good will
emerge out of this." She took Jason's hand and walked up the
aisle toward the sunlight to greet her friends.

I watched. Chills traveled through my body.

AFTER STEVE'S FUNERAL, I lingered in the empty sanctuary. Cathy's words, "One day something good will emerge out
of this," rung in my ears over and over again. I stared at the
gold cross and the vases of flowers. She already understands
the faith of those who lament. Even while her feet are slogging
through the deepest darkest pit of her life, she knows that one
day... She knows that those who've been wounded, crushed,
betrayed and slammed in the face with life speak of it — a
light, a word of hope, a spark of love, or a taste of peace. It may
take months; it may take years, but she knows it comes. God, I
thank you for reaching into her heart and soul with that assurance. Reach into mine.

The Smell of Freshly Baked Cookies

THE PLANE LANDED LATE in Boston. I waited for my luggage and then found my car in the parking deck where Ken and I had left it for our flight to New Orleans and the wedding of the daughter of one of our long time friends. Ken stayed in New Orleans to party with our friends. I returned to preach the next day.

As I drove home I floated on the joy of old friends and memories of our son's wedding just two weeks ago. After 9/11 and our son's serious illness a month before his wedding, celebrating joyous times lightened the load.

I parked in the driveway and gathered my bags. I shoved the back door open and Ebony greeted me with a wet nose and a thumping tail. I dropped my luggage and pushed the button on the answering machine. "You have three new messages." The machine rewound and the first message began.

I heard the sobbing, spent voice of my sister, Barb. "Marsh, call me as soon as you get in from the wedding."

The second message played. It was Barb's voice again. "If you are there, pick up." And finally the third message, "Marcia, I hate to leave this message but there has been a terrible accident. David Opiela is dead."

MY HANDS SHOOK AND knees trembled as I dialed Barb's number. David dead. How? Why? "Barb, I can't believe this. David. Dead." Alone in the house I steadied myself by leaning heavily into the kitchen counter. Ebony came and sat on my feet.

"Marsh, sorry to have left the news, but I didn't know what else to do." I could not take it in. David dead. Dead at thirty-seven. My niece Jen now a widow. Elizabeth and Katherine, no daddy. My sister, Marge, Jen's mother…My mother…

"What happened?"

"The family was camping and David went into the camper to do the dishes. Jen heard a gun shot. She and his brother jumped to their feet and opened the trailer door and found David on the floor dead with a gun shot wound in the front of his neck near his collar bone."

I pulled out the kitchen chair. My body folded into it.

"Barb, I don't understand. Why did he have a gun?"

"When they camp outside of Austin, Texas, he carries a gun in case of snakes."

"A shot in the front of his neck." I repeated still paralyzed in disbelief of the reality Barb was sharing.

"The police concluded that the gun fell to the floor as David pushed the holster aside to do the dishes and it went off."

"Right into the front of his neck. What are the chances of that?"

"A million to one. The weight of the gun hitting the floor caused it to fire…there was no mercy." My stomach turned and I felt sick as Barb talked.

"What about Jen and the kids? Marge and Marv? Mother?" I whispered, nearly exhausted from the news.

"All are devastated. Marge and Marv are on their way to Texas. Jen has her church family around her. Mother's neighbors are with her."

After hanging up I sat for a long time in the stillness of the house. Stunned, I offered no prayer. I had no words. Ebony moved closer and leaned her head on my lap.

I called Jen. A friend answered. "I'll see if she can talk."

"Jen, I'm sorry." Shock filled the air between us as grief had shattered Jen and her two girls, Elizabeth and Katherine.

"You will come, won't you?"

"I'll be there."

I called Ken who was still at the wedding in New Orleans. After his initial shock he said, "You are making arrangements to go, aren't you? Do you want me to call the kids?"

"No. I need to call them. See you tomorrow." I made a cup of coffee and settled in the TV room on the sofa and called our adult children. They all responded with shock and then questions, "What can we do?" "Should we come?" "I'll call Jen and go see her later." "Give her our love."

I called my travel agent friend. She found me a flight for the next evening. I dragged my travel bags upstairs and unpacked my wedding clothes and packed my funeral clothes. I slept fitfully dreading the face-to-face reality of David's death..

JEN'S FATHER, MY BROTHER-IN-LAW met me at the airport. I hugged him and asked, "Marv, how are you doing?"

"Okay." And then he rattled on and on about this and that

on our drive to Jen and David's house. "The town is devastated. Scholarship funds have been set up for the kids. Jen's back is in terrible condition. The shock of the death, they say. The chiropractor called and offered to see her free of charge for the next year. Their church friends have cleaned up the yard, set up meals, and offered rooms for family. I've never been around Christians that put their words into action so well." His emotions were too raw to speak directly of David's death.

Marge greeted me at the door with a long hug. Food covered every available space in the kitchen and flowers filled every table and shelf in the dining room and living room. I found five-year-old Katherine in the backyard tree house. "I'm drawing pictures of Daddy. Daddy built this tree house," she told me. I sat while she continued her drawing in silence.

I knocked on Elizabeth's bedroom door. "Come in, Aunt Marcia." Elizabeth sat on her bed surrounded by her stuffed animals. "Here's one I bought in Ohio last summer." She held out a small bear with a bright yellow hat.

"Yes, I remember that." I patted the bear. "On my flight I remembered the fun we had at the playground and hiking in the Gorge Park."

"Daddy was pretty silly, wasn't he?"

"Yes. Your Daddy had more fun than anyone I know." Quiet settled over us. I remembered David playing inside out and backwards on the monkey bars and adventuring off the marked hiking trails.

The door to Elizabeth's room squeaked. Marge looked in. "Jen's ready to see you, Marcia. She's sitting in the front yard."

"Thanks." I squeezed Elizabeth's hands and stood. I walked slowly out of her room and down the hall. As I opened the front door I breathed in a prayer, "God be with me." Jen sat in a low yard chair. I leaned over and hugged her. As I pulled another chair closer, she asked,

"Did you bring your Halloween outfit?"

"Yes, because you asked." I remembered feeling weird packing clothes for visiting hours, the funeral and Halloween.

"I want the kids to go to the Halloween party at the church tonight. They need to do something normal. Will you help them with their makeup?" It wasn't long before Elizabeth, Katherine, and I were sitting on the floor in front of mirror in a cramped hall with our faces decorated for the evening.

Jen held herself high as she walked among church friends at the party. Marge and Marv stayed close, watching for the signal that she needed to escape. The kids and I played games and bobbed for apples. By the time I settled for the night I was exhausted.

THE NEXT MORNING, JEN invited me into her bedroom. The room, dark and warm, seemed devoid of air. I couldn't breathe. "Marcia, will you speak for our family?"

Surprised at her request, I hesitated for a moment. Their church has a different theological position from mine. Will my words be appropriate? Jen had already said to the children, "Jesus needed your Daddy." I cringed at her words and wanted to shout, "Jen, it was an accident and it's terrible. What kind of God would snatch David up?" I pictured God with David as the bullet entered his neck, holding him as tears flooded both their eyes. I looked into her swollen red eyes. "Yes. It will be an honor."

THE CALLING HOURS — I feared them; yet, as we entered the funeral home, the smell of freshly baked cookies welcomed us instead of the scent of gladiolas…the funeral flower. A large woman in a brightly colored dress led us to a side room with tables and chairs and snacks and warm cookies. "I am here to be with the children." Katherine and Elizabeth were immediately drawn to her. Because of her size, her arms enveloped them and because of the warmth that showed in her eyes, her body provided a refuge.

Taking her love with us, we walked into the viewing room. Flowers and pictures of David decorated every available space. The girls hung around the casket and often leaned over and talked with their Daddy. Jen greeted hundreds of town and church folks. Each time the greeting and meeting became too much to bear, the children, and many of us, were drawn to the smell of the freshly baked cookies and this large woman.

I remembered Luke 13:34b. "Jesus replied to the sorrow-filled disciples, "How often have I longed to gather your children together, as a hen gathers her brood under her wings…!" She became the mother hen holding us in the shelter of her embrace.

THE DAY BETWEEN THE calling hours and the funeral was filled with sorrow and laughter; with chatter and silence; with busyness and stillness. Jen's sister arrived with her five-week old baby, Taylor. The joy of Taylor took the edge off of many moments. Sometime the hours seemed normal; other times black with grief.

THE SERVICE FOR DAVID began with praise songs, words of assurance and prayers. The minister shared a story that David related to his Bible study group earlier that week.

> David said, "I noticed the light reflecting off the communion cups onto the ceiling of the room. Each little, seemingly insignificant cup has the potential to reflect the bright light above in a thousand different directions. The reflection of dancing lights witnesses to us that we all have the potential to be lights to God's world."

The pastor introduced me. "We welcome Reverend Marcia Cham, Jen's aunt. She will speak for Jen's family." I stood in the middle of the preaching stage and looked at Jen. Her face was cast down. I could not catch her eye. I spoke,

> Light sparked from David to Jen when they danced the cowboy dances before their wedding. Light glistened in his eyes as he saw the miracle of his children. Light sparkled from David to everyone he met. David was a brilliant light in God's world.

> He lived abundantly. His hug spoke from a deep place in his heart and his eyes could see into your soul. His life force rubbed off on other people. He lived more in thirty-seven years than most people do in eighty-seven years, and he talked more in his thirty-seven years than most people do in one hundred seven years.

> David, we will miss the physical presence of
> your light but our faith tells us that your light
> will continue to shine and will bring us joy
> and laughter at unexpected moments of our
> lives. We thank God for the gift of your life.

Jen glanced at me. Tears glistened in her eyes.

THE SPIRIT WORKED HARD as it moved in and through all who touched the lives of Jen and her family, not just during the immediacy of the tragedy but for years after David's death. There were black days, but I can only imagine how much blacker they would have been for Jen without her personal faith and her church community.

Jen declared, "At age thirty-three I am not going to remain a widow the rest of my life." A few years later Jen remarried and the family moved the tree house that David built for the children to their new home.

DAVID'S DEATH RIPPED HOLES in my soul. Shock and disbelief jammed into my heart. Confusion, frustration and exhaustion poured in and fears burrowed into my being through my privacy window. When I reached out to others, some offered platitudes; "God knows best." "God has a plan." Some judged me and said; "Your faith isn't strong enough to understand God's ways."

To which I responded, "God's ways…were Dean's, Steve's and David's death's ordained by God? Is that God's way?" Questions tumbled through my prayer. "Where is your mercy? Am I, your servant, supposed to understand? Are there words for this kind of pain?"

No answers came, only silence hung between me and God. God's silence angered me. But then through the frustration I found the words, "God is silent, catching breath because our Creator is crying, hurting along with you. Be silent. Can you feel God's tears in your heart?" I felt God's tears in my heart.

The Gift
of Laughter

*Where does laughter come from? It comes from
as deep a place as tears come from,
and in a way
it comes from the same place.*

*With laughter something new breaks
into our darkness,
something so unexpected and preposterous
and glad that we can
only laugh at it in astonishment.* [2]

A Wax Job!

I'D HAD A QUIET day at home catching up with laundry, writing thank you notes, and reading a mystery. The phone rang. I marked my place in the book, reached over the arm of the sofa, and picked up the receiver. I heard the voice of my friend Betsy. "Barbara's dead."

"Oh, Betsy, your friend gone, I can't imagine."

"Last week, when we said goodbye, our final goodbye, she threw her arms toward the ceiling in her bedroom as if it were open to the heavens and said,. 'From somewhere out there, I promise to call you everyday at 8:30.' She turned to me. 'The kids will be off to school so we can really yak.' Then she cupped her hands around her mouth. 'I'll yell loudly so you can hear.' We laughed and fell into each others arms, holding on tight. Marcia, as I held her, I told her if I could take my strength and give it to her to help fight the cancer, I would do it in a heartbeat. Barbara mumbled, 'I know.'"

I cried and choked out, "I'm sorry." Colon cancer had eaten Barbara's life away in three months; black, self-deprecating humor had kept her sane. My heart broke for Barbara and my friend.

WE MET IN BARBARA'S kitchen to plan her service. Bobby, Barbara's significant other came in as Betsy put down her beer. She hugged Bobby and stayed standing ready to act out a 'Barbara-drama' as she talked.

"On one particular day during the throes of her battle, she rubbed her bald head and exclaimed to me, 'As long as the hair on my head is gone, what about the rest of it? And, anyway, I know there will be something sexy in it for my Bobby.' She put her hands on her hips and gyrated." Betsy mimicked Barbara as she took a sip of her beer.

"I drove Barbara to get the wax job. When they called her name, she sashayed into the office. A half hour later with her Scarlett O'Hara-like wide-brimmed hat dramatically cocked to one side of her head. She stood in the middle of the room with no one paying attention to her, looked around, pulled off the hat and screamed, 'Look what they've done to me,' then roared with laughter.'" Betsy, Bobby and I laughed until we cried.

HUNDREDS CROWDED THE CHURCH for the service to celebrate her life — family, teachers, students, friends and clients from the Ninety-Nine Restaurant where she tended bar. I introduced Betsy. She walked up the steps to the lectern and spoke.

> Barbara talked loudly, laughed heartily and spoke with a freedom that left most of us speechless.
>
> She faced cancer with more courage and strength than I knew existed inside of her being. She told me on the Fourth of July she was not afraid to die but she did not want to leave those she loved.
>
> She was Scarlett O'Hara. She loved to make an entrance. She knew the proper way to execute the perfect "Pout and Stomp."
>
> She was Our Miss Brooks. The youth whose lives she touched learned not just about Social Studies, but about the people they were trying to become. The kids not only knew they could talk to Ms. Kenney and she'd listen, they trusted her. She was...
>
> I've only scratched the surface of who the B-Girl was. Now I can almost hear Barbara saying, 'Get the hook.' Betsy paused and shifted her position and sighed.
>
> Well, it's easy for me to celebrate Barbara's life with you today, but like the rest of you, I must deal with her death.
>
> I am thankful that Barbara is no longer suffering, but I am frightened about not having her here for me.

Betsy returned to her seat and her husband, John pulled her close to him. A pregnant silence permeated the room.

At the beginning notes of Louis Armstrong's, "It's a Wonderful World," eyes filled. As he sang, "I see friends shaking hands saying how do you do. They're really saying I love you," tears flooded the room. Purses snapped. Tissues passed from one to the other. Noses honked, here and there. Comic nose blowing sounds traveled from one side of the worship room to the other. Unexpected laughter broke out. That's when we knew Barbara's spirit was sweeping and diving through the sanctuary, bringing with it holy laughter that balanced the depths of our despair.

Moments later, the laughter faded to a profound silence. I stepped to the lectern and prayed a prayer sent to Betsy anonymously.

> Our teacher, friend, mom, sister, bartender,
> O God, the one I loved is now with you. I do
> not know "how" or "where," but I can say it
> because it makes no sense that so rich and
> full a life would come to an abrupt end…
> except for memories. Still I am bereft for she
> is not with me. I listen to all the clichés of my
> friends, spoken to console me: "She is better
> off." "She is past her pain and suffering." "She
> is in heaven," whatever that means. I listen
> and am not consoled.
>
> My grief is selfish. I want to feel her touch,
> hear her voice, and see her smile. I am
> confident she is with You and I am just as
> confident, O Lord, that you understand how
> it is with me. I cannot help recalling the
> times I might have been gentler, softer, and
> more thoughtful. I wish I could live some
> hours over. I would like to say, "I love you"
> one more time.
>
> They say, "Time heals all things." I do not
> believe that time does a thing. You, O God,
> are healer and helper. You can heal me in

time…help me through lonely days and long
nights. You can give me renewed zest for
going on and entering life once more, but
right now I grieve, I hurt, I am bereft. Amen.

LATER THAT DAY, I sat in my office and repeated Betsy's words. "It's easy for me to celebrate Barbara's life with you today, but like the rest of you, I must deal with Barbara's death." I leaned back and ticked off what I had done after Betsy's call. I'd contacted the funeral home, coordinated with the organist and custodian and arranged for sound to be piped into the fellowship hall for the expected overflow crowd. I'd listened to her family and friends, designed the service, guided the celebration of Barbara's life, greeted the hundreds of guests, circulated during the reception and heard more stories and held their sorrow. I leaned forward with my elbows on my desk holding my head, I talked right out loud. "Betsy, you are right. The busyness is over, now I must deal with Barbara's death."

I remembered that's what I had to do after my dad's death. When the calls and visitors stopped and the cards only dribbled in, I had to face his death. I filed the folder marked, "Service for Barbara," turned off the lights in my office, locked the door, drove home and changed clothes. I needed to push down my privacy window and tend to me.

I drove to the beach and walked. I found the words I'd prayed at the service repeating themselves in my head, "my grief is selfish," and boring into me. I realized my grief for Barbara was selfish. I felt cheated that Barbara died so young. I wanted time to absorb her unorthodox look at life. I wanted more of her black humor. I cried and an old proverb suddenly popped into my head, "Laughter is God's hand on the shoulder of a troubled world."

I looked around — a goofy gull with its wings ruffled to catch the wind was strutting with pomp and stomp down the beach. I laughed and shouted after the gull.

"Thanks to you Barbara, I've felt that hand."

I knelt and dug my knees into the sand. "God, hold me in my grief for Barbara and my sadness for Betsy. Strengthen me for the next crisis."

The Coat

IT WAS FEBRUARY AND I was getting around to putting the Christmas decorations away. I'd promised myself to have them put away in the attic before Ash Wednesday. And I'd decided to organize them into categories, so boxes were scattered all over the house. I found the phone on the third ring. "Hello."

"Marcia, its Sally Dade. Judy's prayer was granted. Hospice settled her in her own room two days ago and she died this morning. She went out as she lived ... getting her way." Sally laughed and then I heard her sob and I cried.

I'D BUMPED INTO JUDY in the aisle of the local bookstore. "Hey, Judy, how are you doing?"

As she turned I noticed a yellow cast to her skin. "Not so good...I just came from the doctor's and I have gastric cancer and in his words, 'Judy, it's ripping through your body.'" I stammered as I searched for words.

Judy looked directly at me. "I've been in your place before, searching for words to say. And already, having shared this with a couple of friends, I find it's easier to be on my end telling you my story, than it is to be on your end silently searching for a reply...for there is really so little to say."

Throughout her three-month bout with cancer, Judy controlled calls and visitors; whose calls she'd accept and which visitors she'd see. After Christmas she gave me permission to come over. I settled in a chair and she leaned forward to the edge of the sofa.

"In October Walt presented me with a full length mink." A picture immediately popped into my head. Judy all five feet of her weighed down and almost lost in the fur.

Judy continued. "I said to Walt are you doing this because I'm going to die? He said, 'You've always wanted one. I just want you to have it.'"

My throat felt tightened as Judy leaned back and struggled for a full breath. When she had full control, she spoke with a wry expression, "I expect Walt to find another companion."

"Really."

"Yes really, but Marcia, I don't want that bitch to have

my mink."

We laughed. She clapped her hands to her face. "I'm serious." We talked a little longer and as I pulled on my coat Judy shook her finger at me. "And remember, I'll haunt the church, if there are any cold cucumber sandwiches at the reception after my funeral."

"I'll pass the word."

She grinned. "I am really serious about the sandwiches." I turned to leave and heard Judy's parched voice. "Marcia, I'm worried about my sons at the viewing."

I walked a few steps back to her place on the sofa. "I know." Her eyes closed and I carefully closed the door and left.

Now on this icy February morning, I met Walt as I walked up their driveway from parking my car some distance away from their house. "Marcia. This morning I greeted the hospice nurse, kissed Judy and drove into town to make a deposit for the hardware store. When I returned, as the garage door opened, I saw the feet of my boys. I knew she'd died." He pointed to the house. "Friends are crowded into our living room. They know what I want and need. I'm going for a walk." Walt walked off as I called to him,

"Walt, I'm sorry." I opened the front door and heard frenzied conversation about the funeral and the burial arrangements. Out of the chaos one request was clear, the family needed the burial to be right after the celebration of Judy's life. I left that message with the funeral director.

Eddie, the funeral director and my friend, returned my call in the midst of the high powered confusion. "Marcia, we've got a problem. The ground is frozen and we are going to have to put Judy in a vault until spring. There is no way to bury her now."

"Eddie, you must find a way."

"You know my hands are tied."

"Eddie, the Catholics dig graves all winter. Contact the Catholic cemetery and borrow the back hoe."

"Now, Marcia, you know how difficult and costly that can be."

"I know, but my job for the family is to make sure we have a burial. They do not want Judy waiting for the spring thaw."

"But…"

"Eddie, here's the picture. Eight women are standing here in Judy's living room. They are ready to break out picks and shovels from Judy's hardware store, call the evening news, rig up spotlights and dig that grave."

Eddie made the arrangements. Walt gave Eddie Judy's clothes for the viewing.

As I ENTERED THE funeral home for the calling hours, lightness filled the air. I greeted the family. I walked around the corner where the casket sat out of sight from Judy's boys and looked.

Then I understood...there was Judy decked out in her full length mink. I laughed and felt the mink as I knelt before Judy.

THE NEXT DAY EIGHT women in full-length fur coats carried Judy's casket out of the church to the hearse and then hoisted the casket to its resting place at the cemetery. Three wild geese flew over squawking with what sounded like laughter. The eight pallbearers pointed to the geese. I heard one say in a stage whisper, "It's a sign. Judy's at peace. She knows that bitch, whoever she may be, will never have the coat."

At the reception, I inspected the tables for cucumber sandwiches. Not a one. I breathed a sigh of relief. I looked at Judy's boys and found sorrow in their eyes. Humor did not eliminate the darkness but it kept it away to be dealt with more gently as the days unfolded.

Robe Flying — Another Judy

THE GUEST SPEAKER DRONED on and on. I watched the congregation getting restless as they stretched and yawned and looked at their watches. I heard choir robes brush against the metal chairs as the choir shifted in their seats. I tried to stay attentive. When the back door opened and Judy's brother waved, I eased up the side aisle to meet him.

"Judy passed an hour ago." He reached out and hugged me.

"I'm sorry. You stood by her and allowed her to keep her dignity," I whispered in his ear as we held one another.

"I'm glad it's finally over and she's free." He breathed in deeply and let go of the door to his emotions.

JUDY, A DAUGHTER OF THE fire chief, knew everyone in town. She worked tirelessly creating a narrative history of Hingham. At 40 she was diagnosed with breast cancer, and for ten years squeezed every extra ounce of living out of the time she had left. I met her in the ninth year of her struggle. With a brace holding her neck and her dauntless determination, she attended my ordination. "Nothing will keep me away. I want to see the rafters of that old building shake when they lay hands on you — a woman."

Now at home and confined to her small bedroom that overlooked the Hingham Center Cemetery, caregivers kept her involved in everyday life. One read to her. One wrote as she dictated her history of the town. Her brother helped her write checks, even though her signature was no longer legible. The family knew that the act of signing the checks gave her some sense of control in her life. The checks were rewritten later.

Her mother, Mildred, fixed trays for her meals. Bright cloth napkins. China plates and teacups. Crystal glassware. One evening Mildred observed me noticing the tray. She hunched her shoulders and whispered, "To keep Judy's spirits up."

I hugged Mildred. "If I get sick, I want to move in with you." She gave me a half-smile, lowered her head and carried the tray downstairs to the kitchen.

I visited daily. One day when I walked in, her sister lay on the floor reaching for boxes in Judy's closet and pulling them out in a pile at the foot of the bed. Judy's head hung over the side of the bed, vomiting in a bucket. From her 'hanging over the bed position,' Judy noticed my feet. "Your feet are about the same size as mine. Take my *almost new* loafers home with you." At first I felt strange walking in her shoes, but gradually I became proud as I learned more about the life through which she had walked.

TWO WEEKS BEFORE HER death, she called at 3 a.m. and asked for communion. I dressed and filled a small glass bottle with wine, wrapped a piece of pita bread and a pottery chalice in a colorful cloth napkin and packed them in a wicker basket. In the pitch black of night, I drove the few blocks to Judy's.

Her mother opened the door. She leaned into me for a few moments. "I'm sorry she called you out in the middle of the night."

"It's okay."

I walked up the stairs and into Judy's room, put my basket on the stand next to her bed and sat on the edge. She took my hand, her eyes opened as wide as saucers. "I'm scared. I dreamed the cancer was eating my face and my fingers. I saw my sister standing beside a dark highway with bus after bus whizzing by. She looked desperate. I'm worried that no one is going to care about her when I die." She sobbed. I turned and took the lilac lotion from the table next to her bed and squeezed some on my hands. I lifted her gown and covered her back with circular motions and listened. The sobs quieted.

"Sometimes I'm ready to die; other times I'm scared, scared of what it will be like, the dying itself. Marcia, I don't want to feel any more pain. Is God really with me?"

"Yes, Judy, God is with you. I am sure of it."

"I believe I will see Dad in heaven." A slight laugh cut through the seriousness of the moment when Judy added, "I told my brother today that when he gets to heaven, he will be as bald as a billiard ball." The emotional tension of this middle of the night visit broke. Her devilish eyes darted and she touched my arm.

"Will you give me communion now?"

I laid the cloth napkin on the table tray at the foot of the bed. I set the pottery chalice and the pita on the napkin and while pouring the wine into the chalice said, "Judy, Jesus promised to be with us in our brokenness. He is with you in your pain, your fears, and your questions. Take this bread and remember his great love for you." I broke the bread and we both ate.

I cupped the pottery chalice in my hands. "Our lives are held in the hands of God. Jesus promised that with God one day all things will be made new. Take and drink and remember his promise of new life." We held the cup together and drank.

I returned home feeling blessed by my time with Judy and drained from sitting so close to death and digging for words to comfort and support Judy.

A few nights later she called again. Mildred met me at the door, filled with apologies. "We removed the telephone from Judy's room so she would not call you again, but she managed to get out of bed and made the call from the hall."

I shrugged. "Judy is one determined lady." Mildred walked to her first floor bedroom and shut the door.

I climbed the stairs. Judy's broad smile greeted me. "I have an idea for my burial."

"You do?" I threw my coat on the end of the bed and started to sit down when Judy interrupted me.

"Marcia, before you sit, look out my window. See the plot in the cemetery where I will be buried." I moved to the window and looked down at the tiny gravestones below.

"Well," hardly being able to talk through her excitement, Judy continued, "during the night I remembered your fear of amusement rides and especially the ones that take you high into the air." I nodded in agreement.

Judy continued. "A vision came to me of Eddie embalming me here in this room, placing me in the coffin, and rigging up a slide from my window to my grave. Then one of Eddie's guys helps you climb on and straddle the casket and gives you a little push." She demonstrated for effect. "And then — can you see it?" She threw her arms up. "There you'll be hanging on for dear life, with your robes just a-flying, as we swoop down to the cemetery below." We laughed until we cried.

DURING MY LAST VISIT with Judy, I prayed for the angels to come and release her. She squeezed my hand. "Thanks."

ON A COLD WINTER day at the graveside service, I looked up at Judy's window. I imagined that I heard her laughter through my despair. The memory of her holy laughter lifted me.

MY MOTHER WAS VISITING at the time of Judy's death. She caught the ear of Amy, a church member at a pre-Christmas party. Mother wrung her hands and touched Amy's shoulder to get her attention. "I feel so bad that Marcia has to deal with death all the time."

"Why? It's her job." Amy shot back. Mother, startled by Amy's response, fingered the chords around the sofa pillow.

"Well, I mean it must be so hard." Mother said still a bit rattled. She moved to a chair across the room.

Later Mother and I continued the conversation around the kitchen table at home. "It's hard, but it's the most sacred thing I do," I told her.

Mother twisted her hands in her lap. "Do you really like seeing the bodies and being so near the sick and dying? Do you get used to it?"

"I never get used to it. Seeing the bodies and being near the folks is hard at first, but then I get focused on the families and my pastoral ministry with them. The body and smells of death fade into the background while I listen to their stories and concerns."

She fiddled with the flowers in the middle of the table. "I still don't see how you do it." Mother struggled with death and its unpredictability.

"I know Mother. But you know what's amazing? The dying help me. They welcome me to their bedsides. They ask about how I am doing. They are interested in life outside their personal situation. When I feel weak and powerless, when I wonder if I have anything more to give or to say, their love pulls me through. They minister to me."

Mother's voice grew more confident. "I've seen your friends support you."

"Yes. They are invaluable to me. Addie and Jan pray for me. They, in particular, know what I do is not easy. Their prayers give me strength. I feel and see God at work in the worst situations and I'm amazed. It's a privilege."

"I don't want it to wear you out."

I accepted mother's concern. We sat quiet for a while and I wondered, will the dying wear me out?

Stranger
Needs a Stranger

Love the stranger,
for you were once strangers in Egypt.
Deuteronomy 10:19

Remember always to welcome strangers
for by doing this
some people have entertained angels
without knowing it.
Hebrews 13:2

"Not a Woman!"

I RETURNED TO THE office from lunch with my daughter. I moved a pile of books from my desk to the floor to clear some space to plan a new Bible Study. Betty Ann buzzed.

"You have a call from a funeral director in western Massachusetts."

"Reverend Cham. Jerry Eifert here. Funeral Director at the Peace Funeral Home in Amherst. I need a clergy person to do a gravesite service for Maude Denning in the Hingham Center Cemetery on Thursday." He paused and pleaded. "I am at the end of my list of possible clergy in your area. Can you help on Thursday?"

I looked at my calendar. "I'm available."

I heard him breathe a sigh of relief. "Thank you. Is eleven on Thursday morning good with you?"

"Eleven will be fine. Now what can you to tell me about Maude?"

"Ms. Denning attended Boston University in the early twenties. And she worked in a corporate job until she retired at seventy and then volunteered her services to help other women in the business world."

"Ms. Denning sounds like a woman ahead of her time. Thanks, Jerry. I'll see you on Thursday." I hung up feeling honored with the idea of celebrating Maude Denning's life, even for the ten-minute graveside service.

ON THAT ICY JANUARY day, I walked to the gravesite in my black ministerial coat. As I approached the small group gathered near the open grave, I heard gasps. I shrugged and extended my hand to Jerry, the funeral director.

Jerry introduced me to the family. In their cold red faces I saw sorrow and sadness. I conducted the service complete with readings from the Book of Proverbs and personal remarks about Maude — a woman ahead of her time.

After the benediction, family members spoke to me. "Thank you." "You did a nice job." "Maude would have been surprised to see you here."

As I turned to walk back to the office, Jerry stopped me. "Did you notice the gasps as you approached?"

"Yes. What was that about?"

"Ms. Denning did everything in her power to avoid having a woman do her service. 'Not a woman!' She instructed. She insisted her last hospitalization be in a Catholic Hospital. She thought, surely, one of the priests would take pity on her and bury her, even though she was not Catholic. So the gasp was an expression of surprise."

"Didn't they know I was a woman?"

"Honestly, when I talked to you, I'd been on the phone looking for someone to do her service for hours. I was so grateful when you said 'Yes,' I only told the family that your name was Reverend Cham. I let them discover that you were a woman."

"Well, some of the most forward looking people, women included, hang onto the traditional image of male clergy. Sometimes they're convinced it's biblical. Sometimes they haven't experienced a woman in the pulpit. Sometimes with constant change in their lives, they cling to male pastors, as anchors in this fast-changing world."

Jerry and I shook hands and he walked to the hearse. As he pulled away he waved from his open window and made a fist with his thumb up. I'm sure he meant, "You go, girl."

I felt the cold and pulled up the collar on my coat and headed back to the church. I laughed to myself as I pictured the relatives on their ride back to western Massachusetts shaking their heads.

"Can you believe it? With all her plans — a woman."

TWO WEEKS LATER, THE local Catholic funeral home called. "Reverend Cham, Richard Byers from Pine Funeral Home."

"Hey. Richard. How's the Catholic world of wakes and funerals?"

He laughed. "I have an unusual request. Gus Franchetti, my friend for years, called me to his house the other day. He said, 'Richard, you know my mind is clear and I'm not dead yet, right?' I nodded and saw the glint in his eye. 'I want a Protestant clergy woman to conduct my service in your funeral home.'"

"Really?" I straightened up in my chair.

"Yes. Then Gus laughed and elbowed my side. 'All I need,

Richard, is a simple service — a few prayers and the Twenty-third Psalm. With the shock of a woman, the family won't hear any other words.'"

"He's probably right." I agreed.

"Reverend Cham, are you available to do his service?"

"Sure, I'll do the service." I paused while we both enjoyed the idea of Gus's rebellious act. "I'm sorry I never knew Gus. I think we would have had a laugh or two."

"You've got that right. Is ten on Friday morning good with you?"

"That's fine. I'll be there robed and collared." I saved wearing a collar for special occasions when I needed to let others know that I was ordained clergy.

I put together the service and practiced crossing myself and showed up at the Catholic funeral home. I knelt before Gus. I rose and faced the assembled friends and family. Richard introduced me.

"I'm honored to be here to celebrate the life of Gus Franchetti. The Lord be with you."

"And also with you." Some eyes rolled, and others stared wondering, "What is she doing here?" Others grinned and elbowed each other as if they knew some secret. I shared readings and prayers. The group stumbled through the words to the Twenty-third Psalm.

After the service, several guests greeted me with "Nice service." Others scooted out as quickly as possible, maybe feeling like they needed confession for even sitting through the service with a Protestant, and a woman, no less. One older gentleman waited until all were gone. With his large rosary wrapped through his fingers he stepped toward me with his walker and shook my hand. "Gus got in one last shot, didn't he? I knew he'd find a way of getting back at the church for having to eat fish every Friday." He winked and went on his way

Richard helped me with my coat. I left feeling Gus by my side saying, "Thanks." I wondered if Gus had met up with Maude Denning yet.

NOT A WOMAN! A lifetime earlier I would have said, "Not a woman!" too. Church had always been a positive in my life even though it was dominated by men...men pastors, ushers and deacons. I said, "God the Father," like the rest of the church.

When I entered seminary and heard the sound of shrill whistles each time the professors used the male gender for God, I bristled. Raising three children in a small town in Iowa, I was out of the feminist loop, but the first time a man asked me what I wear under my robes, I joined the movement.

When I counseled a woman who had been abused by her father, she said, "I can have nothing to do with a God called Father. The word father creates for me only negative feelings. I need to call God something else." After her personal struggle I rarely referred to God as Father in worship. I introduced the congregation to the hundreds of other images of God in scripture.

YEARS LATER, A CATHOLIC man came early to a wedding I was officiating to see a woman minister. He sat in the back pew. Before the service I was tending to details in the sanctuary. Dressed in my street clothes, I welcomed him. He said, "I came to see a woman do this service. I'm sitting here in case I want to leave early."

After the service, with me all decked out in my robes, he stood close. "I attend mass each morning. I'm going to tell the guys we need to support women to be priests in the Catholic Church." He patted my shoulder and using his cane walked down the front steps of the church.

THE NAMES OF GUS FRANCHETTI and Maude Denning bring a smile to my heart with their differing opinions of women clergy. Did their variety of needs bother me? No. I admired their chutzpah.

No One Knew Her

I LINGERED AT MY desk contemplating the weekend. My eldest son Mike was coming home from college and we had tickets to see the Red Sox. I'd been to the grocery and bought his favorites and I could hear his siblings, Maureen and Dave tease, "Special food for Mike, huh?" I grabbed my purse, stood and reached for the switch to turn out the lights when the phone rang. I sat back down and answered.

"Reverend, we are not part of your church. A friend told us you would help us. A hospice worker is with our mother Lily, so we thought we'd better call." The caller rattled off these words without a breath.

"I'm so sorry. How can I help?"

Silence.

I added, "I know this is hard. Would it be easier if I came over?"

The voice shot back. "Oh, no, if you came, we'd know she's dying. We will call you on Monday." I shrugged, turned off my office lights and headed home.

Sunday afternoon the call came. Lily had died a few hours before and they wanted me to meet with them at one the next afternoon.

MONDAY AT 1 P.M. I parked in front of their white Cape Cod house with navy shutters and admired a well-trimmed yard. The daughter, son and husband welcomed me at the door with cool handshakes. They directed me to a chair. The father sat across from me in a tall wing chair. Son and daughter shared the sofa to my left, one at each end. I looked around. No signs of death. No flowers. No casserole dishes in the kitchen. As I settled into my chair, I spoke softly and carefully. "I'm sorry for your loss."

Heads moved a little, and the father opened his mouth to speak but stopped. The daughter rescued him. "We talked with our friends at the funeral home. They will take care of mother."

"What arrangements have you made?"

"No visiting hours. A service at the church. The casket will stay at the funeral home and she will be cremated later." The daughter recited as if she had rehearsed the lines.

I sensed in their body language their shock at Lily's death. I decided not to pry. The conversation went on for thirty minutes about the hot summer, how long I'd been a pastor, and the brother's interest in film. With the mention of the brother producing a film, their bodies relaxed a little. The conversation left me knowing little about the one who had died.

BACK AT THE OFFICE, I found a message on my desk. "Call me. I knew Lily. Bobbie."

As I dialed Bobbie, a church member who knew something about almost everyone in town, I stared at the word 'Lily' at the top of a blank pad on my desk. "Hi Bobbie, how are you?"

Bobbie dismissed small talk and shot directly to the reason she'd called. "Lily was quiet. She played golf with the ladies at the club for years and was always pleasant. Lily was very nice."

"Bobbie, don't you have a story or an experience you've had with Lily? Isn't there more to her than nice?" Bobbie stammered.

"That's it, I guess. I thought I knew more about her, but I really don't know what to add."

I wrote nice and pleasant under the word Lily. "Are there others at the golf club that might have more to tell me about Lily?" Bobbie gave me several names and phone numbers of women who might have known Lily better. I called each of them. "Lily was such a nice person." They offered nothing more.

I REFUSED TO GIVE up. I called the family and invited myself over for another visit. Again the house was spotless. Again no signs that anyone had died. I searched for common ground to build some trust and generate easier conversation. I asked them about their work, where they lived and how long they had lived in town. They responded to these questions, but after every inquiry about Lily, a wall of silence went up and the stiffness of their bodies read: PRIVATE.

As I sat stymied, I noticed a painting that reminded me of Isak Dinesen author of *Out of Africa*. I stood and walked over to the painting. The daughter joined me. "That's our mother, a self-portrait. She was an artist, you know." I didn't know.

Very gently I asked permission to see her studio. I spent several hours in the studio of a woman whom no one seemed to know, but everyone thought was 'a very nice person.'

The room caught the light of early morning. Her working palette, covered with earthy colors of browns and greens and a tube of blue, lay on a table. I found her portfolio on the well-ordered shelves that lined her studio. Gentle brush strokes created soft images on each canvas. The warm landscapes and the shy eyes looking out from each portrait gave hints about the soul of the artist. I soaked in what my senses told me was the essence of Lily…their mother…his wife.

The day before the funeral I drove over and checked in with the family. "I know you have requested no visiting at the funeral home and you have said that you have no need to view the body, but would you mind if I went to see Lily?"

The daughter said, "Do you really want to?"

"Yes, seeing Lily will give me a more complete picture of her."

The husband, son, and daughter passed nervous glances at each other. The daughter whispered, "That will be fine."

THE MORNING OF THE service I rose early to review my notes. The family had mentioned nothing of their faith or belief. I relied on my own understanding of God to affirm the resurrection of Lily's soul. I chose words of comfort and assurance from scripture and special readings. I hoped I had captured Lily.

I dressed and was about to leave the house for the funeral home when the telephone rang. "Reverend Cham. We've decided to meet you at the funeral home."

As I climbed out of my car into the parking lot, I met the family. We walked in silence to the door where their friend, the funeral director, met us and ushered us inside. They stood barely inside the door. I asked, "Would you like to approach the casket with me?"

They froze out of fear, out of grief, out of what I don't know, but I hugged each of them and assured them it was okay. I went forward and had a few minutes with Lily, small and even in death, a beautiful woman who looked as if she'd walked out of one of Dinesen's books.

At the church I robed while they waited in the vestry. We climbed the back stairs to the sanctuary. I escorted them in and they sat in the front row. I glanced out as I climbed the three stairs to the pulpit. To my surprise the church was full. I took my seat. The organist played Handel's *Water Music.* I shared words of greeting from the United Church of Christ Book of Worship

> Friends, we gather here in the protective shelter of God's healing love. We are free to pour out our grief, release our anger, face our emptiness, and know that God cares.
>
> We gather here as God's people, conscious of others who have died and of the frailty of our own existence on earth. We come to comfort and to support one another in our common loss.
>
> We gather to hear God's word of hope that can drive away our despair and move us to offer God our praise.
>
> We gather to commend to God with thanksgiving the life of Lily, as we celebrate the good news of Christ's resurrection.
>
> For whether we live or whether we die, we belong to Christ who is Lord both of the dead and of the living.3

And I added my chosen scriptures. To honor Lily's artist's eye, I read from Dinesen. To describe Lily, as I came to know her, I shared,

A Portrait

by Elizabeth Barrett Browning

> And her voice, it murmurs lowly,
> As a silver stream may run,
> Which yet feels (you feel) the sun.
> And her smile it seems half holy,
> As if drawn from thoughts more far
> Than our common jestings are.
> And if any poet knew her,

He would sing of her with falls
Used in lovely madrigals.
And a stranger, when he sees her
In the street even smiles
Just as you would at a lily.
And all voices that address her,
Soften, sleeken every word,
As if speaking to a bird.
And all fancies yearn to cover
The hard earth, whereon she passes,
With the thyme-scented grasses.
And all hearts do pray, "God love her!"
Ay and always, in good sooth,
We may all be sure He Doth.4

Family and friend left the service saying, "You captured exactly who she was."

I DROVE HOME PLEASED and sad; pleased that I'd captured exactly who she was and sad that no one could tell me about her with their own words.

The Funeral for Anyone

THE SUMMER HEAT HAD taken the air out of my office. I opened the door to the elevated porch and walked out and stood looking at the tops of the two-hundred-year-old trees and then down into the cemetery with graves going back over two centuries. I yelled back to Carol, my secretary. "Carol, come out and feel the fresh air."

"You know that the height of that porch scares me."

"Oh, come on." A call coming in saved her.

"Marcia, it's the Sumner Funeral Home."

I left the door open and returned to my desk. "Reverend Cham. Charlie Sumner."

"Hi, Charlie."

"Margaret Elias died. Roy, a member of your church and one of our greeters, thinks she is connected to your congregation."

"The name isn't familiar. Let me check." I reached for the church roster in the center drawer of my desk. "Charlie, she's not part of our community."

"But can you help us anyhow tomorrow morning?"

"Sure, Charlie. Can you give me some contact numbers so I might arrange to meet or at least talk with the family before the service?"

"They are not interested in talking with whomever I find to do the service. The daughter said, 'Just have the person read words of comfort.'"

I TURNED TO MY computer. A string of prayers, scriptures, and words of comfort filled the screen. I filed the document under the name "The Funeral for Anyone." I saved it. I tried to imagine a family that had no interest in honoring the dead with at least a few personal words or a story. I wondered why.

AT THE FUNERAL HOME the next morning, Roy opened my car door. "Glad you could make it, Rev." He lowered his voice. "Just to clue you in — when I directed the early arrivals where to park, they pulled up and backed in. Then the others arrived and I motioned for them to park next to the last car. The latecomer rolled down the window of his pick-up and yelled, 'I wouldn't park next to that car if you paid me. He's a jerk.'" Roy took my elbow and escorted me to the door.

The funeral director hung up my coat. I walked into the viewing room. Margaret Elias lay there with a string of rosary beads wound through her fingers and holding the huge cross in her hands. I knelt. My gut turned as I clutched onto the pages of the *Funeral for Anyone* I held in my hand. I whispered, "Margaret, I can't do this without knowing something about you."

I stood and walked behind the lectern and looked out. Rows of empty chairs stood between what seemed to be family units. A wide aisle down the center of the room separated the groups even further. I laid my folder on the lectern and walked toward the nearest family unit. I introduced myself with, "I'm sorry for your loss," an icy "Hello," and a simple, "Oh," greeted me.

I crossed the wide aisle to the other group. I met the same cold reception. "Pastor. Oh. Hello." No effect. No physical contact.

I returned to the lectern. I opened my folder, "The Funeral for Anyone." I fingered the papers. I looked toward the isolated pods. Blank eyes stared into space. Sadness for Margaret invaded my spirit. I wanted to shout, "What happened? What happened to divide you? Do you even remember?"

I glanced down. In the front rows sat five small children, legs swinging from their chairs. I bet these young ones have something to say about their great-grandmother. I know my children at a young age would have had stories to share. I approached the children.

"Hi, I'm Reverend Marcia. I'm here to celebrate your Great-grandmother Margaret Elias."

"Hi," they said in unison and squirmed in their seats.

"Can you tell me what you loved about your great-grandmother…what made her special?"

The first two girls squeezed each other hands. "She hugged me when I visited her." "She played games with me."

The little boy in the middle waved his hand to me. "She made special cookies after school."

A bashful girl in pink swung her legs and twisted her fingers and then wound her legs around the chair. "She told me stories."

The child who appeared to be the oldest smiled into my eyes. "She gave me a special doll. I named it Grandma Margaret."

I hugged each of the children and returned to the lectern.

I breathed in a prayer. God, be with me and these children as I honor Margaret. May something said here soften the hearts of the adults.

I read my prepared words and included the phrases from the children. Each child smiled and wiggled more at the mention of their words. The adults remained stoic.

At the end of the service, the parents snatched up their children. Family units filed out of the room and marched to their cars and trucks. Engines revved up. They left as they'd come, family baggage in hand. I prayed for the children to be instruments of healing among their families.

As I EXITED THE funeral home parking lot, I pounded on the steering wheel, frustrated. "Why did they bother to have a service? Nobody showed love or care for Margaret except the children. The words of comfort bounced off the adults and slid down onto the thick carpeting. Couldn't they have pulled together for a moment or two for the children? Did it matter that I cared?"

I gunned out of the parking lot mumbling to myself, "Hey, Marcia you need to calm yourself." I pulled into Dunkin' Donuts. There's nothing like a sweet to soothe my frustrations. I opened the car door and slammed it but my clerical robe, hung haphazardly in the back, caught in the door. I pulled it open, pushed my robe aside and successfully slammed it shut. I stood in line and ordered my coffee and a toasted coconut cake donut. I sat at a table and stared out the window at the traffic crowding its way down Route 18.

The stream of traffic drew me back thirty years, when helpless and angry, I vented to Ken as we drove home from Mom Mitchell's funeral.

"How dare he barely mention MY grandmother's name? Did you see him look at an index card and read her name and then slip the card under his notes? The minister didn't care about Mom. He didn't care about MY grandmother."

Ken tried to interrupt. "I…"

"Wait, I'm not done. I listened for the scriptures she loved. Nothing. I listened for stories about her love of nature. Nothing. For stories about her Bible schools, her sewing for the church, her three sons and grandchildren. Nothing. His eulogy — strung together platitudes — that could have been for anyone." I pounded my feet on the floor of the car.

"Maybe he didn't…" Ken attempted again.

"Our family cared. He could have asked. All of us had stories. He didn't even ask."

"Maybe no one offered."

"He should have asked." I paused, exhausted and my anger as hot as the August day. "He looked pious…miles above the grief that sat in front of him. Didn't he care who she was?"

A man ordering a large coffee with double cream and sugar brought me back to Dunkin' Donuts and the traffic on Route 18. I pulled my donut apart and ate it slowly with alternating gulps of coffee. I mused. "Isn't it ironic that I cared and Margaret's family didn't?" The revelation caught me mid-gulp. I felt a hand on my shoulder and heard Mom's voice.

"I can still feel your anger and frustration at that man. A teaching, wasn't it?"

"Yes, his bad example taught me to work to capture the essence of the ones whose lives I'm privileged to celebrate. I don't want anyone leaving a service wondering who died." My mind spoke to Mom as if she stood right beside me whispering in my ear,

"Honey, you would have done that anyway, but it is a reminder, isn't it?" Mom's presence let go of my shoulder and a breeze fluttered by my eyes. I rummaged through my pocketbook for a pen, a piece of paper, anything I could write on. Through my tears I found a ballpoint and reached for the extra napkin under my donut. I wrote,

> Mom, when you folded paper and made
> a string of paper dolls, and orchestrated
> games like "Thimble, Thimble, who has the
> Thimble" and "Fanny Duster" with simple
> props, you taught me simplicity.

> When you guided walks in the woods to
> see the blossoms under the May apples'
> umbrella leaves and the spores hidden on the
> moss, you showed me the wonders of God's
> creation.

Through your sewing at church and your at-the-farm Bible School, you showed me your heart in action.

Your living faith, joy in the simple things, and strength have mentored me and my life.

I folded the napkin and laid it carefully in my purse. I drove home feeling lighter.

DURING MY PRAYER THE next morning, something, maybe the hand of God or Mom, guided me to two scriptures, two scriptures for me to remember when stranger meets stranger.

Love the stranger,
for you were once strangers in Egypt.
Deuteronomy 10:19

Remember always to welcome strangers, for by
doing that some people have entertained
angels without knowing it.
Hebrews 13:2

I talked to Mom in my heart. Maude, Gus, Lily, and Margaret's great-grandchildren came into my life as strangers. I served them and they, along with you, have lived alongside me these many years…angels in disguise. Thanks.

A Good Death

Life's not a journey to the grave
with the intention of arriving safely
in a pretty and well-preserved body,
but rather to skid in sideways,
thoroughly used up,
totally worn out,
and loudly proclaiming
"Wow- what a Ride!"[5]

A Beer in Twilight Zone

THE CHURCH STAFF CELEBRATED my birthday with a surprise lunch at the Lobster Shack. Back at the office hints of lobster rose to my nose as I worked on a sermon. The intercom buzzed. I heard Betty Ann's voice on the other end. "Two things: I have lemon spray for your hands and you have a call on line two."

"Marcia, this is Matt McNeilly. We've met a couple of times but you may not know me except as one whose name has a permanent place on the prayer list." Betty Ann tiptoed into my office with the lemon spray. I held my hands out; she sprayed, flashed me a pleased look and went back to her office.

Matt cleared his throat. "I don't like to talk about my cancer, but I need to. Can you come this afternoon?"

"I'd be happy to come over." I rubbed my hands and checked for lobster odor.

"I need someone with some God connections."

"God connections, huh? I'll do my best."

I ARRIVED AT MATT'S house late that afternoon. He met me at the door and showed me into the dimly lit living room. He motioned to two blue club chairs and we sat facing each other. He leaned back and clasped his hands behind his head, extended his legs and crossed them at the ankles. "My wife Flo says you're not a typical pastor." Matt looked at me over his glasses. "You know, stiff, pious and humorless — all trussed up in a dark suit and heavy black shoes." His stereotypical description of a pastor amused me as I looked down at my jeans, sweater and western boots. "I've heard you like a good joke and have been known to have a beer or two."

"That's right. And I suppose you've heard me referred to as the irreverent reverend."

"I have." Matt lifted two four-inch blue binders off the table beside him. He placed them on the floor between us. "These notebooks tell my story. Every organ in my body has been invaded by the stuff, the crud as I call it. My insides have been fried by radiation and screwed up by chemo."

I started to interrupt, but Matt was on a roll. I settled back in my chair and listened for nearly three hours as Matt described his career, his marriage and children, and the recent prognosis about his cancer.

"I have dodged the bullets for years. Yesterday I was told the final bullet is in the chamber. Of course, I'd rather have many more years, but I've had a good run." He picked his right thumb nail and unconsciously tapped his left foot on the pile of notebooks. "Flo has the crud too, you know." I didn't know.

He folded his hand over his chest. "Those of us waiting for treatment are a real community. No masks. No pretension. No lies. We talk about our fears and regrets. The black humor is really sick."

Matt scratched at a sore on his arm. "Flo took me to the ocean the other day. I've tried to discuss my death with her, but I just can't. I don't want to bring both of us down." He leaned forward in his chair. "Anyhow, I think I'm coping pretty well. I lean on my 'waiting room family.' They listen and let me stay on the pity pot for a while and then some joker brings me back with a sick joke and the laughter takes the edge off. I don't believe healthy people would understand; they'd be nervous with us making jokes about our burns, our yellow skin and our gaunt eyes."

"I believe you're right. Matt, I can't imagine being this together if death were staring me in the face." He shrugged.

"Say Marcia, did you ever hear the saying, angels can fly because they take themselves lightly?"

I nodded no.

"Going to dark places and falling into depression isn't me. I need to be light. Maybe I'll be an angel one day, albeit one with tarnished wings." He laughed and leaned his head on the back of the chair and then wiped his brow with the handkerchief he found in his back pocket. He winked and picked up the two binders and returned them to the table near his chair. "That's all folks," he said mimicking Bugs Bunny. "Thanks for listening. I'll call you again."

"Thank you for sharing."

Matt showed me out. I chuckled at Matt's Bugs Bunny voice while opening the door to my car. I never expected that conversation from Matt. A level of trust has been established. Must be my jeans, I laughed to myself.

A FEW WEEKS LATER Matt found his way to my office in the basement of the church. He walked around examining little trinkets: a marionette-like witch, a container of shells, and a Buddhist bell. He picked up the bell and stroked it and listened to the tone whisper off into nothing. Then he stood studying the work camp photos on my bookshelf. "Flo told me about the grief you've taken for traveling out of the area with the teens for work camp."

"Yes, some grumble to me that there's plenty of need around here closer to home. Others grouse, about the Navajo Nation and present their stereotypic arguments about alcohol abuse on Reservations. They think the decisions for the work camp should be in their hands and not mine and certainly not with the youth."

"Rough group."

"Yes, they don't care to listen to the value of working in other cultures."

"Flo came unglued over the adults who criticized you for teaching the teens to be open and non-judgmental of kids wearing Jesus jackets."

"Right. Before each work camp I remind our youth that we will be with teens from a wide spectrum of theologies… those who are considering Christ and those who witness by wearing jackets with 'Jesus Saves' across the back. Some of our parents fear the more demonstrative faith will rub off on their kids and then they'll have to talk about their faith. I swear some of them find it easier to talk about sex than faith. So each year the rift continues."

"Those types of squabbles are why I hang around at the fringes of the church. If I got caught up in the politics, I'd lose what faith I do have."

Matt moved to a grouping of chairs in the corner of my office and sat. I pulled a pile of books off the other chair and joined him. He looked serious and rubbed the sores on his balding head. "Does anyone stand outside the love of God?"

An opening for God-talk. The past few weeks he'd skillfully skirted the topic. Now, what to say? I knew platitudes would not do. "Matt, maybe a story will answer your question."

A boy shamed his Dad by demanding his
inheritance and then ran off and squandered
Dad's hard earned money on drink and
wild living. He ended up on the street in
tattered clothes. When threatened with jail,
he thought of his Dad. He yelled. "I can't
live like this. I am going home. I'll take my
punishment." As he came along the familiar
streets, his Dad's friends' saw the young man
and rubbed their hands in delight, thinking
now he would get what's coming to him.
His Dad saw his son, whom he thought was
dead, coming up the road. He grabbed his
robe and picked it up above his knees — an
act in the time of Jesus that robbed him of
his dignity — and ran as fast as he could
down the street to meet his son. He hugged
his son. He gave him a ring and threw a huge
party to welcome him home.

"I've heard that story before but not with your spin. I get
it. No one is outside God's love, are they?"

"No one."

Matt and I met periodically. He wasn't someone to crowd.
He talked and I listened, always in my jeans. One day when I
arrived at his house, his boys were building a wheelchair ramp.
An awkward feeling hung over the yard. Their joke that Dad
could freewheel down the ramp to his car fell flat. While the
boys completed their work, he led me inside and pointed at
the hospital bed that dominated the dining room. "I won't be
horizontal on that bed until the day I die."

THREE DAYS LATER MATT called the office. "Marcia, it's
time we have that beer. I'll pick you up in a few minutes." I lingered at my desk, fiddled with some papers and rearranged the
family photos that rested to one side of a gooseneck desk lamp.
I studied the picture of Ken looking relaxed in a small silver
frame. "Ken, how does he do it? If I were in his shoes…"

My secretary buzzed. I made my way up the stairs to her
office. She said, "Matt's out front." She shrugged her shoulders.
"Can you believe he's still driving?"

Matt and I sipped our beers at Stars on the Harbor. His sparkling eyes met mine. "Isn't this something like out of Twilight Zone? Death is on my door step and yet, here we are having a beer as if I had all the time in the world."

"It's weird. Here's to how you are living your dying." We raised our mugs, touched them lightly against each other and drank.

"This is the way I wanted life to end, not going inch by inch in a bed with tubes, but drinking beer with friends."

TWO DAYS PASSED AND Flo called. "Matt died a few hours ago. He sat at the table with us and picked at the spaghetti and sipped a little beer. He climbed into the hospital bed and said, 'I feel a little weak.' He died a few hours later."

As Flo talked an image of Matt meeting God flashed in my mind, and I heard Matt say, "Thanks for the blessing of a good death. Where's the beer?"

That evening as I watched TV with Ken, I pondered to myself, would I ever think of death as good?

Gladys and the Crocus

I WALKED THROUGH THE snow from the mailbox to the parsonage flipping through a seed catalog. I opened the door and answered the phone on the first ring. I heard Jean's voice. "Mom's gone."

"I'll be right over."

"It's okay. Take your time. We're alright."

I SAT ON THE SOFA with the latest seed catalogs and thought about the first time I'd met Gladys. She was in her mid-eighties, officially a shut-in according to our church list. She looked at me from her recliner that sat near the picture window of her house. Devilment shone through the lenses of her overlarge glasses that magnified her eyes. "Women pastors. I don't know what the church is coming to."

She decorated her house with family photos, hand-hooked rugs created by her sister, and original paintings by her daughter. Her recliner sat where she could keep an eye on the street and anyone coming into the driveway. A table placed conveniently next to her recliner held recent correspondence, a box of stationery, the local paper opened to the obituaries, and the telephone, her primary connection to the outside world.

Conversations always included something about gardening. "The latest seed catalogues arrived." "Did you see the bulbs poking through the ground as you walked up the driveway? See how the Amaryllis is growing. It will be in bloom soon." When I admitted to never having tasted a fresh pea right out of the garden, she looked aghast. "Never." She laughed and slapped her knee in disbelief.

On my walks that passed Gladys' house on the hottest days of the summer, I'd stand and watch her use her walker to reach one of the white plastic chairs, she'd strategically set throughout her yard and gardens. She'd back into the chair and put her walker to one side then proceed to weed and trim. After a while I'd say, "Gladys, you're not supposed to be out here in this heat." She'd shrug her shoulders and grin at me through her glasses that had slipped down her nose wet with perspiration.

"Don't tell Jean on me."

Gladys was as hard-packed as the New England soil in the heat of summer, as prickly as the wild blackberry plants that stretched out along the fences in her back yard and as sneaky as the rabbits that ate the roots of her bulbs.

I SET THE SEED CATALOG aside and went into the kitchen and warmed a cup of coffee in the microwave. I returned to the sofa and reviewed the last few days with Gladys.

After the hospital bed arrived and hospice came, Gladys curled up on the bed in what had been her dining room. "It's not good. I wanted to see the bulbs bloom once again." She closed her almost 95-year-old eyes. "Oh well..." Jean and I looked at each other knowing what she said was true. Discouragement lay heavy on her.

The next day her granddaughter Laurie arrived. She hugged Jean and sat near Gladys. Gladys listened to Laurie's stories of life in San Diego. "I'm going to miss the spring bulbs showing off in my yard," Gladys told her and slipped into sleep. Laurie unpacked her bags and we shared lunch.

LATER THAT AFTERNOON LAURIE noticed the bright yellow boot-shaped ceramic planter on top of the television set. She brought it near Gladys. "Gram, look at the crocus Lenore brought you."

Gladys raised her eyebrows. "Lenore?"

"Lenore, you know, the church deacon who visits you." Gladys acknowledged the tightly budded crocus with a fragile smile.

After a restless night, she awoke agitated with fright in her eyes. She spoke to Laurie and Jean in a low parched voice. "You're treating me special. I'm not special." Her eyes widened and a deep sadness set in.

Laurie and Jean huddled on the edge of the bed. Laurie reached under Gladys and hugged her weak body next to hers. "You are special, Gram. I am here because of you." Jean touched her mother's face.

"Mom, you've supported me all my life. You stay in contact with your friends. And think of all the time you spend with Duke, your man-friend. I know he sees you as his special friend."

Gladys squeezed Jean's hand. "Really, I'm special?"

Laurie rolled her back on the bed and fixed her pillow. Gladys glowed and her face relaxed. A paraphrase of II Corinthians 4:16 floated through my mind. Her outer nature was wasting away, but her inner nature was being renewed and revealed. Somehow this hard-packed, prickly New Englander was opening her private emotions to be seen by those she loved.

The next morning she woke with a calmer countenance. "I saw the light. It's beautiful! It's beautiful! Tell everybody I saw people. I saw my parents. It's okay."

As I leaned over her bed, she waved her hands around her face. "Marcia, I saw angels. Some angels buzzed close to my eyes, some floated far away, some looked like doctors, and others prevented me from moving."

Later in the afternoon Laurie noticed the fear again deep in her grandmother's eyes. She climbed into bed with her and held her. Gladys turned her head to the side and checked the crocus.

I STRETCHED AND PULLED myself from the sofa. Those had been amazing few days for Gladys, Jean, Laurie and me. Now I needed to go to the house and hear the story of last moments of Gladys's life.

I returned my coffee cup to the kitchen and pulled on my coat and boots. I walked up the driveway dodging the deep snow and down the almost cleared sidewalk to Gladys' house. Jean saw me coming and opened the door. We hugged. "Thanks for coming. Throw your coat on the chair and let me tell you about this morning."

I took off my coat and walked over to Gladys' still body. Laurie and Jean stood behind me. I reached for Gladys' hand. "I'll miss your quick spirit and your eyes that sparkled with devilment. I'll miss your gardens and those white plastic chairs." I turned and we walked to the sofa where I sat with Jean. Laurie took Gladys' recliner. Jean picked up a throw pillow and held it on her lap.

"The hospice nurse checked Mom's signs early this morning and said it would be soon. After a few minutes of the reality sinking in, I noticed the crocus had opened. I held the boot-shaped pot where Mom could see it." Jean paused. "Her eyes focused on it for a moment. The sun broke through the cloud cover. I looked down and she was gone." A tear coursed down Jean's face as she reached for my hand. "Mom had a good death."

A FEW DAYS AFTER the funeral, Jean met me in the church parking lot. She moved a case of Brooklyn Lager Beer from her trunk to mine. "Wouldn't it be something if the East Bridgewater police drove up now?"

I shut my trunk and leaned on the lid. "I'd just point to you and say, 'she's trying to give up beer. I'm keeping it for her.'" I leaned against my car, she against her truck.

"How are you doing?"

"Right now I am doing fine. Those last days were pretty special." She looked down and kicked her feet against the wheel of her truck. "I'd never seen anything like it."

"That doesn't happen all the time. My body chills every time I picture Gladys' face lighting up, realizing she really mattered."

Jean rubbed her hands together and we stood in silence. Then she said, "Join me for lunch in a couple of weeks. My treat."

"Sounds good." My eyes followed Jean as she climbed in her truck and I waved as she turned out of the driveway.

I looked at my watch. I'm late. I drove to the Rectory of St. John's Catholic Church. Father Jack and Bernie, the deacon, stood in the parking lot with their hands on the kneeler we were borrowing for confirmation.

"Hey, Reverend," Bernie directed me to a particular parking spot. "Open your trunk." I stopped as I reached for the automatic trunk opening button. The beer. Oh well. The trunk popped open. By the time I joined Bernie and Jack, they were in stitches.

"The Reverend is now carrying cases of beer." Bernie quipped with an English accent. "Is that a Protestant thing?"

I started to explain but they waved away my explanation. "We'll create our own story." They loaded a kneeler in my trunk and were bent over laughing when I looked at them in my rear view window.

Gladys, are you enjoying this?

Life — A Curious Adventure

KEN AND I JUMPED for the telephone each time it rang. We were expecting our first grandchildren — twins. When it rang, I grabbed it. "Are they here?"

"No, they aren't here yet." Mike announced. "But Mom can you come down to Stamford and sit with Maggie?"

"Sure. What day do you want me?"

"Tomorrow?"

"I'll be there on the 4 p.m. train." I packed and Ken drove me to the train.

I joined Maggie, now confined to bed rest for fear of an early delivery. She and I visited and watched TV. The next morning, she noticed some contractions. We called the doctor, put her suitcase in the car and headed to the hospital. Mike met us there. The babies were born a few hours later. Mike came out to the waiting room still in his scrubs. "Mom, come with me I want to introduce you to the BOYS."

Arm in arm we walked to the viewing window. "That one all stretched out under the warming lamp is Bertram Mitchell Cham. And the little guy scrunched up in the blanket is Harrison Edward." I cannot explain the emotions that stirred deep in my heart.

"They're perfect, Mike." I stood with my nose and hands pressed on the viewing window. Mike touched my shoulder.

"Grandma, I need to be with Maggie. Have you called Dad?"

I turned and smiled, enjoying my new name. "I've been keeping him informed. He's on his way. I'll call and let him know they're here. I'll check in with Maggie's folks, too."

In the waiting room, I made the calls. Ken and I celebrated over the phone and Ken added. "I'm in Connecticut only a few more exits to go. By the way Doris called. Ernie died early this morning. I told her you'd call as soon as you could." In the excitement I didn't call Doris until the next day.

"Doris, I'm sorry. How were his last few hours?"

"Quiet and peaceful" Silence filled the space between us.

"Doris, remember the day when Ernie said, 'I've been in a warm bright tunnel of light. I thought I might see the spirits of the twins coming into life."

Doris, without a pause, followed right on my words. "Yes.

He knew the twins were expected soon and with his curious nature..." I heard Doris crying and waited.

I finished Doris' sentence. "...the close connection of him leaving this life and the twins coming made him wonder. I'll keep you in my prayers and see you in a few days."

"I know you will," Doris sighed.

Before leaving Connecticut to be with Doris, I held the twins and wondered if they'd seen Ernie's spirit as they came into this world. I marveled at the miracle of birth and returned home to the reality of death.

ERNIE AND DORIS ATTENDED the church where I served as Christian Educator while I studied for the ordained ministry. Ernie sang pieces from Mendelssohn's *Elijah* when I gave my first sermon and also at my ordination to become Associate Pastor of the church. Ken and I sat next to Doris the first time we visited the church and over the years became like family. Each time I stopped at their home for lunch, Ernie cooked, honoring a retirement agreement between them.

"I have turkey sandwiches today, and we'll have ice cream with a little crème de menthe on top for dessert." He winked. "I can't be serving you too much since you have to go back to work." Conversation included political controversies in the *Boston Globe*, stories of their latest trip to the symphony and what they saw at the theater. We talked as we sat at the kitchen table looking out the window watching the trees turn with the seasons.

On a visit during the last months of Ernie's life, he sat in the gold wingback chair angled in the corner of their living room in his uniform, a white dress shirt, slacks and a light yellow golf sweater. Ernie quoted words from Mendelssohn's, *Elijah*,[6]

> It is enough, O Lord. Now take away my
> life. I desire to live no longer. Let me die.
> Yet...I am on my way on the strength of the
> Lord. O, that, I now might die. O, that, I now
> might die.

I listened from a rocker across the room. He let some silence rest between us. Then he sang in a weak but lovely voice,

O rest in the Lord, Wait patiently for him,
and he shall give thee thy hearts desire...
Commit thy ways unto him and trust him.
O rest in the Lord. Wait patiently for him.

My heart skipped as I rocked. He leaned his head back and removed his glasses, wiped them on a white linen handkerchief and replaced them on his face adjusting the ear pieces. "Now that I have made peace, I can think of dying as another curious adventure, another curious part of the movie of my life that God set in motion some 85 years ago. As the movie comes to a close, I don't want to miss anything. I want to understand the changes in my body and understand how it shuts down. I want to plan the service. I want to hear something of what will be said about me."

Doris shared his curiosity, welcomed visiting guests, and arranged for his niece to write his eulogy and read it to Ernie. She found a friend to bathe him and Ernie and Doris lingered longer in bed. "Savoring the time," they both said.

Hospice workers kept him informed about the changes in his body, from the gradual shutting down to the end. "We love our time with Ernie and Doris. Their warm welcome and genuine curiosity is a blessing in our work," they said.

During the last weeks of his life, as Ernie slept one afternoon, Doris and I visited on the sun porch with our coffee. Doris took a paper from the table. "I wrote this while I watched Ernie sleep yesterday." She read.

As I look at my husband
Who is nearing the end of his life
Who knows so many things
About so much...
Names of actors, playwrights, music,
Answers to Jeopardy, how to build a house
I know that all that does not, cannot
Just disappear with ashes.
Somewhere there is a plan
That only God knows.

Stillness filled the sun room. Doris folded the paper and laid it back on the table. "Do you think it will all disappear? You were a biology teacher and now a pastor. Does the essence of the person become energy in the universe?"

"Possibly. Science says that matter and energy can be neither created nor destroyed. And the prophets declare that God is creating all things new. So with all the kinds of energies that we know, and other forms of energy we have yet to discover, I hope that Ernie's energy and spirit will be part of and affect the universe for a long time to come."

"I want to believe that. I sure hope we get some answers to our questions when we die." Doris picked up her coffee and held the warm cup in her hands.

Now a few days after Ernie's death, with pictures of the twins spread over the table where Doris and Ernie and I lunched, Doris shared her immediate thoughts following Ernie's death. "In only a few moments it seemed that his physical body changed so much that I knew it was not my husband any more. His soul was set free." She paused as if letting me take this in. "Seeing the essence of Ernie leave his body made the dread of the undertaker arriving easier. He had a good death."

We sat looking at the barren trees outside the window. Doris cleared her throat and pushed her chair back and stood. "Tell me about the twins and Mike and Maggie while I make a pot of fresh coffee." I shared about holding the boys for the first time and the joy of the parents and grandparents. I told Doris about examining their feet to see if they had the Fulmer Foot, one webbed toe, from Ken's mother's side of the family.

She carried two cups of coffee to the table and sat down with a broad smile on her face. "After we knew Ernie was dead, my daughter and I observed a slight movement in his body. Startled, Meredith, a nurse you know, checked again — no vital signs. He moved again ever so slightly and by then we were really wondering what was happening. Then we looked under the sheet, and guess what?" She took a sip of coffee making me wait. "The air mattress was pulsing, the one that kept him comfortable. It was making him move. Meredith and I laughed with great relief. In death as in life Ernie provided us with humor."

"I love it. Ernie had the last word, didn't he?"

"And that didn't happen too much around here." Doris and I cleared the table and with a lingering hug, I left. While pulling away from their house, another car pulled up and I waved to other friends as they started up to the door to visit with Doris.

THE DAY OF THE funeral I filed into the pew with Doris's family. At the appropriate time, I walked to the lectern and told the story of Ernie in the yard with his super soaker water gun shooting at squirrels. And I shared Ernie's excitement over the annual Ernie Golf Tournament and his delight as he rolled out his first pastry crust in our kitchen.

At the end I said, "I'll miss Ernie, his curiosity, his zest for life, his presence in the choir. He lived the faith of which he sang. He rested in the Lord. He committed his life to the ways of God with patience, gentleness, compassion and generosity. He trusted God with his life. He knew when he'd had enough. His humor and love touched the soul of all he met. He had a good death. I thank God for Ernie's life and all he was and will continue to be to each of us."

AFTER THE FUNERAL, I returned home and sat in the quiet of our living room listening to Mendelssohn's *Elijah* and felt memories of Ernie finding a place to lodge in my soul. The chairs that I sit on for dinner each night are the same chairs where Ernie, Doris and I shared lunch and many talks. They are a reminder of the joy and warmth of this man and when the twins come and sit in them, I will wonder again if they saw each other as they entered this world and Ernie left it for another.

A Little Bourbon and A Little Water

B ARBARA'S CALL FOUND ME in the office of my new church. "Marcia, Mother died this morning."

Tears welled up in my eyes; I heard Helen's voice in my mind. "You have what it takes to be solo pastor. Good humor. Compassion. Empathy. A questioning mind."

Barbara, Helen's daughter, waited. "She loved you. Remember in the hallway after funeral service for Ernie, she made you promise to officiate at hers?"

"I remember, but Barbara, with my move and with your new pastor, officiating might be difficult. She has the right to deny my presence."

"Not if I insist on it."

HELEN SERVED ON THE committee that guided and supported my road to ordination. She read and critiqued my ordination paper. She participated in the Wednesday morning Bible study group. She and her friend Mary argued whenever they had the opportunity. "Is it faith before works or works before faith?"

She loved the prophets. "The original sandwich board boys," she called them. "They holler at us for justice. We need more justice education. A musical like *Jesus Christ Superstar* made from the prophet's fire and brimstone speeches might wake us up." Through faith-based and humorous discussions, we created a deep relationship of trust during her eight years in the Bible study group.

On a cold Saturday South Shore Hospital tracked me down and found me working with youth in Boston. "Helen Wollan is in the ICU with a heart attack. She's asking for you."

"What happened?"

"She was at a convenience store; a wind blew the door into her and knocked her down, all eighty pounds of her. They don't know if that caused the heart attack or not."

"I'll be there as soon as possible." I talked with the other adult leaders and then made my way to the hospital.

Helen grabbed for my hands the moment she heard my voice. I leaned against her bed. "You came." A little tear crept down her cheek. "I'm scared. They said I've had a heart attack."

She looked at me for confirmation of the news they'd given her.

With one hand I unzipped my jacket and threw it on the chair next to Helen's bed, while she kept the other in her grasp. "Yes, they told me you'd had a minor heart attack. A bit of a warning, I'd guess."

"I hope it's minor. It might be time for me to move to The Village at Duxbury. My house is getting to be too much and I don't want to be a burden to my children."

"I'm sure you aren't." She released my hands and motioned for the cup with a straw on her tray. I held it while she took a small drink.

"This must be a warning. When I get home, I'll see about selling my house." Her fearful eyes took on a sparkle. "Could be the beginning of another adventure?"

Helen recovered from her heart attack and settled into the senior living center. I visited her a few months after her move. In the beautifully appointed parlor we sat around a small table. After some pleasantries, she leaned across the table. "Let's talk about politics and the Bible. The management here thinks we might rise up against each other or something if we engage in these two subjects. It is completely unreasonable; some heated discussion groups will help our minds and prevent depression."

We talked for several hours about the controversies in the book of Genesis and needs around special education. At the door, Helen hugged me. "Now that was the best kind of exercise." I watched her walk to the elevator and push the button for her floor.

Now after Barbara's call announcing Helen's death, I reached into my file drawer and took out Helen's file. During her 89th year, she sent me the first of several letters. I spread the letters over my desk. I held the first one in my hands and leaned back in my chair and read.

> Dear Marcia,
> I know you will plan a eulogy for my service
> that will be wonderful. I want you to use this
> letter for part of my eulogy, too.
>
> I was born a Lutheran where religion
> was a wordy study of the rote catechism,

and finding the study dreary, sad, and foreboding, I rebelled! At one point during confirmation I skipped a class with a friend enough times to be chastised and threatened.

I fell in love with and married a Lutheran minister who aspired to a Ph.D. in theology feeling he could instill his ideas in his church. His career path changed to work with troubled kids and youth.

We became Congregationalists. With my lack of background in Bible and religion I took many, many Bible classes and became part of many discussion groups. I learned that being a Christian can be a happy adventure. There can be laughter and joy together with all the difficulties and seriousness of troubling responsibilities.

I am not a good Christian or maybe not even a Christian. I don't pray on my knees (it always hurts.) But usually when I find myself in a situation that I feel requires God's help, I ask. I try to live my life with love for all, whether it be in the workplace, socially or politically and to stand up for my beliefs.

I have trouble with the hereafter. I believe it is what we leave behind — how we lived with our family, children, friends and our deeds in the work place — that are the legacies of each life.

Being almost 90 years old, I do not worry myself with new experiences of dying. I have been blessed with reasonably good health, a wonderful marriage and family and a long and happy time together.

Love,

Helen

I PUT THE LETTER down and remembered calling Helen the afternoon I received the letter. She invited me to lunch. She met me in the luxurious entry of the Village at Duxbury. I walked next to her as she negotiated with her cane. "We are eating in the snack bar. It's more private and I'm craving a plain old toasted cheese sandwich." We ordered and I carried our tray behind Helen to a table at the far side of the room.

"How's everything at your new church?" I told church stories as Helen ate. Then I thanked Helen for the letter and said, "I've put it in a safe place."

"I trust you completely with my service but I needed to write some of it as an exercise for me. At night I review our Bible classes and laugh at many of the stories. Remember Marge's fundamental friend who advised her to stop the heretical class?"

I nodded and cut my sandwich in half and arranged it around the chips on my plate. Helen continued, "I loved Gene's reaction when the telephone rang. Remember he whipped to his feet, trotted to the phone and before answering turned to us and said, 'It must be the Almighty.'" After a laugh, Helen's eyes grew misty. "I miss Gene. Remember shortly after his death, when the phone rang and I shouted, 'it must be Gene reporting on the Almighty.'" We sat in an easy silence, each with our shared memories.

Helen grasped my hands in her arthritic fingers. "We had special times, didn't we? And we learned so much through our different opinions, Bible translations and the laughter, always the laughter."

I REACHED FOR ANOTHER envelope on my desk. I opened it and pulled out the Christmas card tucked inside. I turned to the back where Helen had written.

> In addition to my cane, I have added a small wagon with wheels, which allows me to walk easily and farther both indoors and out-of-doors. I can no longer manage trips to the symphony or the theater, but the Village offers so much in the way of activities. This year I have joined a poetry class and a series of lectures on American history, as well as continuing to volunteer in our library.

My waning years would be happier if, as a
nation, we had more concern for children,
health care, and education than for sending
the news of the pornographic intimacies of
our sex scandals around the world. As I face
with sorrow and horror the actions of our
nation's leaders, I search for the Christmas
Season's message of hope and joy that could
alleviate the rampant hatred and vengeance
of humankind.

I do not dwell upon death. I have lived my
life — good and bad — that I cannot change.
After Christmas I am going to re-read the
book of Luke. What will it say about this
adventure of diminishment? I am also going
to read *Angela's Ashes* and *The Pentagon
Murder* for variety.

Love, Helen

I SWIVELED IN MY chair and stood looking at the bulletin
board behind my desk. I pulled out the push pins and laid a
picture on my desk. I studied the picture of the Bible study
group dressed in my collection of hats at the luncheon before I
left their church where we'd studied together for eleven years. I
spotted Helen in the front row with a small black brimmed hat
perched on her head with a wide grin on her face. I focused
my eyes on Helen, always interested in the world, in bettering
life for others and involving herself in new experiences. She
made a difference with her droll humor and her sharp mind.

I placed the Christmas card back in the envelope and unfolded the last letter, a short note that she wrote from Hopewell
House where she transferred to early in her 93rd year.

Dear Marcia,
The five years at the Village were wonderful
for me, and I feel like it was my home. But
now I realize that the process of growing old
has its phases, and I am now in another.

My journey to the next life: a happening, an
adventure. Have you ever thought of that?
Love, Helen

An adventure? Helen, you are remarkable. My heart lightened when I remembered my last visit with her. In a weakened
voice she said, "I agreed to come to the Hopewell House as
long as they agreed to serve me my bourbon and water every
day at 4 p.m."

I returned the letters to their folder and held the picture
against the bulletin board and push-pinned it back in its place.
I studied each of the thirty individuals in the picture. A whole
generation gradually leaving us. I was so privileged to work
with them.

HELEN'S DAUGHTER CONTACTED THE new pastor at Helen's
church, the one who struggled with my participation in the
service for Helen. The pastor was caught between establish-
ing herself as the pastor and allowing me to return and work
with her. When pastors move to another church, we agree to a
Code of Ethics that we will not interfere with the ministry of
the next pastor.

Within the strict black and white reading of the Code of
Ethics, I would be guilty of invading the territory of the new
pastor if I participated in Helen's service. But I promised Helen.
So my options were to violate the Code of Ethics or break my
promise to Helen. No contest. I violated the Code of Ethics. I
participated at the reluctant invitation of the pastor through
pressure from Helen's daughter.

AT THE SERVICE WE celebrated Helen's ninety-four years.
I shared her letters and placed a small bottle of bourbon and a
little water on the pulpit. During the reception, the Bible study
group reminisced. Doris related the pet burial story. "Helen
said they dug a hole for every pet. She and the family gathered
around the hole. Her husband held the pet over the hole and
said, 'In the name of the Father, the Son and into the hole he
goes.'" Jan remembered her line, "All are chosen, but most are
frozen." Janice shared, "Helen's eyes sparkled with curiosity. I
hope to remember that as I age."

After the last person left the hall, I climbed the stairs to the worship room and reached for the small bottle of bourbon and carried it home. I searched in the cabinet for an old-fashion glass and set it on the counter. I opened the small bottle of bourbon and poured an inch in the glass. I mixed in a little water and raised the glass up in a toast.

"To Helen, you touched my life with your curiosity and your integrity. You introduced me to thinking about death as an adventure. Put in a good word with the Almighty for me. Thanks."

Celebrations of Life

Each life indeed is a gift,
No matter how short
No matter how fragile
Each life is a gift
To be held in our hearts forever
A celebration of God's love. [7]

Daddy's Quilt

"The producers did a good job the film." I turned the key in the lock. We'd been to a matinee performance of *Mystic River*.

Ken shut the door behind us. "I enjoyed the views around Boston. Was the movie as good as the book?"

I hung up my jacket. "Yes, just as thrilling."

"The light on the answering machine is flashing. It's probably for you." Ken opened the freezer and took out the ice cream.

I dropped my purse on the counter and hit the message button. "Marcia, David died today. I'm relieved. The kids want you to come over and plan the service with them."

Ken dished ice cream. "Another death. I'm sorry." Licking the spoon, Ken continued. "Have you noticed that many calls about a death come when we are at the movies?" He picked up the newspaper and his ice cream and disappeared into the family room.

I leaned on the counter and stared out the window. Ebony, my black lab, came over and rubbed against me and pushed into my leg. She sensed when the calls were about death. I loved David and Jodi and the kids. Sadness rolled over me.

I returned the call. "Jodi, I'm sorry. When do you want me to come?" Sadness caught in my voice as I heard strength in Jodi's voice.

"The kids are eager to see you. Will you join us for pizza and beer?"

"Of course, I'll be by in an hour or so."

I sat at the kitchen table with Ebony lying on my feet and thought about my first meeting with David, Jodi, Amy, Sarah, and their dog Luther. The kids stood shyly behind their parents' legs, but warmed to sharing stories and making jokes. At summer worship, David, all six foot plus of him, clapped and danced to the music geared for children. The family enjoyed the energetic yet laid back services with little to no pretense. We were a good fit.

I moved in the chair and Ebony looked back at me with sorrowful eyes and stretched. I scratched her ears. "Ebony, I'm going to make myself a cup of tea. The tea will warm my body;

I'm feeling cold with the news of David's death." She looked at me as if she understood every word and reluctantly got up and stood waiting for me to fix my tea.

With tea in hand, I turned toward Ebony. "Let's go and sit in a more comfortable place." She plodded after me and sat as close to me as she could on the floor near the sofa in the living room. My thoughts shifted to David. He'd struggled with his brain tumor for years. When the tumor seemed to be arrested, he and Jodi decided to have children. I remembered David's words.

"I was healthy when Amy was born but it was not long after Sarah's birth when the tumor activated again. Some days and weeks were more difficult than others, but we continued to live — camping, fishing, and partying with our friends. Amy and Sarah are the joys of our lives. Jodi's been fantastic through all my hospitalizations. I am disappointed I will not see them grow up."

I sipped my tea and mused over one of my last visits with David at their home. David had lost his ability to speak and pointed to letters and pictures on a chart to 'speak.' When he couldn't find a sign that would communicate his thoughts or, most times a joke, he hunched his shoulders, ran his hand over his balding head, and smiled, a smile filled with love and life — not a smile of resignation and self- pity.

I remembered David's eyes shining with joy over little things like a drawing from his kids or a kiss from his pastor, even as his body was wracked with pain and his mind filled with confusion. My heart broke as I recalled listening to Jodi as she struggled with David's decline. "Marcia, David's needs are beyond me. I need to place him in a care facility for his own safety and comfort." I felt her struggle with this heart-wrenching, but necessary decision.

Ebony nuzzled my arm with her nose and looked at me with unconditional love. I let my body relax into the sofa and stretched. I'd needed time to absorb the reality of David's death before I was ready to meet Jodi, Amy and Sarah.

I GATHERED MY FUNERAL and memorial service materials and went into the family room. "Ken, I'm off to Jodi's."

"Give her a hug for me." He stood and hugged me.

I drove through the country, passed the lake near their house and pulled into their driveway. Luther barked as I opened my car door and the kids came running out. We hugged for a long time before Luther nudged me off balance onto the ground. The kids and I laughed.

Jodi came out. We hung onto each other. She collected my sorrow.

"Let's eat." Amy and Sarah announced. They ran into the house and we gathered around the table as if it were a normal evening enjoying the pizza.

After she finished her pizza, Amy jumped up from the table, ran across the room, stood on a chair and took down the poster-story-quilt school project Jodi had had framed.

"Look Marcia, remember this?"

"I do, Amy." She handed her framed art work to her mother.

"Hold this please." Amy stood next to the picture and pointed to each square. "I filled the squares with the earth, a cheetah, a butterfly, dots and paisley designs copied from Daddy's shirts and ties and one square with the word 'ballet.'" She moved to stand on the other side of her work. "And on this side I wrote, 'I will never forget when my Dad dies. When he does, I will cut squares out of all his shirts and pants for a quilt, and I will never forget. On Halloween, I was wearing a cheetah costume. It had black and orange on it. My mom put black and orange on my face. Mom said, 'You look great!' Then she took a picture of me. I will never forget it.'"

When she finished, she hunched her shoulders, as if becoming a little shy. Her comfort with death bowled me over.

WHILE AMY AND SARAH played outside after dinner, Jodi talked. "David's parents want to be part of the funeral. Of course they want to pay for it. I know he's their son, but they haven't bothered with us except over their own selfish needs for years."

Jodi stopped and chewed on the pizza crust for a minute. "They drove the staff at the care facility mad with suggestions of how to prolong his life. Last week they demanded another speech therapist. They clamored for more social services. And you'll love this. On some days when David heard them coming, he pretended sleep."

"Knowing how he loved to laugh, I'm surprised he could keep a straight face." We laughed and then Jodi turned serious.

"They'll be part of the funeral, but then they will disappear again."

"I don't understand the reasons for their distance." I remarked.

Jodi took a deep breath and looked out the front window at the girls. "I do. First, they've never really liked me. And they wanted our life to be lived on their own terms. When they wanted to see us, they expected us to drop everything and be with them. They rarely concerned themselves with our lives, our schedules and needs. And since we didn't comply with their demands, they ignored the girls and offered little help over the eighteen years of David's illness." Her eyes shifted to the front window and she added, "The girls are coming in."

She turned back to me and reached her hand across the table. "I've dealt with David's illness and have prepared myself for his death. I don't need the funeral, but the girls do. I've talked with them about planning it with you. I want the service to be a celebration of their Daddy's life."

Jodi had lived with David's brain tumor for eighteen years. She'd struggled through the ups and downs, the almosts and maybes. She grieved the many losses as they came up. I believed her statement that she didn't need the funeral.

THE GIRLS BOUNDED OVEr to the table and joined Jodi and me. "Marcia, we're ready to plan Daddy's service."

Amy, a second grader, shuffled through the papers and books I'd spread over the table. "Daddy loved that thing you have about balloons." She found the book with the reading about balloons in church. She stood and read it as if she knew it by heart.

"Where did we get the idea that balloons don't belong in church? Where did we get the idea that God loves gray and "Sh-h-h" and drab? So celebrate! Bring your balloons and your butterflies, your bouquets of flowers, dance your dances, paint your feelings, and sing your songs, whistle, and laugh. Life is a celebration, an..." She stopped and pointed to the next big word. "Marcia, how do you pronounce that one?"

I told her and she went on. "...an affirmation of God's love. Where did we ever get the idea that balloons don't belong in church?"[8] Amy rocked back and forth on her heels.

"That's one of David's favorites." Jodi reached for Amy.

After Amy's performance, Sarah looked up at Jodi with her impish look.

"Mom, when you marry again, I want that daddy to have lots of black hair with lots of gel." Jodi's eyes rolled up and we tried not to make eye contact. Neither of us wanted to diminish Sarah's comment with some adult remark that might squelch her enthusiasm and innocence.

Sarah shifted her focus to me. "What can I read?"

"Here's one about there is a season for everything." I suggested and handed the reading to Sarah, a beginning reader.

"Marcia, what does this mean?" She looked at me all serious.

"It means there is a balance to everything like good and bad."

"And happy and sad, right and left...I get it." Sarah bounced from one foot to the other.

"I'll read some of the lines and you repeat after me."

Sarah followed my cue and traced each word with her finger and again bounced from one foot to the other as we read Ecclesiastes 3.

> There is a season for everything,
> A time for every occupation under heaven:
> A time for giving birth, a time for dying;
> A time for tears, a time for laughter;
> A time for mourning, a time for dancing.
> A time for tearing, a time for sewing.
> A time for loving, a time for hating.
> A time for war, a time for peace.

"I'll read that." Sarah practiced the piece again sounding out all the words. Amy came over and leaned on me.

"What else can I do?" I picked up "An Old English Blessing" and read it to her.

> Take time to be friendly,
> it is the road to happiness.
> Take time to dream,
> it is hitching your wagon to a star.
> Take time to love and to be loved,
> it is the privilege of the gods.
> Take time to look around,

it is too short a day to be selfish.
Take time to laugh,
it is the music of the soul.[9]

She giggled. "I'll read it. Daddy loved to laugh." We squeezed each other and she jumped off my lap.

We continued planning — choosing songs with actions and a scripture for me to read. I left feeling excited about the service the girls created for their Daddy...a service that would be filled with joy and laughter, a service that might be a little irreverent for some.

THE SERVICE OPENED WITH "Balloons in Church" by Ann Weems. Then six-year-old Sarah and her cousin ran up the steps, climbed up on a chair, and peeked over the lectern. Together she and her cousin led the congregation in Ecclesiastes 3 complete with Sarah's finger following each word and her shifting from one foot to the other as they read. They looked up at the audience with impetuous grins and skipped and scooted back to their seats.

The congregation sang "Jesus Loves Me." Shrill children's voices rose above the adults. I read Second Timothy 4.

I have fought the good fight.
I have run the race to the finish.
I have kept the faith.
And all there is for me now is the
shouting and God's applause.

Friends shared anecdotes, laughter filled the room. David's father stood in the center aisle and tried to be warm as he thanked everyone for coming.

Amy and Sarah ran up to the top of the pulpit area with their cousins following and led the congregation in the hymn "I've Got Peace like a River." Their daddy enjoyed singing this song and loved to exaggerate the movements. He formed his six-foot-plus frame into a fountain for the verse, "I've got joy like a fountain." The children mimicked their daddy's gestures.

With clarity and pride, eight-year-old Amy read "An Old English Blessing." After the closing hymn, "In the Bulb, there is a Flower," the girls skipped to the front and picked up the hand bells and rang them to be sure their daddy received his angel wings. Their innocent faces brought a lump to my throat.

The service ended with everyone joining in Jodi's suggested affirmation,

> There is a joyous celebration in our
> Father's house today as one so dearly
> loved is welcomed home.

After the funeral I continued to visit Jodi and the kids. On one of these visits, Jodi showed me two boxes of David's shirts, ties, and pants. "Marcia, the girls want quilts made from them. I cannot sew and have no creative talent, so we packed them up until later when I'll find someone to make them."

The girls dug in the boxes and showed me their favorites. Their excitement overwhelmed me. "Jodi, I want the girls to have the quilts to hold their memories of David. We have a quilters group at the church. I know the women will make quilts for the girls. Let me take the boxes with me."

"Mommy, let Marcia take the boxes." Amy pleaded while jumping up and down with excitement.

A few days later I lugged the two boxes to the basement of the church. I heaved them on the table where the quilters worked and explained about the quilts. One of the quilters, Martha, looked at the boxes and said, "I will take these home and make the quilts for the girls."

Martha worked on the quilts for a year — a year when she had severe health problems. As she handed me the completed quilts, she said, "The creative energy I put into the quilts gave me strength to face each day."

I held them and tried to take in their beauty. "A work of love, Martha, a work of love."

During Sunday worship, I presented the quilts to the family. I am sure David was hovering around the sanctuary proud and pleased with the creative beauty made from his funky ties and crazy shirts.

DAVID AT FORTY-TWO was too young to die. According to scripture our bodies are "fearfully and wonderfully made." I struggle with this scripture each time I am faced with the death of the young and the death of those ravaged with disease. On good days I understand the biology of the human body; on other days, I hate how disease runs rampant over life.

A Sharp Little Bell

I HUNG THE HEDGE trimmer in the garage and walked across the yard to the porch. I dropped into the hammock. The red and yellow tulips bobbed in a slight breeze that cooled the air. A drink of cold lemonade sounded good so I pulled myself out of my prone position and went inside. I dropped the ice into the glass and caught the phone on the third ring.

Dorna talked fast, so I had to listen fast. "Chet's taken a turn. The doctor called me to the hospital today and told me Chet's heart has deteriorated and he doesn't have long. We've contacted the nursing facility and added hospice."

"I'm sorry Dorna. What can I do? Where..."

She continued without taking a breath. "I've contacted the family. They consulted their calendars and decided a funeral on the first Saturday of August would do everyone just fine. Is that good with you?"

I said, "Sure. But are you..."

"Good. I've got a few more calls to make." Hanging up and catching my breath, I completed my question to the window over the kitchen sink, "certain he will be dead by then?"

ON MY INITIAL PASTORAL visit Chet talked of economics and investments. "Anyone immigrating to the United States should be required to have $25,000 and an I.Q. of 125. The foreign governments destabilize the value of the dollar. Welfare has ruined the poor. Their children need the rod."

A harder man I'd never met. I'd run into a solid brick wall with no way into his hardened heart. His soliloquy criticized the poor even though his parents came as uneducated immigrants to the United States. His flat judgments and his black and white world view made him difficult to be around. I listened and left feeling stymied.

On a later visit I promised Chet I'd bring him a new book on economics. Too busy to take it to Chet, I asked my son, Dave. "Sure, I'll go." He took the book and grabbed his keys and turned as he rushed out the door. "Mom, I've heard you mention your frustrations with Chet. He can't be that bad." He smiled a confident smile.

Later I heard a car in our gravel driveway. Dave came in and tossed his keys on the counter. "Mom, I can't believe him. His brick wall is more like steel. Why is he so hard and unlikable?"

"I don't know. I don't think I'll ever know."

ROUTINELY, WHEN I VISITED with Chet, Dorna escaped to the porch off the kitchen to have a peaceful cup of tea. I took a chair across from Chet who commanded the middle cushion of the sofa surrounded by *Barron's, The Financial Times* and *The Wall Street Journal*. At the beginning of one visit Chet stopped Dorna as she was making her escape. "Dorna sit down."

Dorna snapped to attention, halted her steps, and perched in the ladder back chair under the wall clock. Chet cleared his throat. "Listen. Hear the agenda for my death. Number 1. Cremation. Number 2. No visiting hours. Number 3. Burial. Private. Family only. Number 4. Silence. No readings." He stared at Dorna daring a response. The clock ticked. Dorna stood. I joined her and walked with her to the door. Looking defeated, she shrugged. We shared a quick hug and she trotted off as he called for his lunch. I stamped out to my car. I opened the door and slammed it and pounded the steering wheel.

"Bastard."

The next morning, Dorna came to my office. She took the chair next to my desk and propped her elbows on the corner holding her chin in her arthritic fingers. "Chet's callous announcement startled me. Why doesn't he see that I'm part of this too? He's so selfish. Always puts himself first. I've had it with him. I need to tell you what I need." Dorna stopped for a moment and laid her hands on the desk. "I'm going to need a gathering with family and friends to thank them for their support and friendship, in spite of Chet."

I touched Dorna's hands. "We will work around Chet's demands." With a sigh of relief Dorna straightened out of the chair and gave me a thankful look of trust and walked out of my office. I leaned back in my chair. A pastoral dilemma: Whose needs to meet — the dying or the living?

CHET'S HEALTH DETERIORATED. Bedridden, he demanded a bell. He rang that high-pitched little bell each time he wanted attention from Dorna. When someone telephoned or a visitor called, he struck that little bell so it rang with an extra sharpness, piercing the air with a non-negotiable demand. Thankfully, when

Dorna moved him to the nursing facility at the end of May, the bell stayed behind on a shelf in the kitchen.

In early June, Dorna cleaned out their house to put it on the market. The house sold in July. She delayed the closing on their home until mid-August. She knew it would upset Chet if by some chance he'd learned she started moving things out of the house. And more importantly the house would be intact for the reception after Chet's funeral still scheduled on the first Saturday of August. She also made reservations for a "recovery from grief cruise" for October — a respectable time after an August funeral.

AT A TIME WHEN Chet's condition was steady, I approached the subject of his death. "Chet, I've heard your desire for cremation and no visiting hours and a private burial, but Flo has requested a gathering with her friends. What do you..."

He raised his arms and pointed both index fingers in my face. "I told you a cremation, no visiting hours and a private burial."

My stomach knotted. With pastoral determination and a fear for his physical strength, I touched his arm. "Regardless of your orders, Chet, there will be a gathering for Dorna."

His breathing slowed and his body slunk into the bed. He shrugged and mumbled, and looked away from me. "I wouldn't want anyone to go to the bother to do anything for me." I could hardly take what Chet just said — an opening into his hard heart, a crack in his brick wall.

Take it slow...measure your words, I whispered to my soul. I leaned in closer. "As long as there will be a service for Dorna, is there anything I can do or say for you?"

Almost without a pause, he began, his fingers gesturing as he talked. "I love classical music. When I listen, I trace the moods of the music from anger to love, from despair to hope. The rhythms and changes remind me of the moods of the sea, from the churning to the gentle lapping of waves."

He continued in a warm reflective voice that was unfamiliar to my ears. "For me the service would have no words, only three classical pieces. A violin version of *Schubert's Ave Maria*. The start of life is beautiful and innocent, you know. A piano version of *Beethoven's Moonlight Sonata* to recognize the rhythm of living and dying. And for the finale, a full orchestra playing *Verdi's Triumphal March from Aida*, a piece that is not mournful or sad, but a piece of commanding determination to go forth and conquer. There you are." He half smiled and turned away.

I lingered there beside his bed — a witness to a glimpse of a human spirit lodged and hidden inside his bricked wall. Sadness flooded over me. Chet's soul trapped, fearful of revealing itself. Why?

At home I opened my journal and wrote down his requests and prayed. My God, you've blessed me by these sacred moments with Chet. My God, why me? Why, the privilege? Has Dorna seen it? His daughter? What happened to Chet that he's lived bricked in from the stuff of life? When the time comes, show me how to share this glimpse into the heart of this son of yours. Amen.

THE FIRST SATURDAY IN August, *the day that would do everyone in the family just fine for a funeral for Chet*, came and went. Chet did not die on schedule. The not-yet-to-be-a-widow's plans were foiled.

In fact, by early September his situation improved. Dorna panicked. Chet didn't know that she had sold the house. He didn't know she was preparing to move into a condo. And, certainly, he didn't know of the "recovery from grief cruise" coming up.

The social workers called a family meeting. "Dorna, you are aware that Chet's condition has improved and we feel health workers can handle Chet's needs at home. As soon as you can arrange for a hospital bed to be delivered, we will release him."

Dorna pleaded with them. "I've sold my house. I've planned a cruise. I need you to keep him a little longer, so I can work out a way to tell him all that I've hidden."

Out of their compassion for Dorna, they extended Chet's stay and the not-yet-a-widow went on her cruise, now christened, "my cruise-to-prepare-to-share my new condo with Chet."

When she returned, Dorna told Chet about the sale of their house. He frowned and stewed. His body language showed belligerence. They moved into the condo in early November, and that shrill little bell that had been shelved in the kitchen began to ring once more. It rang continuously for the next ten months, every time the telephone rang, or every time a friend came to call, and every time he wanted Dorna's attention.

"I can't take this." Dorna called me in frustration. "How long will this go on? He gets more demanding every day. I have no peace."

I tried to soothe her, but she was beyond soothing. I visited and tried to intercede, but Chet's demands trumped any constructive plans to negotiate the use of the bell. Dorna lived tired, worn and fearful that if she didn't respond to the bell, "it might be real distress, a real need." Home health care personnel came and went — fired by Chet for not meeting his particular needs — his paper folded properly and placed on the corner of the table next to his bed, fresh clothes laid out in a particular way on his bed, rushing to his bedside almost before he rang the bell for help.

EXACTLY ONE YEAR AFTER the date of the scheduled funeral, the date that had suited everyone's schedule, Dorna called. "Chet died this morning." The not-yet-widow finally became a widow, and the sharp little bell was silenced.

During the memorial service to celebrate Chet's life, professional musicians played Chet's requested music. I honored him by connecting the music with his brief words about each piece. Jan, a family friend, crafted a homily about Chet, the hard-hearted one, the curmudgeon, yet one of God's own. The church held a reception in the fellowship hall. Dorna greeted her friends and thanked them for being with her on the journey, in spite of Chet.

I HATED THAT I couldn't like Chet. I hated his bell ringing abuse of his wife. I hated being caught in the conundrum — a pastoral struggle between Chet and Dorna. Most times the desires around death are not so diametrically opposed; most times I can honor the dead and serve the living with little compromise. But every once in a while there is a Chet.

I still wonder about the privilege I'd had being a witness inside Chet's brick wall, moments on holy ground. I don't know why I had that glimpse. All I know is that I didn't dream it. It really happened and it allowed me to witness the seed of God in Chet, in spite of himself.

Show Me the Way to Go Home[10]

Ruby Righteous, one of my teaching personas, needed to make an appearance to loosen the church community's frozen ideas about the 'right way to pray.' Ken found me in the attic deep in a costume box searching for Ruby's hat and glasses. "Didn't you hear the telephone?"

"No. I probably didn't want to hear it." I slid on Ruby's hat.[11]

Ken gave me his usual, 'you are not really going to wear that' look and handed me the phone. "It's Suzanne. She sounds teary."

I took a deep breath. I wondered what happened. She rarely calls. Is it Chuck or one of the kids? "Hey, Suzanne."

"Mother died last night."

I cried. I felt the loss of a friend as I slipped off Ruby's hat and sat on the attic steps. I heard Suzanne crying as she waited for me to absorb the news. "Would you conduct the memorial service for us?"

"Of course, for Charlotte and for you, I'd be honored." I regained my strength.

"I am relieved that we will have someone we know do the service." Suzanne let out a sigh. We talked about travel arrangements, and then Suzanne added, "I have many others to call. Let's talk tomorrow."

"I'll give you a call. Go gently."

The next day I called Suzanne to begin our plans for Charlotte's service. "Suzanne, I've been remembering our college days. Remember Mother's Weekend when our seven mothers took over the attic space in the sorority house. They created more of a mess throwing their clothes around than we ever did."

Suzanne laughed. "Remember the afternoon tea when our mothers made a grand entry dressed in our blue and white sorority nightshirts with rollers twisted haphazardly in their hair and performed a skit and sang about our lives in the attic room?"

"Charlotte instigated the performance." I choked up as I pictured the scene and my thoughts wandered to Charlotte's love of music. The image of evenings with Charlotte playing the piano as the rest of us sang and danced with the dogs, Sophie and Bugger (pronounced "Booger"), passed through my mind.

Suzanne's voice broke in. "Are you okay?"

My words caught in my breath. "During college your mother was a gift to me with her open-mindedness and acceptance of the college spirit of testing and change. Her delightful spirit, keen insights, and sense for the zany tapped unknown parts of my curiosity about life." We stayed quiet for a few moments, each of us hanging onto the receiver remembering.

Suzanne cleared her throat. "Alzheimer's changed her life. The disease affected her short-term memory but left her with a peaceful spirit. I placed mother in assisted living nearby so I could monitor her care and needs before they became a problem. Eventually I moved her to more home-like setting. The staff and nurses became family and guarded her dignity. Toward the end, she hummed, "Show me the Way to Go Home.""

"I can see your mother swinging and swaying to that music." I hummed a few bars to myself as Suzanne continued.

"The staff said the song became a theme song for many of those suffering from this form of dementia."

I imagined the words of the song as a prayerful plea, "Is there any way for you, God, to take pity on me and show me the way to go home to you, now?"

Suzanne interrupted me and changed the subject. "Marcia, at a recent funeral the pastor invited people to come forward to share personal remembrances. I know many had something to say but could not get up to talk."

"I know what you mean. When families ask me to have an open microphone, I worry that no one will step forward and I think about those who would like to speak but can't."

"So, how about a handout for the service, a separate sheet titled, 'A Memory or Anecdote about Charlotte.' It would give an opportunity to those who would never dare to speak, to share something that would be read in the service, and we would have these additional memories to treasure."

"Suzanne, that's a wonderful idea. Let's do it." I knew it would be a bit of a challenge for me to decipher some of the handwriting and to do justice in reading the written memories without preparation, but I understood as I recalled the comfort I'd received from the notes and cards after Dad's death which I had saved and read for years after.

THE CELEBRATION OF CHARLOTTE's life took place in a glorious interfaith chapel. The music director agreed to play Charlotte's original composition — "Memories of You." But she balked at the family's request for "Show Me the Way to Go Home" to be included in the service. "We have guidelines for appropriate music for memorial services, and they do not include popular music." She lectured from the altar.

"You mean you can't honor the request of a bereaved family?" I tried to control my anger and see her point of view, but I confess my personal relationship with the family blinded me as I ran into the organist's wall of resistance and the chapel's reasonable guidelines. I climbed the steps to the altar.

"You do understand that according to caregivers in the Alzheimer Care Center, "Show Me the Way to Go Home" was a theme song for Charlotte and other Alzheimer's victims."

"Yes, the family told me that, but I still cannot do it. I will not do it within the service, but I can play it softly as the family leaves the chapel."

I backed down and thanked her for her compromise.

THE CHAPEL SUITED CHARLOTTE with its clean majestic lines and warm interior. Friends wrote anecdotes as they listened to Charlotte's original composition. I read the scriptures and prayed the prayers buoyed by Charlotte's hope-filled spirit. Family members spoke as I sat behind the pulpit and arranged the hand-outs. I puffed up with joy as I shared the stories and memories in the honor of Charlotte.

The organist played the theme song quietly as we filed out and crossed the marble floors into the sunshine. I shot up a prayer. Spirit of God, swoop in and zap the organ so that it blasts out Charlotte's prayer request, "SHOW ME THE WAY TO GO HOME, PLEASE."

God neglected my prayer request.

DURING MY FLIGHT HOME from Charlotte's service, I whispered words at the cloud bank that hung outside the window of the plane. "God, you know my prayer was a prayer of desperation and frustration over protocol. I didn't expect a response; I needed only to give voice to my anger. And speaking of anger, questions about dementia have flooded my heart. Why, God? Why Charlotte, my friend's mother, my mentor during college? God, how am I to understand this disease? Is there any purpose to it? Is there anything of You to be found in their repetitive stories, their incessant pacing and wandering? Addie, a gentle friend, became vicious and angry when attacked by this disease. Why? Why do some victims remain gentle and others have to be bound for their own safety? Why is the memory wiped out, erased? When will there be a medical breakthrough?"

ARRIVING AT THE OFFICE and still carrying my anger over Charlotte, my secretary stopped me. "Marcia, Florence is in Norwell Knoll."

I sat in the chair in next to Betty Ann's desk. "Why?"

"Her friend Irene went to pick her up for church and found her pacing around her house all dressed up for church, purse in hand. She didn't know Irene."

"Florence was just fine two weeks ago."

"They are calling it rapid onset Alzheimer's."

I checked my messages and left the office. I drove to Norwell Knoll. I asked for Florence's room. I passed wheelchair after wheelchair of patients staring into space. I found her room and looked in. Florence was seated on the side of her bed, dressed for church, her purse in her lap. "Have you come to pick me up for church?"

"I'll take you to church." She rose and took my arm. We walked out the door to the hall. She held onto my arm and the hall railing until the end of the hall. We turned and her eyes fixed.

"Where am I? Who are you?" She tore her arm away from me and froze in place. A nurse rescued us and escorted Florence to her room.

I asked the nurse. "Two weeks ago she knew me. Now she is wandering the halls with her purse and cannot find her room. Why?"

The nurse shrugged, looking as frustrated as I felt.

STILL FEELING FRUSTRATED, I drove to see Florence's friend, Miriam. I pulled in the driveway and parked in front of the barn where milk cows lived for years. I knocked and waited for Miriam to come to the door. At ninety I knew she walked with care. "Marcia. What a pleasant surprise! Come in. The tea kettle is boiling. Will you join me?"

I followed Miriam into the kitchen and we engaged in small talk while she made tea. I carried the tray into the sitting room. Miriam, always a lady, sat erect in her navy dress with a white sweater around her shoulders. She stretched her arm across the table and with her age-spotted hand patted mine.

I sipped my tea. "Miriam, I came home from the funeral for a friend's mother who suffered from Alzheimer's to the news about Florence. I don't understand. I know you visit your sister-in-law with dementia. How do you cope with the disease?"

Miriam set her tea cup down and folded her hands in her lap. "Marcia this is how I think of it." She leaned forward in her chair. "Dear, my sister-in-law skipped over her adolescence right to marriage. She is living those years now. She has shut out the world, as we know it, to do that work before she dies." Miriam closed her eyes and sighed. "She isn't the only person I've watched through Alzheimer's."

I waited for her eyes to open. "Miriam, where is God in all this?"

"God hugs them to his bosom and never lets them go. He gives them a comfort we don't understand."

"I hope so Miriam, I hope so. I must believe that God has not abandoned them."

Family Deaths

God, we praise you for the good gift of life,
for its wonder and mystery,
its interests and joys,
its friendships and fellowships.

We give thanks for the meanings
that lie hidden in the very heart of all our experiences,
so that we learn even through pain and sorrow,
and we feel your guiding hand
during the pilgrimage of life.[12]

Sudden Death

TWO NIGHTS AFTER MY return from Charlotte's service, Ken arrived home from a business trip. After he finished his dinner he pushed back his chair. "How did things go after your run-in with the music director?"

"I calmed down and it felt like a family reunion with Suzanne's kids and her sister-in-law's family. Suzanne and I stayed up and talked about college and Mom and Dad's weekends."

"Did both of your Dads come to Dad's Weekend?"

"Yes, they had great fun with their girls." I pushed the bites of chicken around my plate. "Suzanne asked about Dad's death. The last two nights I've struggled with memories of Dad. Grief is pouring over me again."

Ken took my hand. "I'm sorry."

That night I tossed and turned. I didn't want to disturb Ken so I headed down to the sofa. I pushed my back against the pillows, a position in which I usually fell asleep almost instantly but this night it was not to happen. Instead my sleep was fretful, reliving Dad's death.

I HAD POURED A GLASS of wine. When I answered the phone, I heard Mother's voice from Florida where she and Dad had gone for the winter. "Marcia, we were walking on the beach with your Uncle John when your dad said he felt sick. We rushed him to the hospital. They are going to do the balloon thing, angioplasty. I'll call you later." She hung up. Filled with shock, I called two friends and asked them to pray.

Later, my sister Barb called. "Dad made it. He's doing fine. He's asking for his glasses to see the pretty nurses." I went to bed feeling relief.

At 4 a.m., five hours after my sister's call of assurance, the phone woke me from a restless sleep. "Your dad didn't make it. He's gone."

"What?" I sat up in disbelief, shock, confusion. Was this a dream? No, Mother's on the phone. Ken's stirring next to me. Dad's dead. He couldn't have died. In my mind, I could hear Dad boasting, "I'll outlive your mother."

"Mother, what happened?"

"I'm not sure. Complications set in and he had a massive

heart attack and died."

"Are Aunt Mary and Uncle John still with you?"

"Mary is but John has been admitted to the hospital with a heart problem too."

"I'm glad you are not alone."

"I need to call Marge and Barb."

"Okay." I put the phone down and reached for Ken, pounded the sheets, gasped for breath between the floods of tears. "Dad's dead. It can't be. No."

IN THE MORNING I faced two of our three teenagers, Maureen and David. "Papa died last night." Tears coursed down our cheeks and onto our clothing as we hugged. David choked out, "He couldn't have. He was just here at my football game." Maureen sighed, "He promised me he'd be at my graduation. How could this have happened? I don't understand." David asked, "Have you called Mike?"

"Not yet." Hurting deep inside for having to tell Mike the news over the phone, I called Carnegie Mellon University where Mike was in his first year of college.

"Mike."

"Mom? Is that you?"

"Yes, Papa died last night." Silence and then Mike's words came.

"Is Grandma all right?"

"Barb's flying down to be with her. She's in shock like the rest of us."

"But Papa was always healthy. What happened?"

I knew his heart was breaking. I wanted to be with him. I couldn't talk anymore. Ken took over giving Mike the details.

After Ken's talk with Mike, I called two friends, Connie and Doris. They came over.

"Don't worry; we'll take care of things on this end." They chimed as they came in with hot coffee and donuts.

"You take care of your family and get to Ohio to meet your mother before she arrives from Florida." Doris ordered.

Connie called Earl, a former pastor. He came over and found Maureen and David in their rooms and listened to them.

Ken made flight arrangements. I contacted a couple of long distance friends. I repeated the words. "Mother called.

My Dad's dead. They were walking the beach. Dad felt ill. Dad died. He's dead." I listened to their shock and kind words.

Judie called. "I'll take care of your house."

EARLY SUNDAY MORNING I flew from Boston to Ohio, while Ken stayed behind to organize the children, make calls to his family and other friends, and arrange to be away from work.

During the flight, my mind stayed busy with continual self-talk and disbelief at the reality that I had to face. Dad died. I'm flying to Ohio. A heart attack. Were there signs? Was he having pain or other symptoms? Mother's crushed. Barb's with her. Dad's body, right now, is in the same plane with Mother and Barb. His body cold. Me cold with shock.

AUNT ANN AND UNCLE DEAN met me at the airport. "We can't believe it. Bill! Always robust." As we waited at the gate for mother's flight, they comforted me with their presence.

Sadness…no, more than sadness…deep grief stabbed my being when mother came through the gate, leaning heavily on my sister's arm, instead of striding out of the gate with Dad, full of smiles and energy for yet another visit. My heart and mind could hardly take it in.

Mother, Barb, and I climbed in Uncle Dean's car for the drive to Jackson, Ohio, my parents' home of 22 years. Time stretched and strained. Traffic lights lasted forever. At last the bright red apple-shaped water tower appeared in the distance. The downtown looked as drained as I felt.

A right turn off Main Street brought us to the hill and to Redondo Drive. There sat the home they'd left a month earlier for a fun-filled winter in the Florida trailer park. No signs of welcome. No American flag flying. No garage door open. My breath stood still as I watched Mother enter their house, alone.

IN THE CONFUSION AND emotional upheaval we must have unpacked and someone must have contacted the funeral home because in no time we were sitting with the funeral director talking about Dad in the past tense. In no way were we prepared for this. No plans made. No casket picked. No burial plot purchased. With too loud a voice and fear sitting alive in my gut I said, "We are not going to have to see Dad now, are we?"

"No. We are preparing him for the viewing." He walked us through the necessary arrangements. The obituary. Notification of the church. Discussion of a burial plot. He led us up an endless flight of stairs to the casket showroom. Row after row after row of long rectangular boxes with flashy satin linings bombarded my sight. A mind-chilling thought gripped me, "The next time I see Dad, he'll be laid out in one of these." My body shuddered.

The next morning the director picked us up and drove us to the cemetery. He showed us the new section; it looked flat and exposed with no character. We moved to an older section of the cemetery where one plot looked at Jackson's bright red apple-shaped water tower. The funeral director pointed to the water tower. "I think this is the right spot for my friend Bill." We agreed, for Dad was proud of Jackson, Ohio, the Apple Capital of the World.

LAUGHTER ARRIVED THAT AFTERNOON with the grand entry of Aunt Jeanne and Uncle Clark after a two-day drive from Texas. Aunt Jean burst into the house, winked at Uncle Clark and said to us, "Do you know why my face is red?"

After a well-timed pause she said, "Well, when I get in a motel room with your Uncle Clark, I can't keep my hands off him. I stay red-faced for days afterward." My Aunt Jeanne's warm, zany presence and huge hugs brought us laughter.

KEN PICKED MIKE UP FROM college and drove to Jackson with Maureen and David and settled in with neighbors. They came to the house. Sadness gripped them as they gathered on the sofa with their grandmother. Eventually she straightened up. "Now it's time to get to work. Go into the garage and put out the flag. Your papa would want it flying."

Time rushed on. Casseroles arrived. Flowers were delivered. My sister Marge arrived. We caught her up on the plans. The mantra, "Bill Mitchell, I can't believe it," shattered the air as it traveled through Jackson. Calls, visits and hugs filled us with a strange energy. Perhaps the energy came from shared grief over this well-loved man.

The Methodist pastor — a pale, proper preacher man — visited. He sat stiffly in the living room. He knew Dad, for Dad was one of his always-ready volunteers. He went over the plans for the funeral as if he were sharing a pre-recorded message. He talked. He left. I wondered. "Did he care that much or that little?"

The calling hours brought us a step closer to the reality that Dad was dead. Mother announced, "I will not stand next to the casket." But she stayed near the body all evening. I looked on from far away. All the guests said, "He looks so good." We agreed. I half expected Dad to look over at us, as he did when he lay down for a nap, and say, 'I'm just resting my eyes.'

My sisters and I went into our Bill Mitchell mode of meeting and greeting folks, making the guests feel warm and welcome. At times one would have thought we were at a sorority rush party. Meeting. Greeting. Absorbing the shock for others.

THE DAY OF THE funeral my nephew Steve and I arrived early at the funeral home. Numb with grief, yet, determined to celebrate Dad's life, I worked on Dad's eulogy within eye view of the casket. Steve practiced his music on the funeral home organ.

"Aunt Marcia, no hymns during the service, right?"

"Right, Steve. Mother says that singing makes her cry."

Steve turned to face me from his seat at the organ. "Are you doing okay?"

"I have no idea. I just know I need to do this for Dad. Being busy takes me away from the reality of his death." I doodled on the paper in front of me. "Does that make sense with his body right over there?"

"I think so. Maybe that's why I need to play." Steve returned to his practice.

As the time for the funeral approached, friends and relatives arrived and listened to Steve's music. Mother and we three daughters and our husbands and children sat in the front rows. The preacher man entered and stood like a statue at the front. The room settled to a quiet hush except for the stage whisper of my maternal grandmother, Gertie, to Aunt Jeanne. "I can't believe it...my Billie Boy, my Billie Mitchell."

The preacher laid his notebook on the lectern and switched on the light. "Welcome. We're shocked and saddened to be here to remember and celebrate the life of William Mark Mitchell." His eyes followed his script and never acknowledged my mother. His voice read words of scripture and said words of prayer. He introduced me. Ken grasped my hand and squeezed.

I stood and walked to the lectern. I put my papers down and looked over the crowd. So many people sitting quiet with expectant faces. I found Ken's eyes and he smiled. This is unbelievable. I wish this were a dream. My heart aches. I took a deep breath and shared my eulogy.

First, I want to thank the people of Jackson for the warm reception of our family. You have greeted each of us with care and affection. It has felt great to be Bill Mitchell's daughter.

For each of us gathered here, the last several days have represented the experience of Good Friday — the shock, the disbelief, the questions of Why Bill? Why Dad? Why Papa? Anger, tears and sorrow have filled us.

But for Dad, Bill, Papa the last several days have been an Easter experience — the resurrection — the change — the moving on — the freedom to soar in God's love to greater heights to new experiences with God.

I believe Dad is with God. I even allow myself to think that God and Dad may be thinking and talking about all of us and deciding on who now will take care of the bluebirds.

Of course the experience of Easter is nothing new to Dad. Dad lived every day with vitality and enthusiasm. Every day was Easter for him. Every day was new life, joyous and challenging.

Some people greet each morning with "Good God, its morning!" but Dad greeted each morning with "Good morning, God, what do you have for me to do today?"

No, Dad was not a Good Friday person but an Easter person. And I thank God for that

model in my life. However, the model is not
Dad alone. Rarely do I think of Dad without
Mother — Mother and Dad, Evelyn and Bill,
Grandma and Papa, a team for some 56 years.

A few years ago I gave Mother and Dad a
book by Shel Silverstein entitled *The Giving
Tree*, a parable of a boy and a tree. During
the boy's young life the tree enjoyed the boy
climbing and playing in its branches and
leaves. Later, during the dating years the tree
was happy when the boy carved initials in its
trunk. When the boy needed some money,
the tree happily gave all its apples to the boy
so the boy could have the money he needed.

Again years later the boy came to the tree
with another need—the boy needed a house.
The tree gave all its branches to the boy to
build the house and the tree was happy.
When the boy was a man, he came to the
tree needing a boat—and yes, again the tree
happily gave its trunk. And then a long time
later the man came back to the tree and the
tree wondered what it had to give to the boy
who was now old, it gave the old man the
stump as a resting place.

Mother and Dad in combination have lived
their lives as givers to each of us as family
and to you as friends. Mother and Dad, Papa
and Grandma, Evelyn and Bill have lived
their lives as giving trees. I celebrate their gift
of giving to each of us and I thank God for
gracing our lives with their presence.

Today I come asking for the power and
strength of God's love to enter each of us and
empower us to move from Good Friday to
Easter and to celebrate life as Dad did with
vitality and enthusiasm. Amen.

As I returned to my seat, Dad's spirit touched me. "Thanks, Marsh."

THE FUNERAL PROCESSION WOUND through Jackson. Some flags were at half-mast. Some police saluted the hearse as Dad went by. Some shopkeepers doffed their hats. The burial made his death final.

We gathered at the house for a reception. Somewhere during the visiting my Aunt Annie commented on the scarf I was wearing. She wanted a lesson in scarf tying. So, there in the middle of our grief, my sisters and aunts practiced the latest fashion trends in scarf art. The scarf-tying was the first of many interruptions that took our hearts away from the reality of Dad's death for a few brief moments.

At the sound of the last car leaving the driveway, we collapsed into chairs in the living room. Mother relaxed for a brief moment then stood with arms on hips. "Girls, I have to go to the bank, court house, and the insurance office tomorrow." We watched her go to her room alone. Lumps stuck in our throats.

Barb, Marge and I made our way to the kitchen. Barb made coffee, poured it and took a few sips before setting her cup on the counter. "Mother hasn't driven in years."

Marge opened the refrigerator and removed the carton of orange juice box. She reached into the cabinet for a glass and poured. "How is she going to get around when we leave?"

I dunked a cookie from the reception in my coffee and let the treat comfort me. "What if we make her drive tomorrow?"

IN THE MORNING AFTER breakfast, the three of us hurried to the car. Climbed in the back seat. Belted ourselves in tight. Mother locked the front door and walked toward the car. She stared at us. Her look said, "Do I have to?" but she knew she must. She slid into the driver's seat, checked the mirrors and with determination in her eyes backed out of the driveway.

The three of us stayed a week with mother. During the week, mother played over and over again in her mind the hours at the emergency room. She questioned. "In the confusion did I miss something? Should I have allowed the procedure?" At times she nagged at Dad as if he were right in front of her. "Why did you stop taking an aspirin a day? One little aspirin wouldn't have hurt you."

Her friend Louise stopped by and comforted us all with her warm smile and her love for Dad and Mother. Before leaving she hugged each of us and whispered. "I'll call your mother every day to see how she is doing."

My sisters and I left one by one so the house would not be empty for mother all at once.

ON MY RETURN FLIGHT I fantasized that Dad met God during the emergency surgery. I pictured God leaning close to Dad and saying, "Bill, you've had a great life. But the reality is your heart has been severely damaged. You'll be hospitalized for a long time. And you'll have to curb your activities."

"God, you know I hate hospitals. I turn green in nursing homes. Let me go now." Then I know God gave Dad a loving nod and said, "Welcome home, Bill Mitchell, my good and faith-filled servant."

ON MY FIRST DAY back home the alarm woke me at 6:30 a.m. I stretched and reached for Ken, but remembered he was on a business trip. I pulled myself out of bed. I threw on my robe and made my way downstairs. As I made coffee I heard two more alarms and footsteps and showers. Maureen, with David not far behind, ran down the stairs, grabbed a quick breakfast and they said almost in unison, "Glad you are back, Mom," and ran out the door to school. The quiet of the house settled around me.

I carried a cup of hot coffee upstairs to my home office. I settled in my gold overstuffed chair and picked up my journal. The date January 30 stared at me. January 30 the day Dad died. I flipped through the empty pages — January 31, February 1, February 2....February 13. I studied the empty pages. I underlined today's date *February 13, 1988.* I underlined it again pushing hard on my pen. I waited. Nothing.

I reached for the button on my CD player and listened to string music. The room became cold. I folded my robe around me and fell into a deep sleep. I woke with a start as my journal slid from my lap. I stretched and pulled myself upright. I looked at the clock. 10:30 a.m. Marcia, get up, take a shower and get dressed.

Dressed, I carried the laundry basket to the basement. I

dropped the basket on the floor by the washer and lumbered back upstairs. I looked through the pantry and attempted a grocery list. I pushed the pad aside. I tried to return a few phone calls but my fingers couldn't punch in even the first number. I made my way to the sofa in the TV room. The next sounds I heard were Maureen and David coming in from school. They fixed dinner. I pushed the spaghetti around my plate.

Maureen cleared my plate. "Mom, you look exhausted. Why don't you go to bed?"

I pushed back my chair. "I haven't done anything all day."

"You need rest, Mom." Dave pulled me from the chair, gave me a long squeeze and I made my way upstairs.

THE NEXT MORNING I propped up two pillows against the wall behind my bed and leaned back and opened my journal. I wrote.

> *February 14, 1988. Lord, how long? I'm*
> *burned out and angry with Dad's death.*

I STRUGGLED INTO MY robe and went downstairs. Valentine greetings decorated the kitchen. I fell into a chair and cried. The phone rang. I let the answering machine take the call. Ken's voice. "It's me. If you are home, pickup." I picked up.

"Hi."

"Happy Valentine's Day. I'll be home by 5. If you feel like it, let's go out for a Valentine treat tonight."

"I'll try."

"If not we'll order out and celebrate at home."

I tried but I couldn't do either.

My friend Jan called the next day. "Ron's making peanut butter sandwiches. Join us for lunch." I ventured out. The quiet presence of Jan and Ron allowed me to absorb their strength and love. After lunch Jan sat at one end of the sofa and I at the other.

I rubbed my legs. "I feel like I've been flattened by a fleet of trucks." I sobbed. Jan stayed at her end of the sofa and let me sob. Through her hospice work she knew to let me go, to not reach out. She knew that human touch at that moment would have stopped my need to cry.

"It takes a long time to grieve." She paused. "Your grief will be good grief. It may not feel that way to you, but it will be good because of the love you shared with your Dad. You have no resentments, no hurts to heal, no unfinished business other than not being able to say good bye." She scooted over next to me. "Take it a day at a time. Don't rush it. Grief is work, but good work. Know I love you and will be here for you."

Jan stood and I unfolded and let her take me in her arms and we hugged. At home I curled in the comfortable chair in my home office and wrote in my journal.

> *February 16, 1988. How many trucks*
> *will roll over me?*

DAYS ROLLED ON. I returned to work and drew in energy from cards, notes and words of comfort. On most days I functioned well but at unexpected moments with a look, a word, a sound, a bird sitting on the bird house the tide of grief rolled over me.

> *March 3, 1988. I'm still raw. This morning*
> *someone said, "Haven't you grieved long*
> *enough?" I wanted to belt them. Phrases*
> *from the grief seminar that I think will help*
> *me. Let the steam out of the kettle. You are*
> *not going to get over it. Do something for*
> *yourself everyday. Give yourself permission*
> *to care for yourself. Open the pain and see*
> *what pain can teach you. You must be kid-*
> *ding. Open the pain? I can't shut it off.*

When I turned the calendar to May, my heart took a dive. Mother and Dad's wedding anniversary month — 56 years. Dad thought we'd gone too far with silliness on the day we celebrated their 50th. I found the photo album for 1985 and studied each photo — Dad in a green top hat and Mother in a quickly assembled bridal veil perched on the backseat of a Mustang convertible. Joy and sadness gripped me.

> *May 25, 1988. I can't imagine Mother's pain.*
> *I only know mine and the emptiness. The old*
> *joke of Dad taking mother for a Coney Island*
> *Hot Dog on their first anniversary falls flat.*

In September, Mother came to our house for her 75th birthday, her first birthday without dad. We had a three-quarter party to celebrate her three-quarters of a century. We cut a quarter from each sandwich and each paper plate to make three-quarter sandwiches and plates. The Webster's came in three-quarter dress; George had cut off one fourth of his tie; Addie, the bottom fourth of her dress. Doris presented Mother with first three-quarters of a paperback book and Bud gave her one-fourth of a pound of candy apologizing for having eaten the other three-quarters. The craziness balanced the reality of Dad's absence.

Days and weeks passed; grief came and went like the tides.

Grief Work

CLOSE TO THE FIRST anniversary of Dad's death, I contacted my spiritual director, Rosemary Brennan, a Sister of St. Joseph of Boston. Over the last year and a half I'd worked with Rosemary about things of the Spirit, how it was with me, the church and God. Every time I drove through the brick pillared entry to the retreat house, calmness came over me.

This day I parked in the back and while crossing the expansive yard, I slowed my step to take in the beauty of the trees silhouetted against the sky. Standing on the rocky cliff overlooking the Atlantic, I breathed in the sea air with gratitude that I had such a place to come. Sister Pat Logan met me at the door with a warm hug. "Welcome. Long time no see. How's the family?"

"All are well."

"Good. Rosemary's just coming down."

Rosemary greeted me at the foot of the winding staircase. She escorted me to the small room where we usually met. A room with a TV, a fireplace, and two windows; one that looked onto the lawn where the Statue of St Joseph stood and the other faced the driveway with a view of the farmers' porch that wound around to the side of the house. She slid onto the sofa and placed a small notebook beside her. I flopped into a swivel-rocker. I rocked for a moment. "The 30th is coming. The day of Dad's death. I'm dreading the day, the time of the call. I'm dreading reliving it all, the call of hope saying it looked like he was going to make it and then the call announcing his death. How can I get through the day?"

"Take it gently. Sadly others may not remember the day, so remind Ken and the kids that it is coming." Rosemary's eyes stayed focused on mine.

"I never thought that they might not remember." I swiveled and fussed with the cording on the arms of the chair.

"Remind them so you do not set yourself up with false expectations." Her soft smile lit up her face. "Don't schedule a full day. In fact, take the day off if you can. Do something for yourself."

"I just don't know what to expect. I think it's the not knowing that has me anxious." I stopped swiveling and leaned forward with my elbows on my knees.

"Be open as the day unfolds. Journal your feelings. Let them teach you. I'll be praying for you and I'm only a call away." We shared a warm hug and Rosemary walked me to the door.

Before opening the door, Sister Pat touched my arm. "Some freshly baked ginger cookies." I took the cookies. The warmth and love of these two women settled in my heart on my drive home.

> *January 30, 1989. The anniversary of Dad's death. I watched the old home movies and nibbled on Pat's cookies. The day passed softly. I hung onto warm memories. No new pain — just a deeper longing to accept sudden death.*

IN LATE FEBRUARY I met again with Rosemary. She settled on the sofa and I in my chair. "We've been meeting for over a year. You are working hard on your grief and the ministry issues at the church. My gut tells me that you're ready for our September eight-day silent directed retreat. I mention it to you now so you can think about it and prepare for it during the next months."

I leaned forward and about tumbled out of the swivel-rocker. "A time-out sounds good, but eight days of silence?"

"Yes. You come to rest, to read, to knit, to paint, to walk, to sit and take in. You come to pray and open yourself to God. The sea does soul-shaping while you are here."

"Why eight days?"

"St. Ignatius found that eight days of silence with direction each day will bring your prayer from utter confusion to deep trust and the seed of something new...a resurrection if you will."

"Will there be others on retreat, too?"

"Yes, the house has room for eight." Rosemary settled back and I relaxed with the idea.

I trusted Rosemary's intuition and began to arrange to attend the retreat in the fall. When I told friends and family the majority laughed. "You? Eight days of silence? You must be kidding."

SPRING CAME AND NEW life and warm winds filled the air. My strength returned and days filled with routine. Then on April 4, my mother called. "Gertie wants to die. I don't need my mother to die so soon after your Dad's death."

I flew to Ohio. I stayed in Gertie's room for three days. For three days I rubbed her back while her housekeeper brought us meals. For three days our conversation repeated.

"Gertie, we need to you to stay alive. We've just lost Dad."

"I know, but I hate seeing my little Evelyn sad. It's just not right. I'm the one who should have died, not my Billie Boy."

"We need you. Please don't leave us." Over the three days Gertie's strength gradually returned as she struggled to free herself from the paralyzing grief. I returned home exhausted from care giving and carrying Gertie's grief and my own.

MOTHER CAME TO OUR house for Maureen's June high school graduation. My sister Barb helped her to the bleacher seats. "I can do this myself." She squirmed with Barb's hand on her back.

"I know, but we don't need an accident to spoil Maureen's day." Barb guided her to her seat. We all did fine until it was time for graduation photos — No papa! Special times like this, Dad would be missed even more.

Several days after Maureen's graduation, Mother and I sat on the porch. Mother rocked. "Did I do the right thing at the hospital letting them do that balloon thing? If I'd only insisted, he takes an aspirin a day..."

I took a drink from my lemonade. "Mother you did everything you could."

"Your Dad was stubborn when it came to doctors and pills." We'd had this conversation before. I hoped with each telling she might begin to believe it.

SEPTEMBER ARRIVED AND THE busyness of the church year started. Meetings, youth group, committees and Bible study all began at the same time. I felt exhausted by the end of the first week, but I knew that my eight days of silence were coming. Each day I packed a few things. I didn't know what I'd need so I packed and packed — books, pens, pencils, two Bibles, drawing paper and pastels, camera and boxes of film, warm clothes and cool clothes.

On September 18, I crammed all my luggage and odds and ends into the car trunk and drove to the retreat center. I lugged my stuff up three flights of stairs. I entered my room and stopped. Through the three windows in front of me, I looked on a full view of the ocean and the rugged shoreline.

I luxuriated in the silence, the simple yet hearty meals prepared by Sister Pat and Sister Catherine, and the lack of demands on my time. I loved not having to make conversation or answer questions or tend to anyone. Twenty-three and a half hours each day were mine. The only conversation was with Rosemary for thirty minutes of direction each day. I talked and she guided my prayer with the Psalms and the Gospel of Mark.

Each morning the shore birds fluttered here and there filled with excitement of a new day. Their sounds drew me to my opened window to witness the dawn creeping into view. The birds talked and talked as they cruised near the black surface of the water searching for insects and sea plants. When the sun rose over the horizon, a stream of brilliant light lit a path across the water and bathed my room. Lingering in my rocker, I watched the rocky shoreline appear through the early morning light; its tide and storm shaped inlets visible here and there for a mile or more down the shore.

After drawing in the freshness of the morning, I followed the smell of brewing coffee down the three flights of stairs to the kitchen. With coffee in my hand, I walked to the main room. I turned the white wicker rocker to face the view and picked up a headset and listened to John Michael Talbot or Phil Coulter or the Monks of Weston Priory and cupped my hands around the mug and let the warmth, the view and the music draw me into a time of prayer.

Back in my room, I pulled on my jeans and a sweat shirt, my typical retreat wear, and picked up my journal and met with Rosemary for thirty minutes. She sat back in her soft pink overstuffed chair. "How is your prayer?"

I leaned forward in my chair. "Lines from Psalm 139 challenge me. 'O God, you've searched and known me. Where could I go to escape your spirit?' Is there no place to hide? I'm not sure I want God to know all of me."

Rosemary smiled and folded her hands. "Isn't it a bit comforting, too?"

"Yes, but what about my warts and all?"

"This time of silence is a place to offer your questions to God. Maybe it's time for a walk." I took her advice and grabbed my jacket and my camera.

I walked listening to the gulls, the wind, the ocean and the cars along Jerusalem Road in Cohasset to Sandy Beach. I knelt on the beach and studied the stones made smooth by the pounding of the tide. I photographed the wet ones that glistened blue, red, and purple in the sun. On my way back to the retreat center, I climbed a hillside and my eye caught the orange of bittersweet showing off among some blue and purple berries close to the ground. I sat on a boulder that was some 300 million years old. It anchored me to the foundations of creation. I picked at the moss and the lichens that clung to the rock. "God, I need to let you in, to see all of me so that I can move to a greater freedom."

That night I listened to the tide washing up on the rocky beach and the scratching sound it made as it returned to the sea through the rocks and sand. I woke up to grief clutching me. I watched the clock until it was my time to be with Rosemary for direction. We settled into the two facing chairs in her room. Her eyes met mine. "How are you doing?"

"Grief has its hold on me, consuming my prayer."

"Your Dad?"

"Yes." I played with the trim on the chair, holding my emotions in check.

"Sometimes, writing a letter to someone that you didn't get to say good-bye to can help." Rosemary held my gaze. "I know your hurt is deep, why don't you give it a try." I chewed on my lip.

I flew down the stairs, flung open the door, and raced across the yard to the rocks overlooking the ocean. I climbed the rocks. I jumped from one to the other. I listened to the pound of the waves as a storm approached. The wind gusts blew my perspiration dry. I yelled to the heavens, "Help me." I returned to my room, threw my coat on the bed, grabbed a pen and my yellow-lined journal and wrote.

Dear Dad,
I remember the letter you wrote to me when
you were in Arizona when I was six years old

*and in grade school. I treasured that letter for
years. I am sorry I don't have that letter now.
I am thinking of my Christmas ornament
wood carving years and how you came to my
rescue and made the wooden skate boards for
Snoopy. Gosh, Dad you were always involved.
I miss you so. I can at times hear your
greeting, "Hi, Marsh."*

*I loved your part of telephone conversations.
How you shared what you saw outside the
window or reported on your tomato plants
or the gooseberries or the speaker at Rotary.
Dave hugged me with your elbow hug the
other day. I found one of your "Shuttleworth"
handyman outfits in the basement a few
weeks ago. It still had your smell. Thanks
again for all the odd jobs you did for us over
the years.*

*How do you feel about Mother's move back
to Akron, or do you know of those changes?
Three blimps flew in formation over Akron as
we arrived with the moving truck. Did you
arrange that? Was it an affirmation to Mother
that you knew of the change in her location?
It was no coincidence.*

*Were Mom and Pop Mitchell there to greet
you? I remember Mom telling me when Pop
died how he was putting in a good word for
her. Dad, what's it like to be in God's presence?*

*I realize I am still angry and frustrated with
how you died. I wish you could have held on
for a while, so I could say good-bye. Now, as
I have had time to reflect, you never liked
hospitals or good-byes, so I guess your way
was appropriate for you.*

Dad, did you know you were going to die?

*I have a difficult time remembering your
last visit with us. I remember meeting you
and Mother at the airport. You were leaning
against a wall and Mother was out looking for
me. Your eyes lit up when you saw me. You
hugged and said, "Hi, Marsh," then we went
to dinner in Boston. You had some wine with
your dinner; that was unlike you. Why did
you do that? Dad, did you know you were
going to die?*

*During that visit we watched family movies.
Remember how excited David was at running
the projector?*

*Right now I hate and fear the word 'died.' As
I look through the sympathy cards and notice
many say "passed on" or "is just away," I
scream to myself, "Don't you get it? He is not
just away; he is dead, cold and dead.*

*So many ways you seem to be present...but
Dad, the emptiness I felt when Mother arrived
in Columbus the day after your death with
only Barb on her arm stabbed my heart. I'll
never forget the fear I experienced when the
funeral director called and wanted us to come
down. I said, "We don't have to see Dad do
we?" He graciously said, "No." Did you see all
this? Dad, was your spirit present as we made
the plans, picked out the casket and selected
your cemetery plot?"*

*Dad, so loved and admired. I loved your
ways—your gentleness, your participation
in projects for the needy. I loved the way you
embraced music. Remember the window
shaking as the organist played "Beast in the
Basement"? And remember the sound of the
old time car horns that would alarm motorists
at our four-way stop."*

*I remember you coming to the hospital for
Moe's birth. The sights and smells mesmerized
you. I remember your love and care and your
reflections on what you missed when we were
born. Thanks for sharing those real feelings.*

*Our kids, Dad, will never forget the Jackson
big apple…your bright red apple-shaped
water storage tank. Those Jackson days were
so important to you. I sensed your spirit being
affirmed. Dad, as we drove through Jackson
to the cemetery, the whole town stopped, even
the police saluted. I was proud. You have
left me with a legacy of gifts. My spiritual
director, Rosemary, refers to these gifts as your
resurrection. You never met Rosemary. She
has a garden built up with wood around it like
yours. I don't know if she counts her tomatoes
as you did, but I do know she doesn't douse
hers with Rapid Grow to compete with the
neighbor.*

*You were great with my kids. You made them
feel unique and special. David talks about
you standing in the school bus shelter on an
extremely cold day watching his football game.
Thanks for the love and concern you showed
to Ken and your interest in his work.*

*Did you help Jerry get his van and your car
out of the mud in West Virginia so he'd be on
time to the funeral? At Suzanne's wedding,
were you in charge of the flickering candles
that made us all laugh with tears in our eyes
as we missed you on her special day? And
did you arrange for the bluebirds to nest in
the birdhouse on the fence outside the kitchen
window? Do you know of the joy our new
black Labrador brings to us? She loves to be
up against us. She reminds me of how you*

*liked to sit close to us. Is that your spiritual
form? What would you have said to Mike
about his college and to Moe as she ventures
off?*

*As I look out the window to the ocean here
on retreat in Cohasset, Massachusetts I feel
us walking in the Cuyahoga Falls River Gorge
and along Lake Superior and I laugh to myself
as I relive the tent collapsing on Barb, you and
me while camping in the Smoky Mountains.
How did you put up with four women in that
nine-by-nine umbrella tent?*

*The bottom line, Dad, is that I wanted you
to keep on living and sharing life's adventures
with us because of your zest for life.*

Love and thanks,

Marsh

At the end of the day I poured a glass of wine, filled the
claw-foot tub with water, climbed in and let my soul rest. That
was enough grief work for now.

Anger

B ACK FROM RETREAT, I shuffled through my retreat photographs. Two of them stopped me; one at high tide with the water sparkling and the rocks showing off beneath the water as rays of sun played on the surface; and one at low tide with six feet of layers of rock and water-drenched sea weed clinging to the rocks, exposed to the air with no place to hide. The days of retreat did that to me. God slowly and lovingly exposed the guts of me, the stuff down deep, the mess I'd covered up out of shame and guilt and said, "I love all of you." I lingered over the photos, amazed at the story they told. I heard the back door open.

"Marcia. I'm home. If you don't have anything planned for supper, do you want to go out?"

"Good idea, Ken. Let me shower and change."

As I came from the shower into our bedroom, Ken was sitting on the bed. "My Dad's doctor called and said if we want to have a last visit with Dad, it's time to come."

Still wrapped in my towel, I sat on the bed beside him. "We've never faced the last visit with a parent." I scooted closer and reached around and hugged his back. "How do you think he will feel with us barging in on him?"

Ken caught my hand and squeezed. "I don't know." Ken's emotions remained buried deep, unknown and unnamed. He stood and rummaged in his closet for his suitcase. Then he went downstairs and I heard him making our flight arrangements.

I lay back on our bed. A last visit to a family member…I'd already witnessed the stages of dying and death. I'd been present at emotionally charged death bed experiences where anger ruled. I'd been there when last minutes phone calls were made by the dying and pent-up venom poured out on unsuspecting friends and family. I'd witnessed the family exchanging years of resentment. And I'd been present at heartwarming and truth-telling death bed scenes. Since his heart attack ten years ago, Ed had changed from an angry, driven man into one who was more humane and less critical. What was waiting for us?

THE NURSES USHERED OUR family, Mike, Maureen, David, Ken and me, into Ed's room. Ed was reading the newspaper.

We stood at the foot of his bed. Ed, with no greeting, looked up from his paper with fire in his eyes. "What are you doing here?" His eyes returned to his paper and with one hand he tugged on the sheet trying to cover his boney shoulder as if the sheet could disguise his fragility. A heavy cold worked through the room. Feeling dismissed by his remark, the kids and I crept out of the room.

A nurse showed us to a waiting room. "Not what I expected." I whispered as I followed closely behind Ed's three grandchildren, my children.

They shrugged. "Us either."

"He didn't even look at us." Maureen added as she picked up a magazine. My heart felt their disappointment and mine.

They sagged into orange plastic chairs. I left the waiting room and stood outside Ed's door. Ken moved from the foot of the bed to his father's side. Ed held the *Wall Street Journal* in front of his face and turned to the financial section. Ken pushed for conversation. "Dad, how are your stocks doing?"

"Don't get into the market unless you can afford it." Ed's eyes did not move from his paper.

Ken rested his hands on the railing around the bed and leaned toward his father. "How are you doing with all this?"

"It's lousy." Ed turned his body away from Ken.

AFTER WE LEFT THE hospital, we joined Ken's mother, Ruth, for dinner. She'd prepared spaghetti and meatballs and all the trimmings. We gathered around the cherry dining room table. Mike and Maureen shared their college adventures with Ruth and Dave talked about football. Ruth fidgeted with the napkins, folding them, shaking them out, and folding them again. "How was Dad?" Ken and I looked at each other.

Ken's gaze shifted down at his hands as he lifted a fork and played with his spaghetti. "He was tired and didn't want to talk." Ken's eyes stayed down.

"Yeah," David announced, "we just hung around the waiting room."

"He's embarrassed to be sick. He's angry. That's why he doesn't say much." Tired and drawn, Ruth sat back in her chair and laid her fork on her plate. She studied the kids as they devoured her homemade cookies. I tried to imagine what she was feeling, what words were stuck in her heart.

Ken glanced at his watch. "Mom, we need to go if we are going to make our flight." Ruth sighed.

As each of the kids gave her a hug, she whispered, "Thanks for coming."

Ken hugged his mother. "Sorry we have to go."

Ruth pushed him an arms' distance away. "Ken I'm glad you came. Ed was tough on you growing up; I'm surprised you keep coming back."

Ken fought back tears. "Will you be all right?"

"Marilyn is coming up this weekend and my friends check on me every day." Ruth stood in the driveway and waved until we turned onto the highway.

DURING OUR FLIGHT HOME, I battled with myself. Could I have done anything to make the visit better? I'd hoped for an opening where we could have thanked him for his generosity. I'd hope we could have said our goodbyes. That was not to be. Ed remained distant. My anger festered. I tried to relax. I turned to Ken.

"Ken, I'm sorry about the visit."

"Me too, I was disappointed by Dad's anger. I guess we were expecting too much. Maybe for him, death had been theoretical until our visit. Maybe our presence confirmed his worst fears."

As the wheels of the plane touched down in Boston, I prayed. God, the visit was awful. Why couldn't Ed rally for the kids? It was the old self-consumed Ed. My anger over his early behavior toward Ken and Mike is welling up from its place buried in my heart. Hurt from his belittlement of Ken and his criticism of Mike. Couldn't he see the pain on Ken's face? Help me to understand.

TWO WEEKS LATER, THE call came. Ed had died. We returned to Ohio for the visiting hours and the funeral. Our children took turns standing with Ruth as visitors filed into the funeral home. We watched Ed's mother, Eleanora kneel at her son's body in disbelief. She touched the word 'son' on the ribbon draped on the flowers to the left of the casket.

Back at the house after the visiting hours at Wilcox Funeral Home, Ken's sisters and brother gathered around the dining room table, snacking and talking, as they caught up with each other. The TV in the living room buzzed as the grandchildren watched their favorite shows. Gradually each person found their bed and the house quieted. The only sound came from Ruth stirring a cup of tea. She motioned for me to take the other chair at the kitchen table. "I've written a few words about Ed. Will you read them for me at the funeral?"

"Sure." We sat in silence for a while. Ruth said good night and made her way down the hall. I watched as she labored to her room, her gait slow and measured because of the bad circulation in her legs. What a lady. I picked up her notes and read them,

> I hope there will be gardens in heaven so
> Ed can go out and spread his seeds and
> watch for the little green shoots. Even last
> summer when he was taking chemotherapy
> treatments every week and not feeling well,
> he had his friend John till the ground so
> he could plant his tomatoes and beans and
> squash. He had a chair by the garden so he
> could sit and watch them grow.

> He started his day by driving over to
> the Giant Eagle for a Wall Street Journal
> and some groceries. When he returned,
> he checked on his stocks and decided
> which broker to call. He was a child of the
> depression, and it was important to him to
> make money so his family would never face
> financial problems. He was proud that all his
> children became financially responsible and
> he was happy to help them out on occasion
> with cash gifts.

> He loved to fix things and make them useful
> again. The nursery school women became
> accustomed to seeing him around the church
> inspecting chairs, toilets, and tending to
> other small tasks. Later Ed came over on
> Thursday nights to work with the trustees.
> His own appliances and cars lasted forever

because of his expert repairs.

He liked to joke and admired people who could get off a one-liner as he called them.

At Westinghouse he had a fresh approach and an inventive solution to electrical problems. The company honored him with 13 patents and 50 disclosures. He became a "fellow" engineer. He always admired and respected his friend Ted who was at home with complicated equations.

He enjoyed his job and his friends at Quality Switch and spent his last productive days there. His mother couldn't believe that he would get up and go to work when he was ill.

He was a man driven by some inner need for useful activity and he often drove his wife and children to do tasks they didn't want to do.

He was often troubled and anxious and prowled about at night. His minister, Phil, and his church attendance helped to calm him and put his life in perspective. He did feel that he'd always been blessed with good luck, and he couldn't understand why he was unlucky enough to contract this fatal illness when he had so much left to do. We will miss you, Ed. Ruth.

I cleaned up the cups from the small table, turned out the lights and found my bed.

OVER BREAKFAST, I SHARED Ruth's notes with Ken. Ruth shuffled into the kitchen. "Have you read my notes?"
"Yes."
"I hope you will add some words of your own."
"Thanks. I will." What will I say with my anger still boiling?

Why was Ed cold at our last visit? Why did he distance himself from the kids? Why was he tough on Ken? Couldn't he have risen above it all?

All day I watched Ruth pondering as she sat on the porch and later as she listened to her children and grandchildren talk on and on around the dining room table. That evening, again with the house quiet, she reminisced with Ken and me. "Ed's life was work, work and more work. Frank and Eleanora, his parents, knew nothing but work as first generation immigrants from Poland. Birthday presents were unknown to Ed as a child. A Christmas present, still in its store bag, was put on a chair with the words, that's your present, Eddie. He fought mental demons from his sterile childhood."

"When we met at college, Ed was a happy adventurous young man who enjoyed flying, but Ken, when you were born, the pressure of fatherhood and World War II caved in on him. He became driven. Ed was tormented that people were out to get him. At times, he drove you kids too hard and yelled too loud. I'm sorry for that." She stood and padded in her slippers to the sink and looked out the window toward the garden.

I wanted to lift Ruth's spirit. "Ruth, remember the summer after we moved from Burlington, Iowa, to Hingham, Mass?" She turned toward me and listened as she leaned into the edge of the sink.

"My friend Carol brought Mike, Maureen, and David's best friends to meet us here for a visit. Dave still talks about Ed helping him and his friend Richie cut down a tree. We enjoyed Ed's fresh corn and beans from the garden. And remember at dinner, when he cleaned the horseradish root and our sinuses cleared instantly and he looked surprised as laughter ran around the table?"

Ruth wiped a tear from her face and made her way to the bedroom.

THE NEXT MORNING QUIET filled the house as the families showered and dressed for the funeral. We drove to the church and I robed with the minister in his study. The pews filled with Ed's friends and family. The pastor read scripture and we sang a hymn. After his words the pastor introduced me.

I stood for a moment. Anger and resentment from our last family visit with Ed lurked below my calm façade. The image of the hurt and downcast faces of my children as they left that hospital room flashed through me. I'd admitted to myself that my expectations for the visit had been too high, yet out of my own frustration, I wanted to get back at Ed and shout to the public, "Ed belittled Ken, planted fear in Mike, and kept Ruth in her place." But this was not the time for me to vent. It was a moment to rise to the level of the occasion.

I read Ruth's well-crafted words about Ed's life that offered no judgment. And then, added my own words addressing the positive little things that were part of Ed too.

> The grandchildren remember Ed slurping watermelon and handing out dollars after each visit. He showed me great kindness. When we visited he made breakfast for the kids to give me a leisurely morning. It touched me when he and Ruth appeared at my Dad's funeral. He visited Carnegie Mellon University with Mike. And Ed and Ruth traveled to Hingham to be with our children as Ken and I ventured to Singapore.

> One curious memory is that each time Ken and I moved, Ed searched out a unique grocery store in our new area. His fetish for grocery shopping amused me. After he checked out these new stores, he'd proudly declare, 'You can't beat the prices in Warren.' Ed loved a bargain.

> Ed's inherited Polish work ethic drove him to perfect attendance at work and eventually to a severe heart attack. After the surgery he walked and adjusted his eating habits according to the doctor's instructions. He became a different person, less driven, more approachable, and more compassionate.

> Last summer while sitting in a webbed lawn chair, looking out toward his garden Ed lamented. "The cancer has frustrated my

plans to take care of Ruth. I'm angry."

Now Ed is free from his anger and welcomed home by a God who loved him.

I offered this prayer.

O God, anger works in us. Mostly our anger originates within our own self-perceived limitations, our own judgments of ourselves. Open us to healthy anger over injustices in your world and in our relationships and within ourselves. Free us from anger that has paralyzed our love.

Lord, we ask for your compassionate arms to surround Ruth and the family and friends, to comfort each of us in our pain. We ask for your spirit of healing to spark deep inside each of us, to slowly ease our anger and lead us to places of peace where we may celebrate in new ways our lives as we lived them with Ed. In the spirit of Christ, the healer and peacemaker, we pray. Amen

I returned to my seat behind the lectern. I prayed, "God transform my anger."

I turned to listen to the soloist sing, "Amazing Grace." In the silence as family and friends recovered from the beauty of the music, I realized I wanted more than Ed could give. The anger I'd witnessed on that last visit was not directed toward Ken and our family. The failure of that visit was about his death. He wasn't angry with us. He was angry at the disease, terrified about death.

Her Solid Cherry Casket

KEN AND I STOOD in the kitchen waiting for our pizza to be delivered. Ken leaned against the counter. "I see you have your witch clothes piled on the window seat. Who is joining you this year?"

"Kate and Rosemary are suiting up as witches and Dave Delano as a clown."

"Kate? Really?"

"Sure. She wants to see what it's like to 'minister' as a witch." The phone rang and I asked Ken to get it. I had spent my day sitting on the rocks, watching and listening to the wave's pound against the shore. It had brought me solace and I didn't want to let go of the contentment just yet.

Ken reached over to the phone and listened. He hung up and spoke with words I could barely hear. "My Mother died a few hours ago. The nurses said she drifted away with a look of peace on her face."

I reached for him. "We should have expected this news. I knew it was bound to happen, yet I'm surprised. I'd hoped she'd go on and on even with her heart problems."

We stood and held each other. Sorrow overwhelmed us.

Ruth and her unconditional love were gone.

YELLOW, RED AND ORANGE trees covered the hills, as Ken and I traveled from Massachusetts to Ohio. I remembered another fall day. Ruth stood on the patio rocking five-week old Maureen in her arms and watching Mike play in the leaves. Ken, Ed and I worked at removing a honey locust tree from the edge of their property to be transported to our yard, a three-hour drive away, and replanted. She walked toward us.

"Maureen, look at how the red of their work shirts pops out against the yellow of the honey locust leaves." In my memory the beauty of that fall day was similar to this one except that on that day Ruth stood there introducing Maureen to life and here we were heading toward the reality of Ruth's death. I sighed and whispered to Ken. "A beautiful day."

He surveyed the trees with his eyes. "The colors are spectacular. I was just picturing you and Mom getting happy sharing blenders of strawberry daiquiris."

"We emptied a few blenders, didn't we?" I added remembering the bond we created over those daiquiris.

Ken shifted in his seat. We let some time elapse, each with our own thoughts.

"Ken, your mother was the first person from whom I felt unconditional love. No judgment. No expectations. I didn't have to earn her love. It was just there." Tears stained my heart.

After a stop for gas and coffee, we switched drivers. Ken finished his coffee. "I'll never forget her call shortly after Dad's death. She asked me to come and assist me in buying a new car. I promised that I would." Ken shrugged. "She didn't need me. She walked right over to the car, a red Buick Park Avenue with all the extras including leather seats and wire wheels. I'm sure Dad rolled over in his grave when she paid cash for the car but it made her feel like a queen."

"For the first time, she took control." Ken paused lost in thought. "Not too long after buying her car she told me she wanted to sponsor family reunions. She wanted to go a place that would lure everyone to come. She did that with the Caribbean cruise and the week at Pink Beach in Bermuda, didn't she?" Ken beamed.

I settled back in my seat and let the hum of the wheels lead me back to the kitchen in Ruth's condo. I sat at the table with my head resting in my hands. The family had raised concern about her health; I offered to spend a week with her. Diabetes, cancer, congestive heart failure and circulation problems curtailed her activities. She needed outside help with meals and a walker to move around her condo. I saw the depression that stalked her even as she fought against it. Such an elegant lady, I hated that age and illness changed her spirit.

I focused on the road and the colors flashing by our car as we drove toward Ohio. My reflections continued. One night, sitting at her dining room table at the end of her living room, I worked on a sermon for the following Sunday. Light from the television flickered. She lay stretched out on the sofa in a pink duster surrounded by magazines that hung on the edge of the cushion. She began to talk in low tones.

"Night after night I re-play my life. Unresolved anger toward Grandma Cham and Ed runs through my night dreams. I relive life with my in-laws. I always felt like an outsider; an English Protestant in a Polish Catholic family." She stopped and her eyes closed. I strained to hear her next words. "I grieve over what could have been. I could have left Ed, yet I decided to stay for the family. Each night I pray for forgiveness for harboring unkind thoughts. I ask God to open the family's hearts to forgive Ed's harshness and anger and to forgive me for not standing up to him, especially with the kids."

A privileged intimate moment. I wiped tears from my eyes remembering those moments and remembering the fullness of her depression.

Then Ken tapped me on the shoulder. "I need a snack." I twisted around and reached into the back seat for the snacks. I noticed my clerical robe hanging from the hook. I had thrown it in along with my notebook on funeral services should I need them for Ruth's service. I prayed a silent prayer. Please, God, let me be family and not the one in charge. Let me be the one comforted instead of the one who comforts. I need to be family. I need to cry over Ruth and the loss of her presence.

When we arrived at the motel, we met Ruth's pastor. "You had a beautiful day to drive."

"We certainly did." Ken stretched and yawned.

"I'm sorry for your loss. The news of Ruth's death has spread throughout the church community."

"She loved the church." I said.

He cleared his throat and adjusted his tie. "I'm sorry to tell you, Marcia, but I can't officiate at Ruth's funeral. She talked with pride of your call to ordained ministry. Will you officiate? You know she'd love for you to do it, don't you?"

My spirit screamed silently, "No, I want to be family," but the words, "I know," came out of my mouth. I slid into the role of officiating pastor for Ruth's celebration and recognized God's strange humor of calling me again to a place I'd rather not go.

Ken and I met with the funeral director. He held a folder with Ruth Cham printed on the cover. He explained, "When we talked, Ruth said, 'I don't want the few who come to my service to feel lost in the sanctuary of the church. Please plan for my service in the mausoleum.'"

Ken slipped into the conversation. "You understand she never wanted to impose on others or have others go out of their way for her. She wasn't the showy sort."

The director opened the folder and glanced over the details of Ruth's preplanned funeral. "She's chosen our most expensive solid cherry casket." He peeked over his glasses at Ken and me.

"Great!! A solid cherry casket!" Joy spread over Ken's face.

"She loved cherry. An expensive solid cherry casket planted right next to Ed. Now that will be a moment." I chimed in.

The director explained their protocol for services. All of the arrangements seemed routine until the last bit of information.

"After the family says their final goodbyes and leaves, the staff will take the casket to the burial site and do the burial." The little hairs on the back of my neck stood stiff.

"Why?"

"We are afraid of a fall or a twisted ankle on the uneven ground around the gravesites."

"You fear a lawsuit, that's what you're saying." He looked away and firmly grasped his pen and tapped it on the edge of his desk.

I leaned forward from my chair and placed both hands on his desk. "It is important for this family to carry Ruth to her resting place. The family needs that journey with Ruth." I spoke as Reverend Cham.

He was reluctant but agreed.

A PERFECT FALL DAY greeted us on the morning of Ruth's funeral. Two ducks on the lawn called their welcome, and we laughed, imagining them to be Ruth and Ed. The deep red beauty of the sweet gum tree and the arrival of her great-grandchildren, Bertram and Harrison, in happy little hats, delighted us.

Inside the darkness of the mausoleum, I stepped to the podium, touched the cherry casket and felt pride grow inside me with the opportunity to facilitate Ruth's service. "We gather in the comfort of this place to pour out our grief, to share in our common loss and to thank God for the life of Ruth Fulmer Cham." I'd taken on the mantel of pastor and her spirit filled me.

After a prayer of thanksgiving and scriptures for our comfort, I pulled a hand-written piece from behind my papers and read the collected memories the grandchildren had gathered.

We remember strawberry jam on toast, pies at Thanksgiving, Grandma Ruth cutting our sandwiches the wrong way and the downstairs bar and shots of Vernor's Ginger Ale, golfing with grandma and the New Year's dress-up costumes, the hooded electric hair dryers and Ruth dancing with Dave at Mike and Maggie's wedding.

I INTRODUCED KEN'S SISTER, Marilyn, Ruth's primary caregiver. She walked to the lectern, unfolded her notes and looked over the crowd.

Ruth was proud of her children and grandchildren. She told me once that when she had Ken she was happy because she knew she would never be lonely again. She was proud of Ken for his accomplishments but I especially think she thought he had married well. She loved to hear Kathy play organ and had high regard for John, Kathy's attorney husband. She bragged about Frank being a college professor. And of course, she bragged about the grandchildren.

The last time I saw her she wanted me to hand her the book she was reading about angels. I've thought since then that maybe she was reading it to get her final instructions on being an angel.

I know how much I'll miss her, but it does give me great comfort to know that she's at peace.

Marilyn returned to her seat as Ken stood. They shared a quick hug. Ken walked behind the lectern and without notes began his story.

She let me arrange trips to the Caribbean
and Bermuda knowing northern Ohio held
little attraction for busy grandchildren. Mom
had three rules for these trips: each person
was responsible for his or her bar bill; all
were expected to be present for dinner; and
guests of the grandchildren paid their own
way unless they were married to one of the
grandchildren."

Ken made us laugh at the picture of Ruth carrying Ed's
sagging threadbare chair out back and burning it to end their
discussion about whether the chair had plenty of life in it. He
remembered her holding her first great grandchildren, Bert
and Harrison, eight months earlier. And he celebrated her solid cherry casket, Ruth's final testament of her freedom.

The sons and grandsons and sons-in-law carried that casket to its resting place. The brilliant fall arrangements of roses
and mums gleamed in the sunlight against the rich deep tones
of the cherry casket. Ken and I lingered. I took a burnished
gold rose and we walked to our car.

A short drive brought us to the Avalon Inn, Ruth's favorite place for lunch. Ruth's presence moved in and through the
family, taking delight in the gossip, seeing the great-grandchildren greeted by all the relatives and meeting Pete, who would
become Ruth's new grandson-in-law.

AFTER THE DETAIL-FILLED DAYS of planning and officiating, I needed to slow down and let Ruth's death settle in my
heart. On the ride home, I found myself pondering as Ruth
often did. I recalled my initial shock and reluctance to conduct
Ruth's service, but now I felt honored to be the pastor for Ruth
as she had been a mentor for me and my studies and my ordination, and always had compliments of how Ken and I were
raising her grandchildren.

At home Ken and I unpacked one of Ruth's cherry arm
chairs and boxes of slides and piles of photograph albums. We
piled the boxes on the dining room table and I sat in the cherry chair for weeks sorting through the picture story of her life
from high school to college, to early marriage and children.

During those days of memory-sorting, I grieved and laughed; I found peace and the blessing that Ruth was and will always be in my life with her unconditional love.

ON SEPTEMBER 26, 2003 Ruth's great-granddaughter Eliza Jane Cham, received her Hebrew name at Simchat Bat, a baby naming ceremony for a Jewish girl. When the rabbi asked Mike and Maggie for Eliza's Hebrew name our daughter-in-law, Maggie said,

> "The Hebrew name we chose for Eliza is Chaya Ruth. In Judaism, chaya means life – the most sacred thing in Judaism. Michael and I knew we wanted a name that meant miracle or life to show our gratitude for our daughter's life.
>
> It was very important to both Michael and me that we honor and remember Grandma Ruth Cham. In Hebrew, Ruth means friend and compassion, both of which she showed me. We shared special one-on-one moments that I'll always be grateful for. She was a very special person and a lady.
>
> And we are grateful to God for life, that of our daughter Eliza, and for the life of Grandma Ruth and we are proud and honored to name Eliza today, Chaya Ruth."

Ruth's memory and unconditional love live on.

Gertie's Parade

D<small>AVE, OUR YOUNGEST, HONKED</small> and we saw his VW rabbit pull into the driveway. He raced across the yard and into the house. He hugged us and picked up Ebony and danced around the kitchen with her. We unloaded his car in no time and sat on the porch catching up with his college adventures. The phone rang. Ken ran into the house and answered it. He choked up as he walked back out on the porch.

"Marsh and Dave, Gertie died today." He held us, knowing of our love for Gertie, my maternal grandmother and Dave's great grandmother.

I cried as I remembered my last visit at the nursing home. I had returned from the errand she instructed me to do. I sat on her bed. I admired her smooth wrinkle-free skin as I watched her rest. An amused look flashed over her face as if she dreamed something funny and her eyes fluttered open. Gertie stroked my hand.

"You've met Joe."

I nodded. She lay back with a contented look on her face. "All is ready then."

O<small>N THE DAY OF MY</small> ordination, Gertie, wrote to me,

> "Congratulations to the Cham family. My Jeanne girl said she sent you a card. Since I haven't one, I called and now I am writing to you. How proud your Dad would be of you. I bet your sermon was beautiful. I remember the one you gave at your Dad's funeral in Jackson. I told Anna Mae I want you to come and say it at my funeral at the Methodist Episcopal Church. OK? I am proud of you. Come see me."

Gertie and I met many times to talk about her funeral. Each time we talked she would say with a little devilment in her voice, "I hope you won't charge me the $25 the local preacher charges." Each time she covered her face like a coy young girl. Each time her gold wedding ring slipped around

144

on her finger, the ring she'd worn for 80 years.

"Ever since my last friend passed on, I've been ready to go, Marcia Janie. All who knowed me when I was young are gone." A faraway look appeared on her face. "I want to go to Joe Humphrey's Funeral Parlor over in Shawnee."

"Gertie, wasn't everyone laid out in your house?"

"They was. Your grandfather, my Ed. Maggie and Jackie. Aunt Amy and Uncle George. Aunt Alice. Grandpa Howe. All of them." She recited from deep in her memory.

Then she puffed up, as she often did. "I am the matriarch of the family and…the town. I want a parade from Methodist Episcopal Church to the cemetery."

When I told my mother of Gertie's plans, she reacted as I knew she would. "Everyone else was laid out at home. Isn't that good enough for her? Why does she have to be different? Does she think she is a queen or something?"

The next time I met with Gertie I replayed my mother's remarks. She put on a mask of indifference and continued with the planning.

In April of 1993 she had one of her spells. She was taken to a nursing care center. I arrived some days later. We hooted and hugged and shared some hard candy. Then she looked at me and said with a parched voice, "It's time, honey. Take your aunts, Novella and sweet little Jeanne girl, to see Joe Humphrey."

That afternoon Novella, Jeanne and I walked up the uneven sidewalk of the Joe E. Humphrey Funeral Parlor and found the bell, hidden under some scraggly ivy near the steps. We rang, but no one came. We tried the door; it opened. We called, "Hello, Hello." "Joe, are you here?" We listened and heard the faint squeak of a chair.

We moved down a dingy hall toward the sound and peeked around a corner into the office. Joe was sitting at a desk among piles of yellowed funeral supply catalogs, stacks of left-behind vases, and nests of odd chairs. He noticed us and pulled himself up out of an ancient chair.

With a nod he directed us to several chairs opposite him, and we sat down. So did Joe. Without a word, he picked at specks of paint on his trousers.

We looked at each other. Novella broke the awkward silence. "Joe, do you remember me? We had a few dates in high school."

"Well,…yes…I…do."

With those words, Joe's energy left him. He looked at his hands, then at his watch, and then fussed with the sleeves of his grayish yellow shirt. He spoke so slowly you could feel the Earth moving on its axis. "So…Gertie's…getting…ready… to…die…is she?"

We nodded.

Again slow words came from his mouth. "She told me… you'd be over…when…the time…came."

He paused and grabbed a toothpick and picked his teeth. "Casket room's…in…the…garage…through…that…door."

WE MADE OUR WAY out the door and across an uneven weed infested path to a rusty metal door with a small sign hanging at an angle from a broken nail. The sign read, "Caskets in here."

Jean took a deep breath. "We have to go in there, don't we?"

Novella grabbed Jean's arm. "I've dreaded this moment for a long time." I pushed the door open and they slid inside. Their eyes popped and to my surprise and theirs, the casket room captivated them. They moved from one box to the other. They ran their hands over the silky interiors, admired each color. Jeanne was about ready to climb in and lie down in one of the caskets to give Novella a better idea of how Gertie would look when Joe's wife came in. She took our order.

GERTIE DIED ON JUNE 13, 1993 at the age of 95 years, 11 months, 14 days.

In the parking lot before the viewing I overheard my mother whispering to her three sisters. "Viewings are old fashioned. I'm going to be cremated. I don't want people to pass my casket saying, doesn't she look good."

Beneath these remarks I heard my mother's avoidance of death. I remembered mother talking about the bodies laid out in her grandmother's house as a child. "Someone sat near the body all night long. Before the preacher came to do the service, I pushed the broom around the casket. They held my dad's body in the house for a few extra days in case Jack and Jimmy could get leave from the service to come home. Dad didn't look at all like himself. I would rather have remembered him alive. I didn't like it then, and I don't like it now."

A push on my elbow jogged my mind back to Gertie's viewing. Mother grabbed my arm as we walked up the path to the funeral home. "Let's get this over with."

Joe's wife met us at the door. Joe was nowhere to be seen. The sisters apprehensively approached the casket but with one look at Gertie they began to play with Gertie's body. "Something doesn't look right. Her glasses are missing. Where are they? They're in her hand. We need to move them. Move her glasses, Jeanne. Put them on her face."

They stepped back. "Something still isn't right. It's the necklace. Take it off." Jeanne lifted Gertie's head, unhooked the necklace, and took it off. "No, now her neck is too bare. But she always loved the shape of her neck. It's too plain. Put it back on."

At that moment I wished for Gertie to have one last muscle reflex to slap her hand at them to say, "Stop your fussing."

THE METHODIST EPISCOPAL CHURCH was full for Gertie's funeral. Ceiling fans clicked. Cardboard funeral fans waved. Guests sat still in an effort to avoid the heat. As I climbed up the stairs to the pulpit, I looked over the gathering of family and friends and thought, Gertie look at this crowd. At almost 96, the church is almost full. I felt Gertie resting her finger on my arm as I did when she said, "Seeing this makes you a believer," while we sat under the cool pines at Linville Falls.

Then as I pulled the chain on the lectern light, something inside me broke. This is my grandmother's life I'm celebrating. My eyes welled up as I spoke the gathering words, "We are gathered here to celebrate the life of Gertrude Edwards Mills."

I looked again at the people sitting there in the heat…my aunts and uncles and cousins…my children and my sisters' children…my mother anticipating my words. For a moment the reality of being pastor to my mother for her mother and being pastor for Gertie's other children, grandchildren and great grandchildren overwhelmed me.

I shifted my weight and read, "I lift my eyes up unto the hills from where I gather my strength," the Spirit intervened. My voice strengthened. I went on with the service dry-eyed and confident as I knew Gertie expected.

When I finished my remarks, my sister Barbara, walked to the pulpit and gazed out at family and friends and read from the collective memories of Gertie's grandchildren.

Gertie, your goodness and spirit lives on, and we all remember…

Your homemade rolls
Your funny high-pitched laughter
A cup to put your teeth in
And "I haven't heard from that Evelyn."

The horn you played through your teeth
Your enjoyment of a joke
Peanut butter fudge
And "I wonder how my angel is."

Early birthday cards,
Lemon meringue pie
The "ha-ha" written in your letters
And "I think I'll call Anne."

Your reaction when one of us called you 'Gert'.
Your bag from O'Neil's
The way you fell asleep in a chair
And "I have a feeling Jack will drop by."

Always having something to take home with us.
Your readiness to go somewhere—anywhere!!
Your liking to dress up
And "Dickie Boy always calls on Sunday."

Mills steak, coconut cream pie
Seven consecutive Ah-choos
Your unconditional love
And "I haven't heard from Novella
this week."

Your clean cotton house dresses and
high-heeled shoes
You chasing us with a shoe or a broom
Those Xs and Os on your letters and cards
And "Do you think my Jeannie will call?"

Trips to the 5 and 10-cent store to buy candy
Getting your grandchildren off the hook
By eating their vegetables and rice pudding
We will remember often
And we'll miss you.

Grandchildren and great-grandchildren carried her casket to Joe's hearse…a Dodge minivan. I rode in the front seat with Joe. Gertie's parade passed Ward's Drug Store, Matthew's bar, and an abandoned coal mine her father had owned, the yellow brick house where she lived her later years, the empty lots where her Aunt Amy's Red and White Store once stood, and the deserted brickworks where her husband Ed had worked.

As the parade struggled up the steep brick hill to the grave, I whispered, "Gertie, did you enjoy your parade?"

THREE MONTHS LATER ON another eight-day directed silent retreat, visions and memories of Gertie broke forth in buckets of tears. My grieving began. I sat in a rocker looking down the rugged shoreline and remembered and wrote.

> *She shuffled to the door or window to wave as we left each time. And when we arrived she always sounded her greeting 'Woo-woo-woo' and followed that with, 'I thought you'd never get here. How long are you going to stay?'*

> *How proud I felt riding in the hearse carrying your body. As Joe drove the few blocks from the church to the cemetery, your long noisy hugs and the taste of your peanut butter fudge flashed through my mind and heart.*

> *I sit here imagining you dancing with your arms folded under your breasts to keep them from jiggling — a grand lady. To be almost 96 and have a church full of family and friends, what a testament to her life.*

Fear Invades

Fear is useless. What is needed is trust.
Mark 5:36

Freedom and independence can't be wrested
from others but only can be
developed painstakingly from within.
Colette Dowling[13]

The other side of every fear is a freedom…
we must take charge of the journey urging
ourselves past our own reluctance
and misgivings and confusions
to new freedom.
M. Ferguson[14]

Calm before the Storm

T HE CHILDREN DECORATED THE house for the holidays. I had been sitting vigil at the hospital for two days with Karen's family. The call came while I put away groceries bought on my way home from the hospital. "It's Jimmy. Mom died. All of us were there. Could you meet us at home tomorrow?"

"Sure, Jimmy."

Again the reality hit hard. Karen, another young mother, ravaged with cancer. Jim, another widower left without a life partner, and their children, Sarah, Megan, Jimmy, and Susan left without a mother for their high school and college years. My heart fell in despair.

I MADE A CUP OF TEA and carried it into the living room. I placed the tea on the table and opened the door to the stereo system and turned on a tape collection of cello music. The deep mellow chords and soul-stirring vibrations carried me back to my first visit with Karen and Jim; Jim in a crisp white shirt and Karen in a fuchsia sweater posed on the sofa in their family room, sunlight slicing through the sky lights.

Jim stacked and restacked a pile of books on the coffee table. "The books we've read about cancer."

Karen pulled more books from under the table. "Here are the books we've read on death."

They seemed ready for death. I struggled to take it in. Ready? Are you ever ready? Where were their anger, their questions, their reaction to the unfairness of it all? Would I ever be that ready for death? Was my own fear of death making it impossible for me to grasp what seemed to be their readiness?

I remembered when I was nineteen years old standing with my back pushed hard against the wall of the Sweeney Funeral Home, my legs weak and my hands clammy. At the other end of the long room, my grandfather's bald head shone above the edge of the coffin even in the dreary light. I didn't want to see more. In fact, I didn't want to see any of it, but I found no way to avoid it. The dark wooden casket with the half-opened lid punctuated with button-quilted silk and a carpet of flowers covering the wood dominated the room. Chills traveled through my body.

From my position against the back wall, I heard bits of conversations as I watched guests filing by Pop's casket. I closed my eyes and talked with him.

"Pop, a woman with a large bosom said to Mom, 'Look how good he looks.' From here I can't tell how you look, but I can't imagine that dead looks good."

"It doesn't," Pop whispered in my ear. "The undertaker did a good job with this old man. He even got the dirt out from under my finger nails." I felt Pop's quiet laughter warm my heart.

"Pop, a couple dressed in matching navy suits just walked in."

"That's the Goddard's." The couple whisked past me along with the cold December wind.

"Pop, they said, 'Such a blessing, he didn't linger.' A blessing that you're dead, how can that be?"

"Marsh, it takes a long time to come to that understanding."

"I'm afraid, afraid to come any closer to your body, afraid that others will die. I'm pinching myself to make sure I'm here."

"I see that. Death is not easy to accept. One day you will be better with it the same as the rest of us. Meanwhile, my spirit will hover around to help you."

The last chords of cello music ended and the tape clicked off. I glanced at the picture of Pop and Mom on the shelf across the room. "Pop, it's been thirty years since your death. Thanks for hovering around. Now, please be with me through Karen's death."

THE NEXT DAY I met with Karen's family. Jim greeted me and pointed to a seat on the sofa. "We want you to see this video with us." Jimmy adjusted the video player on top of the television. The video opened with Karen positioned in a low beach chair next to a pond, wearing a fuchsia sweat suit with a flashy turban around her bald head. Looking directly into the camera, she addressed each of her four children.

> Sarah, since birth you have been in charge.
> You've plowed ahead and made things
> happen. Bring others along with you as you
> challenge the world.

Megan, you zoomed out of the womb.
Excited about life. Remember your curiosity
and your zest for life are blessings to be
shared with others.

Jimmy, you've been the essence of love since
the beginning. Compassion was born in your
eyes. Touch the world with your love.

Susan, you were born with a quiet spirit. As
a little one you discovered life through your
senses. Bless this world by reminding others
to slow down, to touch and feel and breathe
in life.

As I watch you from another place, I know
each of you will make me proud in your own
individual ways. Give back. Bless the world
as you have blessed me.

Then she turned slightly in her chair and crossed her legs.
She threw her head back and laughed.

"Now I want to set the story straight of how
your Dad and I met. Your Dad will have
it all mixed up in no time. We met during
my freshman year at Skidmore College. Jim
had a date with my roommate. I thought
this preppy man was not her type. A year
after college we met again while skiing. A
few weeks later he took me to dinner in
Harvard Square. Two weeks later we wanted
to get married. We waited until November
to please my parents. When it's the right
person, you just know it.

The video ended with the videographer, Karen's doctor
and friend, panning back to where you could barely see Karen
beside the pond.

Tears trailed down each face, dripping from their chins
and clinging to the fibers of their sweaters...a sparkling pres-

ence against the harsh reality of Karen's death. Karen's love silenced the room. It blew me away. Would I ever have that kind of courage in the face of death?

THE DAY BEFORE KAREN's memorial service, Jimmy called. I said, "Jimmy, how are you and your sisters doing?"

"We're doing fine. Our friends are holding us together. Marcia, the movie, *My Life*, starring Michael Keaton is showing. Will you go with Susan and me?"

"I don't know the movie, but I'd be happy to go with you. I'll come by and pick you up."

We bought popcorn and settled to watch the movie. My eyes filled up. I sucked in air. My body heaved as I watched the scenes of a young father recording himself shaving, putting a train together, and doing the ordinary things of life so that his unborn child would know him. The father had terminal cancer.

After the movie, we walked to the car. Jimmy took my arm and Susan with red eyes and runny nose crowded behind me. "Marcia, what did you think?"

I struggled for words but I could only sob. I reached for Jimmy and Susan. They wrapped me in a massive hug. "We had to see it for Mom," Jimmy breathed into our intimate circle of love.

LATER THAT DAY AS I prepared for Karen's service, I couldn't get the movie out of my mind. "What would I do with only a few months left to live?" I sat in the overstuffed chair in my home study and let my imagination run as I talked to the oak tree that stood outside the window.

I'd like to be philosophical about the announcement, skip the anger and the 'pity me part' and say to myself, 'I've had a good life.' But I'll probably be angry, have a pity party, and when I've exhausted family and friends with my ravings, I'll need the unconditional love of a dog to soothe me.

Then, if I make it to the acceptance stage, I'd ask the doctors to make me pain free, yet not so medicated that I won't be alert to visitors. I'd say my goodbyes and then watch humorous movies with friends and family. And in the quiet of the night, I'd review the moments of my life and be grateful. And, most importantly, I'd make the family swear not to tell anyone if I don't do my dying well.

The wind blew and a branch scratched at the frosted design. I prayed, God what's it like to know? Will you be with me all the way? Will you hold me through my questions, fears and emotional explosions? Will you give me courage to do it with dignity and humor?

I heard Ken's footsteps and the sound of the chip bag being opened. I checked the mirror, put on some lipstick and went down the stairs. We hugged. I fixed dinner, and we relaxed in front of the TV.

THE NEXT MORNING I walked the dog to clear my head of the intense emotion of Karen's video and the movie. I sat at my desk to put the final touches on the funeral service and thought of her family. I recalled Susan, Karen's youngest daughter, massaging her mother's back in the hospital room. I remembered the laughter and gentle touches that held them together. I prayed. God continue granting courage and strength to this family. When questions and emotions surface, hold them gently. And God, I ask you to be with me and guide me in the celebration of Karen's life. Amen.

FAMILY AND FRIENDS, TEENS and adults packed the church at the service for this young mother in her forties. After reading scriptures to remind us that God shared in our sorrow, I introduced Karen's children. Each had a prepared speech.

Jimmy, 18, a freshman in college.

> As many of you know beside family and friends, my mother's passion was real estate. Many of you believe that she got into the business for her love of houses and people. For the most part this is true. One Christmas my grandparents gave us the Atari Video Games. It came with many games, one of which was Pac Man. We all got pretty good. She played better than all of us. Being an 8 or 9 year old boy I was in tears with my mother beating me at my own video game. She played while we were at school. One day she was playing and completely forgot to pick up Susan at nursery school. At dinner she said

she was sick of video games and wasting her time, she was getting a job. That's how she got into real estate.

Susan, 15½, a junior in high school.

Something that always stands out about my mother is her ability to redecorate. My mother, as many of you know, loved to move to new houses. She loved to redecorate, not once, but over and over. She really loved to wallpaper. One bathroom in particular in our house on Fulling Mill never had the same wallpaper for more than a week. She'd be in there a while and we'd wonder what she was doing. She'd open the door and would be ripping the wallpaper and leaving to get her steamer to get off the rest. As a result of her wall paper fetish, I was dragged to wallpaper store after wallpaper store. Her favorite was in Lee, Massachusetts at the end of the Mass Pike. I spent so many days there, that to this day, I cringe when I drive through the town. Regardless, I loved the extra time with my mother because I was the youngest.

Megan, 21, a junior in college.

Before my mother started to work, one of her favorite pastimes was rearranging furniture. It was like Christmas to run home after school and run upstairs and find all our belongings someplace new. I can honestly say that I had all six bedrooms in our house on Main Street, at one time or another although much to my chagrin, I had the master bedroom for only one night. Sarah had the master bedroom for three weeks. I'll never forget the look on my father's face as he went to bed for the first night in the dining room. My mother was able to get the queen size bed, two huge bureaus, and essentially every other piece of furniture we had up and down our winding staircase all by herself. After three weeks in the dining room, my father said he couldn't sleep there one more night. And sure enough the next day, we all had new bedrooms and my parents were back in the master bedroom. This sort of episode was a common event and just one of the adventures we endured with our mother, Karen O'Hare.

Sarah, 24 and now working in Boston.

One of the requirements of being an O'Hare child is spending time with the family. Every summer we'd pack up our boat and all of our gear and off the six of us would go to camp at an island on Lake George with no running water. As you can probably imagine, camping as a young child was one of the best things going…campfires, s'mores, swimming, hiking, going to the ranger station to get a treat at night, never having to shower or worry about what your outfit looked like. What could be better? As the years went by and we entered the preteen and teenage years, the shower-less hikes and Dad driving the boat round the lake with his safari hat no longer seemed to have the same effect. To put it simply, I was a teenager.

When I entered college and did not see much of my family, I realized the times I was forced to spend with my family as a teenager are some of my most cherished memories. The look of joy on Mother's face when we were all together as a unit whether it be Christmas Eve, or on top of a mountain, or at Lake George or just having dinner at home is something none of us will ever

forget. I feel we are some of the luckiest in
the world to have had Mother a part of our
lives for as long as we did. She has given us
such a part of her that only her physical body
is being laid to rest today. All the gifts she
has given us and Big Jim will live with us as
long as we live.

The entire congregation sat stunned by the poise of these young people. No tears. No open sorrow. Some guests looked like they knew the children did what Karen expected of them; others had looks of "How did they do that." I knew how they did it; Karen and Jim prepared them.

After the service, family and guests returned to Karen's home for food and drink. I filled my plate with goodies and edged my way between the coffee table and the sofa to a seat next to Penny, a friend. After setting my plate on the table, we hugged. "Marcia, the kids were amazing."

"Yes. I admired their courage. Their stories reminded me that our children actually pay attention to what we do. What do you think our kids will say about us?"

"I am sure yours will say something about your costumes." Penny and I sat quietly as we observed crowds of Karen's friends engaged in conversation all around us.

A FEW MOMENTS LATER exhaustion flowed through me. I felt dizzy and light-headed. I looked around. Was it the pungent scent of the lilies on the table in front of me? My palms began to sweat, and I fussed with my collar. An unreal feeling came over me, and I pinched myself hard. The pinch steadied me for only a moment; then, a horrifying sense of dread sat on my shoulder. The same feeling that I'd experienced at Pop's funeral thirty years earlier where my body lurched, my hands flew forward to grab the pew in front of me. My mother put her hand on my back.

"What's the matter?" she asked. I shrugged. I tried to stay perfectly still and focus on the words spoken by the pastor. Again my body lurched, and I struggled as my hands instinctively reached for the back of the pew in front of me to brace myself. Frightened, my mind went into overdrive. "My breathing…I cannot feel my breath. I'm alone, lost. Pop's dead. Am I dying, too?" Fear took over. "Control your self," I heard some inner voice say. I hid my fear then and now the same feeling of dread hung over me. I tapped Penny's sleeve.

"Penny, I need to get out of here." Penny pressed her body into mine and brought her arm over my shoulder and squeezed me close.

"Hang in there." She looked over the table towards her husband. "John, we need to take Marcia home." John walked over and offered me a hand as Penny held her arm snug around my back. They eased me out of the house and into their car.

Penny sat in the back seat with me. "How are you feeling now?"

"Penny, evil is all around me." Penny held my hands as John drove.

"Take deep slow breaths." Penny breathed along with me. The feeling began to lessen.

They parked in front of my house. Penny helped me out of the back seat of the car, and they both walked me inside to the sofa in the living room. John went to get me a glass of water while Penny sat in a chair near me. "Shall I call Ken?"

"He's out of town. Maureen's number is there next to the phone. She's only a few minutes away. Call her at work." Penny dialed Maureen's number.

"Maureen, your mother isn't feeling well. Can you come home to be with her?"

I watched as Penny listened. "Good. We will see you in a few minutes."

I sipped the water. The ugly feeling eased but fear lurked in every pore of my body. Minutes later, I heard Maureen's car in the driveway. She and Penny and John talked in the kitchen. I heard the door open and shut and John's car start as Maureen came to sit next to me.

"Mom, Penny and John told me what happened. Why don't you rest and then we can talk if you need to ?"

I felt the comfort of my daughter and gradually my body relaxed, but my mind remained on guard, vigilant. It raced with questions. Why now? Why me? Could it be because Judy and Barbara and now Karen are dead from cancer in less than a year? Could it be Karen's death so soon after Gertie's? Could it be because Bob Smith lost his battle with cancer only two weeks ago? Had I had too much death to handle? I tried to analyze —

look at all the reasons, but I kept these questions to myself.

THE NEXT DAY, MY rational self, the self that could manage anything signed up for water aerobics and Weight Watchers. Surely exercise and weight loss will soothe my body and relax my mind.

Weight Watchers became another religion for me. Yet, the fear and anxiety continued, I fretted over each sermon…was it good enough? I feared failure. I feared closing my eyes. Even as I bathed I felt lost in the shower and my fingers almost left finger prints in the tiles as I clung to them. A call came. Another death. After the meeting with the family, I sat in my office and wrote.

> *I'm tired. I need quiet. Yet another death*
> *— this time a hard-to-like person, a needy*
> *daughter, a meek son-in-law and three curious*
> *grandsons, Luke, Neal and Simon. Clear my*
> *mind of judgmental thoughts. Give me energy*
> *to bring your love to the family at the service*
> *tomorrow.*

After the formalities of prayers and scripture at the funeral, I introduced the needy daughter. Cindy climbed the steps to the lectern, arranged a book and said, "I am going to read Shel Silverstein's *The Giving Tree*." Only one guest attended the funeral — my friend Jan. Jan and the meek son-in-law, the three grandsons and I settled back in our seats. Cindy's voice droned on and on. "And the young boy…and the man…and the tree." The grandsons fidgeted, the son-in-law trimmed his finger nails and I kept my pastoral composure, at least I hope I did. At the end of the service, the funeral director escorted the daughter to the limousine. The son-in-law herded the grandsons down the aisle while they kicked and poked at each other.

At the gravesite, I began with the words, "O death where is your sting?" Luke pushed his glasses up on his nose and questioned his Dad.

"When do they put the casket in the ground?"

"Shh!"

"When, Dad?" Neal squealed, rocking from heel to toe in his good shoes.

"Dad, we want to see them put the casket in the ground." Simon pulled at his tie and buttoning the brass button on his navy jacket.

"Shh! They do that after we leave."

After the benediction, the boys ran to my side at the head of the casket and tugged at my sleeve, "Reverend Cham. Can we see the casket lowered into the ground?"

Before I could respond, the funeral director, Eddie Jones interrupted, "Sure, if it is okay with your parents."

"Mother? Daddy? Can we?" The boys shouted in unison. The parents shrugged. I corralled the boys at the side of the casket. Eddie motioned for the cemetery workers to come from their place under a tree out of sight of the family. The workers tipped their ball caps to the family and pierced their shovels into the pile of dirt. They took hold of the straps that supported the casket over the empty vault and slowly lowered the casket.

The boys stood wide-eyed; the parents diverted their eyes. The backhoe ground its way from its hidden place among the trees with the vault lid swinging from the winch. The workers guided the lid in place and clamped it tight to the vault. The boys turned to me. "What's that for?"

"It's environmental. It keeps the decaying fluids from the body from contaminating the surrounding ground and streams."

"Oh."

The workers picked up their shovels. Eddie stopped them as they began to shovel. "The boys want to help with the dirt. Give them each a shovel." They went to work.

Simon leaned on his shovel. "Reverend Cham, can grandmother see us doing this?"

"Sure she can. She's proud that you are not afraid." They looked at me with silent words in their eyes, "What's to fear?"

"You said something about…her returning to earth…"

"Yes, our bodies decay and return to the earth. It's the cycle of life." I saw Neal and Simon chewing on the idea and Luke digesting what I said. Luke wiped at the dirt on his trousers and looked up at me.

"Like the song the 'Circle of Life' in *The Lion King*." Amazement at Luke's understanding jabbed at my heart.

We stood as the backhoe finished the work and the workers cleaned up the site. The boys arranged the baskets of flowers over the mound of dirt. They walked a little taller on their way back to the waiting cars. The daughter and meek son-in-law leaned on each other. The son-in-law touched my sleeve. "Thank you for your patience and understanding with the boys. At their age I couldn't have done that. They loved their grandmother even though others found her unlikeable."

As the family loaded into the waiting limousine and drove off, I groped toward the trees in the distance. Eddie followed me.

"Are you all right?" I clung to the tree.

"I'm struggling with my fear of death."

Eddie leaned against the tree and appeared, as usual, to be in no hurry. "You aren't the first nor will you be the last whom I've seen physically struggle with death. It's not easy, especially when you deal with it so much. It can accumulate. Take care. I'll wait over by the hearse until you are ready to leave."

I watched him walk away. "Is this the way I'm going to be…okay one minute and fearful the next?" A warm presence leaned into me. Pop whispered,

"I know your fear. I am with you. Nothing horrible is going to happen to you." After a few minutes, my weak legs walked me to the hearse.

Later that week I sat in my study and wrote,

> *Water aerobics has rejuvenated me. My weight is down. The Christmas Eve Service was too busy—little time for the holy to come into my heart. Gifts, laughter, pecan rolls, chili and crazy wonderful kids made Christmas Day as zany and wonderful as usual.*

"MOM, PHONE CALL." I heard David yell up the stairs.

"Thanks. I'll take it up here." I uncurled from the chair and moved to my desk. "Hello."

"Reverend Cham, Irene from the ICU at South Shore Hospital. Betty Stallard asked me to call you. She's sorry to interrupt your holiday but she needs you here."

"How's Elbert doing?"

"He's hanging on."

"Tell her I'll be right over." I went downstairs.

"Another death?" My oldest son Mike said.

"Not quite." I pulled on my coat and looked over the

Christmas mess in the kitchen.

"We will take care of the mess, Mom. You take care of you. You have enough to do with this and packing for your sabbatical and taking care of other details before you leave." Mike hugged me as I went out the door.

BETTY'S TIRED EYES AND drawn face greeted me. "Marcia, Elbert's near death. The only thing keeping him alive is the machine. I want to turn it off. I wanted you to be with me."

I held Betty. "I understand." She nodded and rested her hands in mine.

"He's ready to be with *his* Jesus." I felt Betty's body relax with relief.

We heard a soft knock at the door. The doctor pushed it open and took Betty's hand into his. "Betty, I hear you are ready to let Elbert go."

"I am. I'd like to wait until our daughter gets here. She and Elbert have some unresolved issues that need forgiveness but with the Nor'easter approaching, I'm not sure when that will be. I can't let this go on any longer." Exhausted, she leaned on the bed and ruffled Elbert's hair.

The doctor stared directly into Betty's eyes. "If you are ready, I will turn off the support now." She nodded. Mist filled her eyes but a strong determination set in her jaw.

The machines came to a halt. Silence filled the room. Elbert gasped for a breath just as his daughter came in the room, snow dripping off her hat.

"Dad, I made it." She reached for and squeezed his hand.

Elbert whispered, "Forgive me." Robyn choked out, "I forgive you." An aura of light filled the room. Betty and Robyn huddled next to the bed supporting each other with their love and now contentment.

Betty touched my arm. "Will you offer a prayer for us?" I took Betty's hand and we surrounded Elbert's bed. Robyn joined us her eyes red, puffy from tears of sorrow and celebration.

> God, your Love fills us. You give us miracles
> where we least expect them. We thank you
> for Elbert and the transformation of his
> heart. We know that Elbert is free to be held
> in your embrace for all eternity. Be with

us. Be with Betty and Robyn let them feel
your touch as they go through these days of
preparation for and celebration of Elbert's
life. Amen.

We celebrated Elbert's life on December 29.

I BEGAN THE NEW YEAR with a new journal, "Voices: A
Woman's Journal of Self-expression," a gift for my upcoming
sabbatical. I sat in the gold arm chair in my home office surrounded by my suitcase and carry-on bag that were almost
packed. I wrote,

> I've had my shots and my passport's in order.
> I feel revived and peaceful. The months of
> planning for sabbatical have gone smoothly.
> The other week a fear of the distance and the
> political struggles in Israel/Palestine made
> me look into other programs, but the draw of
> three and a half months in the Holy Land won
> out. The kids are excited about my journey
> and Ken's working on internet communication
> for me. I can feel the anxiety of others over
> my decision to be in such a volatile place but
> I know I'm called to be there, to learn and
> experience and then to share. I need to dress
> for the dinner at the Arthurs. Everyone seems
> to want a piece of me before I go.

Ken and I arrived at the dinner party only to discover it
was a surprise party for me. My friends had gathered to send
me on my way with their best wishes. They read poetry, gifted me with practical items like tissues and paper, a candle to
bring their light into my room and a list of their addresses so
I'd be sure and write. The next day I finished my packing and
our family enjoyed a movie matinee. Back home I checked my
itinerary, hugged the kids and Ken drove me to Logan Airport
for my flight to Israel with a stop in Amsterdam.

In Amsterdam relatives of a family at the church met me at
the airport and showed me around including a drive through the
famous "Red Light District." I especially enjoyed the Rembrandt's

and Vermeer's at the Rijksmuseum of Art and the pastry stops where we tried to communicate. Tired, yet stimulated by my few hours in a new place, I returned to the gate for my flight. I rested a couple of hours and boarded the plane through a row of guards and their machine guns stationed at the gate.

SITTING ON THE METAL BED in my room after my first week at Tantur, I lit the candle from my friends, pulled out my journal, glanced at the family pictures on my desk and wrote.

> *At three a.m. I emerged with a sea of strangers through the doors of David Ben Gurion Airport near Tel Aviv on my way to Tantur, an ecumenical study center for their three-month sabbatical study program. A chorus of drivers shouted and gestured for the lady to "come to my taxi." My eyes darted here and there, for I had been instructed to find a shayroot, a van taxi, to Jerusalem.*

> *At last a dark skinned man with a pencil mustache and piercing dark eyes understood my need. He piled my belongings that were to last me for three months on the other bags in his shayroot.*

> *I climbed in, hugging my green Eddie Bauer book bag filled with passport and other essential papers. The book bag sat on my lap as I squeezed in the back next to two students dressed in jeans and sweatshirts with their book bags slung over their backs. The other three bearded passengers dressed in black suits and black hats held business briefcases as we sped along away from the bright lights of Tel Aviv and into the dark.*

> *The van jerked and coughed and chugged up and down the steep hills. Once near Jerusalem, each passenger descended from the van with nary a sound except for the*

slam of the van doors. The driver, much to
my surprise, knew Tantur. As the shayroot
sped to a stop outside the gates of Tantur, he
grabbed my bags, dropped them, rang the bell
and waited with me. It was not long before
brakes screeched to a stop on the other side
of the walled gate. The gate swung open. The
drivers greeted each other with 'mar-ha-ba',
an Arabic hello. Somehow their greeting made
me feel safe. A short steep drive through a
terraced hillside brought me to the door of
Tantur.

Esa, the driver, escorted me through the cold
marble hallways to my second floor room,
opened the door and said good night. I stood
there and surveyed the room. A metal desk
and chair. A metal bookshelf and a metal
framed bed. A metal-framed arm chair sat
next to a slider window that opened to a small
porch. Institutional.

I unpacked a few things. Every sound I made
echoed through the marble floors and cement
block walls. I wondered if I was bothering
anyone or if anyone was even close by. I heard
a quiet knock and a whisper from the door
leading to the shared bath.

"I'm Jean. Are you awake?" Jean introduced
herself as a Sister of Mercy on sabbatical from
Japan. We talked until daybreak. A Middle
Eastern breakfast of sliced meats, vegetables,
and hard rolls with honey and thick coffee
welcomed thirty-two strangers from all over
the world to Tantur.

Still disoriented from our travels, we
boarded a bus and rode through a whirlwind
of images, tastes, smells and sounds
—Palestinians, Israelis, calls to prayer, calls

*of vendors in the streets of the Old City. We
met other Christians — Melkites, Armenians,
Ethiopians, Orthodox, Coptics, Maronites,
Syrians, and Lutherans.*

THE FIRST CLASSES INCLUDED lectures on the Middle East,
the Churches of the Holy Land, and Ecumenism. They were
followed by Palestinian Liberation Theology, Introduction
to Islam, Introduction to Judaism, Peace Studies, Biblical
Geography, The Cultural Background of the Parables,
the Holocaust, and the Parting of the Ways: Judaism and
Christianity. Every day was busy, filled with questions,
challenges, political and religious discussions and tensions.

Exhausted, I opened the sliding door to my room, propped
myself up in a chair, and listened to Phil Coulter's "Serenity" tape
of piano music as I wrote in the warmth of the afternoon sun.

*Sleep is not easy. Daily, fears creep in. I shove
them down. Layers of tension — religious,
political, cultural — rise and fall outside the
walls and inside me each day. My physical
being presses me to weird feelings. I let them
creep in. Then I hustle to cover them. What
if I'd name them? Would they overtake me?
The wind blows on and on. It whips against
the windows and battles the olive trees as my
fear battles inside me. It lifts the black sands
from the desert and the sands cover the sun as
my fears cover me. I hide them. No one here
suspects. I seem so confident.*

I put aside my journal and put on my jacket. I walked
down stairs to the lounge and found my friend, Jim, a priest
from upstate New York.

"How about a walk?" I asked. He grabbed his jacket and
we walked the terraced olive groves around Tantur and the
dusty road to Bethlehem. A Bedouin woman and her son
herding sheep across four lanes of traffic made us wonder if it
was 1995 or 5 BC. We found our way to an Olive Wood Fac-
tory and stood and watched the craftsman create the nativity
figures. After an ice cream we made our way back to the gates

of Tantur. We sat under almond trees and took in the beauty of the land. Jim leaned forward. "Are you doing all right?"

"I'm okay but struggle with a little fear and anxiety." I reached up and pulled down on of the almond branches and smelled the blossom. I had to let someone know.

"The tension inside and outside the walls are enough to raise anxiety in anyone. Let me know if you need my help." We walked to the front door and checked our mail.

He had nothing and I had a fax. I scanned it. Excited, I touched Jim's arm.

"Hey, Jim, let me read this to you." We walked to the dining room and sat at the first table. "It's from Mike."

He made his eye brows jump. "The one who's in love."

"Yes, now listen."

> Well, I wanted to write and tell you what
> has been going on with Maggie and me.
> Things are absolutely wonderful. She and
> I are VERY happy. I bought her a ring last
> week and gave it to her on Friday night. It
> is a round cut, .86 carat diamond mounted
> on a simple 4-prong white gold rind. It is
> very simple and pretty. I also got her a fake
> Christmas ornament engagement ring that
> is big enough to fit around her wrist. When
> I proposed to her I gave her the big one first.
> She says that the fake one is the reason she is
> marrying me. I love her to death, Mom. She
> is kind and fun and wonderful. I just want to
> be with her all the time. Everything seems to
> work out just perfectly with us. I look at her
> and I check how happy I am and I just can't
> believe it sometimes. I just go "WOW"! I
> think that is a good thing.

I folded the fax. "Jim, you can feel his excitement, can't you?"

"Yes, he sounds like you. Does this mean Ken is going to have to tend to all the wedding plans?"

"Yes, I guess he is, but I am sure there will be details when I return."

THE NEXT WEEK PICTURES arrived of Mike and Maggie's engagement. I sat on the flat roof of Tantur looking at the Judean Hills, picturing Mike floating five feet above the ground with excitement. Excitement filled me too. Mike had bought us bath towels for Christmas saying, "Your old ones needed to be replaced and by the way I've invited a friend, Maggie, to visit us before New Year's." I pictured him now grinning from ear-to-ear and just giddy as he waited for Maggie's visit. She arrived with gifts and a sparkle that radiated between her and Mike — a warm and loving young woman. Joy filled me as I looked at the engagement pictures and heard the muezzin call the Moslems to prayer.

TWENTY OF US SLOWED things down again by hiking the Wadi Kelt — the Judean Wilderness from outside Jerusalem to Jericho. The Good Samaritan Story and the stories of Jesus' temptation came alive as I walked. The open air and quiet settled the tensions that had been rising within the walls of Tantur and within me.

Then my busy life came to a halt. I left the dining room feeling sick. Sister Rose, a nun, who served the AIDS community in Kenya, followed me to my room. She touched my head. "You are burning up. Your temperature is about 105." She reported it to the house matron, Vivi, and Vivi piled me in her tiny car. After being grilled by Israeli soldiers at the check-point into Bethlehem, I saw a Palestinian doctor. He diagnosed me with E. coli. For ten days, newly made sabbatical friends tended to me; forcing me to drink water and massaging my sore muscles. The time seemed like a sabbatical within a sabbatical. Now completely relaxed and rested, I noticed my fears were gone. I wondered, am I now free?

IN MID-APRIL, KEN and the kids met me at the airport. We stopped in Boston for Italian food. I longed for a change of diet after the mid-eastern diet of chicken and vegetables and vegetables and vegetables. The family and I hibernated that first weekend. I needed to get my land legs before I faced the inklings of trouble I'd sensed in the last communications I'd received from church members. Mid-week I returned to work to find extreme conflict and chaos in the church between the senior pastor and the choir director and her followers. The anxiety and fear returned. I policed every movement of my body. The florescent lights in stores put me on alert. The perfume samples in magazines triggered fears of poignant smells. Standing and looking into the eyes of people made me fuss and shuffle and sit. My sunny world turned gray. I looked for the shortest line in the grocery store. I scanned rooms for the exits in case I needed to escape. I monitored every normal physical movement — my breathing, any muscle twitch, any ache or pain...and decided they must be signs of death. My hypervigilance fed my anxiety, my anxiety played with my mind, my mind told me to be alert to danger.

I read from Anthony's DeMello's *Awareness* to maintain balance. I practiced meditation with Thich Nat Hahn's *Peace is Every Step*. Burdened by church community and my own obsessive thoughts I went to the retreat center for a day. I pulled an afghan around me and rocked and wrote.

> *I feel bound like the bent woman in Luke 13:10-16.*
> *On the Sabbath day Jesus was teaching in one*
> *of the synagogues. And there before him was*
> *a woman who for eighteen years had been*
> *possessed by a spirit that crippled her.*
>
> *When Jesus saw her, he called her over and said,*
> *"Woman, you are freed from your disability"*
> *and he laid hands on her. At once she stood up*
> *straightened up and she glorified God.*
>
> *Jesus, do for me what you did for her. Free Me!*
> *I demanded.*

My privacy window — like the ones in limousines that separate the driver from the passenger, the one that I operated by the flip of a switch — up and down — no longer worked. I could no longer cut off my inner self from my outer self. I could no longer deal with the intimacy of death and the pressures of life and walk away unscathed. The window that I'd operated unconsciously for so long jerked, started and stopped. It would not let me hide neglected feelings and frustrations. I couldn't control it any more.

AT THE SEPTEMBER WEEKEND of celebration for Mike and Maggie's wedding, I lay in the bed of the hotel clinging to the sheets, bargaining for calm. God let me cover up this fear a while longer. Don't let me ruin this weekend. Keep the fear away.

Back home, I settled into the chair in my home office with my journal.

> *I made it through the wedding and the celebrations. The skits Barb and I did for Maggie and Mike created laughter and relaxed everyone. The connection of friends and family made the wedding time even richer. My attempt at a prayer in Hebrew entertained everyone. Tenderness and fun surrounded the bride and groom and their friends. Thanks. How long before it strikes again?*

The Power of Fear

THREE WEEKS AFTER THE wedding, I met my friends for our weekly breakfast. I ordered scrambled eggs, and I don't even like them. I held onto the edge of the table, I pushed my chair back, I checked my breathing. I excused myself, and I drove home. My sweaty palms clung to the steering wheel as I talked to myself the entire way. "I can make it home. At home I'll be safe."

As I opened the door to my house, the world as I knew it turned black. I was disappearing. I grasped onto the edge of the counter and with tentative steps and hand-over-hand movements made my way to the telephone. With my heart pounding in my ears, I struggled to the phone, picked it up and dropped it and pulled it up by the cord and finally made the call to my friend, Jan.

"I'll be right there."

I stood still, frozen.

I felt the walls closing in. I eased my way out of the house and stood in the yard. I noticed my backyard neighbor. I yelled, "Hello." She waved back.

"Beautiful day."

"Yes. Warm for October."

"Your dog loves to chase that ball, doesn't she?"

I rattled on about something else. She rattled back. At least I knew I was visible to someone. Thoughts jammed my mind. "The world is caving in. Am I still breathing? Jan hurry. Jan hurry. My heart is jumping out of my body." My dog nudged me with her stick. I threw it. "Hurry, Jan."

Jan pulled up. I collapsed into her arms. She guided me onto my porch. We stayed seated on the steps for a long time. "Are you ready to move?" Jan whispered in my ear and I felt her breath on my neck.

"No, if I move I am going to die."

The warmth of her arms and body steadied me and the rhythm of her breathing gave me comfort and a feeling of being safe. Jan hummed a familiar tune that I just couldn't quite name but it soothed me and my mind stopped racing.

"I think I can move now."

Jan managed to get me into the house and into a chair next

to the telephone. She pulled a chair close so her body touched mine. "I am going to call your doctor." She found the number on a list by the telephone and dialed. When the nurse came on the line, Jan's voice sounded calm and strong. "I have Marcia Cham here." Jan handed me the receiver.

"Terry, I'm in trouble." Terry immediately connected me to Kate, my nurse practitioner.

"Marcia?"

I paced back and forth. "Kate, it turned black. I can't be alone. I feel wild-eyed. I think I'm going crazy and will never come back."

Kate breathed into the phone. "Marcia, your voice tells me you are not okay, but you are not crazy. You are having a full panic attack. I am going to prescribe Ativan — a prescription drug that has an immediate calming effect. Let me talk to your friend."

I paced the kitchen as Kate and Jan talked. Jan put down the phone and turned to me and repeated Kate's words. "Marcia, you are not going crazy. The medication will calm you down. I made an appointment for you to see Kate tomorrow."

I paced and Jan kept assuring me. The sharp ring of the telephone interrupted us. Jan answered. "Hello."

Jan put her hand over the receiver. "It's Barb Greer."

"We are to do a stress management talk at the high school on Tuesday." I informed Jan and leaned against the counter. "I'll talk with her." Jan handed me the phone. My voice faltered. "Barb, I've had a strange episode."

Barb paused before responding. "Marcia I can hear it in your voice. What happened?"

"Barb, I've had a panic attack."

Barb spoke slowly and deliberately, "Marcia, I have a psychiatrist friend who can help you. If you don't mind, I'll call her and set up an appointment."

"That's fine." I hung up but kept my hand pressed on the receiver and turned to Jan. "A psychiatrist for me. How strange. I am the consoler, the helper. I hate to admit any needs let alone that I need help."

Jan fixed her eyes on me. "You do try to handle everything yourself, but now you need help. How about a cup of tea?"

Stirring her tea, Jan mused, "Funny isn't it, how Barb called when you needed her." I nodded.

"It is one of those times when the dots of life get connected for a few moments."

We heard Ken's car in our gravel driveway. When Ken opened the door, he saw Jan and me crowded together in the corner of the kitchen. "What's the matter?"

"Marcia's had a full-blown panic attack. There's a prescription at the pharmacy for her." Ken asked no questions. He headed back out and returned in a few minutes with the prescription. I swallowed one of the small white pills. The drug washed over me and within thirty minutes my mind calmed, my body relaxed.

They walked me into the living room. Jan sank into the overstuffed blue chair. I curled up on the sofa. Ken squeezed in next to me. "I've held Marcia through some of her dizzy spells and vertigo attacks and we've had to leave a couple of restaurants over her anxiety, but I didn't expect a panic attack. I don't even know what one is. What caused it?"

I DIDN'T KNOW EITHER. Life as I'd known it had caved in. The conscious and unconscious emotions and fears I'd stuffed inside demanded to be expressed. What a blow to one who always charged forth — a risk taker! One for whom the glass was always half full. One who reached out and touched the pain of others and never looked at her own emotions or pain.

After a restless night Ken drove me to my first visit with Lisa, the psychiatrist. I unfastened my seat belt and fussed with my purse. "Do I really need to do this?"

Ken squeezed my hand. "Yes, I guess you do." He gave me a hug. "Are you sure you don't want me to go in with you?"

"I'm sure."

I opened the door and climbed out and adjusted my purse on my shoulder. I walked to the building along a moss-covered brick walk. A sign by the door read, "Come In." I took the first chair in the waiting room, dumped my purse on the floor as I sat down. I reached down to pick up the mess when a woman appeared in the room.

"Welcome, I'm Lisa. Come in and take any seat you want." I took a padded arm chair that faced a window that looked out on a jumbled garden of white daisies mixed with yellow goldenrod and wild blue asters.

"What's going on?" Lisa sat behind her desk and tapped on a pad.

"What do you want to know?" I squirmed in my chair.

"Barb Greer said you were in the depths of a panic attack."

"I guess so. Although I'm not sure I know what one is and more importantly what you can do about it." I stiffened my back.

"You started Ativan yesterday. That drug will calm you almost instantly but it is addictive."

"Addictive? That's all I need — an addiction with all the other behaviors that have changed and magnified into really weird stuff." I folded my arms high over my chest.

"What do you mean by 'really weird stuff'?" She shuffled papers on her desk.

"I avoid grocery lines and escalators. I hang onto walls and doors. I constantly look for escape paths. I left worship last week and paced the hall. I haven't taken my daily two-mile walk for weeks because I can't get around the corner only a hundred feet or so from my house. What can you do about that?"

"Those are signs of anxiety. They will not harm you."

I stared at the rambles in the garden. "They've already harmed me. They've changed my life. I used to be free, now I'm bound up in knots. I am afraid. I police changes in my breathing and tight muscles send an alarm to my brain saying 'something must be wrong.' I awaken to dreams that I am lost and cannot make my way home."

"I want to prescribe Zoloft — another anti-anxiety, anti-depressant drug. It takes about a month for the drug to kick in, but then you should have better days."

"Is it addictive too?" I played with my hands and noticed my legs tied around each other.

"No. But, with the drug in your system, you will be able to manage the anxiety and have better days."

"Will it help me get to the root cause?" I leaned forward in my chair.

"No, but our talking together may help."

THAT NIGHT AFTER A DINNER of comfort food, French toast and sausage, the phone rang. "It's James. The cancer has metastasized in Marion's brain. Tomorrow she is coming home from the hospital to Hospice. I can't believe it. I thought we'd be together into our old age. Can you come over in the morning around ten?"

"James, I am sorry. I'll be there."

In the morning I prayed for strength to be what the Kaye's needed and put up my privacy window and demanded that God allow me to work with the Kaye's without the panic interfering.

When I arrived the family greeted me with hugs. "Marcia, thanks for coming. We are just toasting bagels. Do you want one?"

"Not now, maybe later." Bakery bags rattled and the smell of toasted bagels rose in the air. Marion motioned me to the side of her bed.

"Hospice is here for me. They are here for me." She repeated with fear in her eyes and then pointed to the family busy slathering cream cheese on their bagels. "They looked relieved when Hospice arrived. I know they'll need the help, but do they know how I feel — knowing it's me they are here for?"

She lay back catching her breath. "I'm angry. Everything is out of my control. I can no longer move on my own. I have to wear diapers." Marion rested for another moment. "I am going to dictate who is going to see me and who is not." Her eyes filled with terror and the family stood still.

The rattle of bags and crunch of toast stopped. Marion motioned for the family to come near her bed. "Now you know how I am feeling. I need to be in charge of something. Kate, get a pencil, here's the list of who is welcome and those who aren't."

"Mom, this is kind of cruel." The entire family took a few steps back from her bed.

"But this is what I want, what I need to face my dying. I need to be in control of something."

James left the room and her daughters made themselves scarce.

Marion took my hand. "Was I too harsh?"

"You did what you needed to do." I shrugged. Anguish for Marian crept down into my heart.

"By the way, how are you? I heard you had a panic attack."

"I'm coping. Thanks for asking."

"I guess that makes two of us coping. Now say a prayer for me and be off, but come back tomorrow, please." After a long hug, I made my way home.

Marion died three days later at 12:10 a.m. A horse-drawn hearse carried her body to the cemetery. We walked behind and then watched yellow balloons released into the air as her body was returned to the ground. A piper piped.

AT MY NEXT APPOINTMENT with Lisa, she began, "I see by the obituaries in the *Ledger* you had a funeral last week. How did you do?"

"I didn't notice any anxiety."

"Why do you think that was?"

"I needed to be present to the family. I couldn't let the thoughts overtake my confidence. But then after a few days, my anxious thoughts took up their repetitive vigil." My body sagged into the chair.

Lisa studied me. "Let me give you a mini-lecture. The sympathetic part of the nervous system releases energy and the parasympathetic restores the body back to normal. Your anxiety, your avoidance behavior, your escape mechanisms, your pacing interrupts the cycle and your large muscles prepare for action that result in shallow breaths. This leads to unpleasant feelings of smothering, dizziness and unreality. Digestive activity decreases and results in a heavy feeling and constipation. Your feelings are trapped. Your mental system is alerted and scans for potential danger. You search for an explanation and finding none, you invent one: 'I must be dying, losing control, going crazy' — all understandable but untrue. We need to work for you to realize the situations are not dangerous; that the fearful thoughts, predictions and images are not accurate. You will learn to become comfortable with stressful and normal changes in your body."

I WORKED WITH LISA on and off for a period of four months. She listened and I talked. She stayed behind her desk tapping on a white pad, while my life felt as jumbled as the garden outside her window that now had aged to dried, prickly confused stems.

At our ninth appointment, she came from behind her desk and sat in a chair across from me. "Is our relationship working for you?"

"Not really. During the last three appointments, you've taken my time to share your work frustrations. I've left here feeling angry that you've imposed your struggles on me. My job is helping people. Right now, I need help. I have no interest in helping you."

"You are right. I've crossed a professional line. I'm sorry. I will contact your physician and she can continue to prescribe the drugs."

Riding home, I felt abandoned by this professional, but I congratulated myself for confronting her directly, for expressing anger, one of my hidden emotions.

FEARFUL OF HAVING NO professional to turn to, I called a therapist friend.

"Gini, Marcia. I'm at home. I'm scared. I dreamed I needed help, but I lay in bed paralyzed—voiceless." I paced as I talked.

"A client just left. I'll be right there."

I paced. I saw Gini pull into the driveway and as she hurried into the house I grabbed her for one of her consuming hugs.

"I'm sorry your anxiety has taken on a life of its own. Let's sit." We sat in my dining room where light streamed in the windows. Our dog Ebony flapped her tail as she plopped herself in the archway. Gini demonstrated a breathing exercise and then guided me through it.

"Place your hands on your abdomen and breathe through your nose to a count of six and watch your hands rise. Then slowly release your breath through your mouth as if blowing through a straw. If you cannot make it to a count of six that's okay, do what you can." We practiced.

"I can't do it. It makes me anxious."

"Start over. There is no perfect way of doing this. Simply do what you can. The oxygen will relax your brain and interrupt the cycle of your fear-raising thoughts." Gini added. "Most of us carry our stress in our shoulders and breathe shallow breaths high in our chests like this." She made quick shallow breaths and I saw her shoulders tighten up. "Moving our breathing to our guts relieves tension. Do some shallow breaths and see what I mean." I did as she asked. "Do you feel the difference?"

"Yes."

"Let's practice again and do it ten times, if you can." We began and Gini counted. "Ten, in and out. Nine, in and out. Eight in and out..."

I reached for her hand. "Thanks."

"Call me any time you need and I'll walk you through it even over the phone." Gini stood and engulfed me in her hug.

"When am I going to feel safe?" I whispered.

"Friend, it has taken time for you to get to this spot in your life, and it will take time to unravel the pieces. Pray for patience."

Working Toward Freedom

As LIFE WOULD HAVE it, my nephew Steve, a social worker serving AIDS and HIV clients in the Boston area, called that afternoon. "Aunt Marcia, Mom tells me you have had some panic attacks."

"Yes, Steve, I feel unsafe, like I'm going crazy."

"I have a book that I recommend to clients, *Overcoming Panic, Anxiety and Phobias* by Carol Goldman and Shirley Babior. I think it might help you."

"I hope so. I need to find out more about this disorder before it eats me up."

"You need some help to understand your body. I have a client coming in right now and I can't talk, but I'll come down this weekend if you are not busy."

"That would be great. Thanks." We set a time for Steve's visit.

I bought and perused the Goldman and Babior book. I discovered that Carol Goldman's practice was in Boston. I contacted her and called a friend Janet who drove me to her office. We parked and walked into the lobby of Carol's building on Commonwealth Avenue. We discovered a steep winding staircase and an elevator. I knew the twists and turns of the staircase would bring on my fears of tight circles. So I pressed the button for the third floor and nudged Janet. "Good thing elevators are not one of my fears. I'd never make it to her office."

We found chairs in the waiting room, quiet except for the white noise. Carol welcomed me into her simple office. "Marcia, take a seat on the sofa. From there is a wonderful view of the city."

Carol pulled the chair from behind her desk and placed it a comfortable distance away from the sofa. "I've been curious to meet you. I can't imagine how hard it would be to be a pastor, meeting everyone's needs."

"Yes, meeting their needs and expectations and finding time for myself is a tight rope walk." I looked down at my fingers.

"On your initial call to me, you described your attack and asked me, 'Am I going crazy?' You said you remembered a woman who had similar problems during menopause and was put away. And I said you are not going crazy and you are not going to be locked up. We have no evidence that panic disorder is driven by menopause. But I can help you overcome your panic and anxiety." She stopped. I let her statements scratch the surface of my well-guarded veneer.

"Marcia, imagine panic and anxiety disorder as a three-legged stool; one leg, your body chemistry; another, your family history and third, the stresses in your life. It will be easier for you to work on the root causes of your anxiety if we boost the levels of serotonin in your body chemistry."

"Can't I do this without the drug?"

"We will do better work if you are on the drug. Will you agree to be on it for six months?"

"Ok. I hate the crazy thoughts and physical feelings that keep me on guard." She listened to personal history about family and jobs. We made another appointment.

On our way down from Carol's office in the elevator, I turned to my friend. "She is not going to let me off the hook. She's going to catch my self-sufficiency and not allow me to fake it through the work we will be doing. I think my psychiatrist let me deceive her."

At my next appointment, Carol asked. "How have you been feeling?"

"Better and safer."

"Remember the three-legged stool of anxiety. The meds, the first leg, are to help your body chemistry. Are the meds giving you some freedom from your anxious thoughts?"

"I think so."

"Marcia, last time you talked about your personal life and described your family with some amusing stories. Now let's look more deeply into the second leg, your family history. Did any of your family members show signs of anxiety or depression?

"My mother and grandmother are afraid to be alone. My mother worries all the time. Mother told me that my dad had a nervous breakdown during the Depression. At times he'd say, 'I need a walk.' He'd leave and upon his return he'd offer no explanation. Other times he'd say, 'My head is tight. I need to go to bed'— never any discussion or explanation, only an uncomfortable silence that scared me. It made me feel edgy about what was really going on. Was Dad sick? Emotionally insecure or what? Now I ask myself, did he have anxiety and panic disorder? Remembering Dad returning from those walks all red in the face raises my anxiety and the fear of my body."

I paused and Carol waited. "Really, in my family, talk of our physical bodies didn't exist. Like sick or weak bodies were embarrassments. I remember waking one night and struggling to the bathroom and looking in the mirror to see if I were still breathing. Mother heard someone up. She came into the open bathroom. 'What's the matter?' Embarrassed I said, 'Seeing if I am alive.' I recall her saying, 'You are fine. Go back to bed.' I accepted that and went back to bed."

On the risers practicing for the Ninth Grade Choral Concert, I had the same experience. When a woman fainted near the soft ice cream counter in Polsky's Department store, mother rushed us away from the scene with 'Girls, move on,' and no explanation. I had the same breathless feeling. I pinched myself to see if I was alive. A simple explanation about the heat and fainting might have given me some comfort."

Carol wrapped her arms around her body and held herself tightly. "Marcia, I see you reliving that fear right now. I am sorry." She paused. "I don't want to make excuses for your mother, but episodes like that were dismissed or referred to as a 'spell' or as a woman's things for a long time. But now we know better. We will get you through this."

Relief flowed over me. After a few minutes Carol asked, "Were there other times in your family that made your fearful or anxious or left questions in your mind?"

"My sister and I shared a bedroom. We each had a teddy bear and at night our teddy bears came to life and performed little shows. After a while, my parents yelled up to us to be quiet and go to sleep. Of course we continued to play. I can still hear the next words shouted from the living room. 'If you two aren't quiet, Marcia Jane we are going to take you back to the home.'"

"That's pretty harsh."

"And that wasn't the end of it. My dad drove a variety of routes to church to bother my mother. Sometimes he drove through an undesirable part of town and mother would say, 'Roll up your windows.' Sometimes he'd drive by the Children's Home. On those drive-bys, Dad would strain his neck and look into the rear view mirror. 'That's where we found you Marcia Jane.' Then he'd grin into the rear view mirror, 'we can take you back anytime.'"

I squirmed in my chair. "I'm sure it was a harmless comment."

Carol offered. "Maybe it was, but how does it make you feel?"

"I think fear of being abandoned lodged itself deep within me with their innocent bantering. The fear forced me to be good, to toe the line, to meet their expectations. At times I thought maybe the story was true, but then I knew that I almost died days after my birth."

"Tell me about it." Carol rolled closer to me in her chair.

"A baby had been born in a taxi and brought into the nursery and developed dysentery. The dysentery spread throughout the nursery. Ten babies died. I survived and I can still see the marks on my stomach where I was fed intravenously. When I was young and noticed the marks, Mother retold the story. 'We brought you home from the hospital. We held you night and day. After two days we knew you were not doing well. We loaded you in the car. Mrs. Hammond came across the street. She took one look at you and said, 'Get ready. She's too weak to make it.' But see, you made it.'"

Carol took in a deep breath and sighed. "She held you night and day and you made it. Take time to feel it, to absorb it. Feel the joy in her remark, you made it." We sat in a comfortable silence. In the silence a tick of the clock announced that my time was up.

"Carol, thanks, I wonder if somewhere in my being I have a memory of that near-death experience."

"Our bodies do hold memory, I'll think about it. Go gently."

ON MY WAY TO the car, I repeated Carol's parting words, 'go gently.' I laughed inside. Over the years Rosemary ended each of our spiritual direction sessions with 'go gently.' And now I repeat the phrase to others, but I rarely practice it myself. Maybe its time I start. As I drove along the southeast expressway towards home, I wondered, am I able to be gentle with myself?

At home over breakfast with Ken, we talked about my visit with Carol. He'd heard the stories of my birth and the children's home, but he hadn't heard my wondering, 'Do you think my body holds any memory of that near-death experience?'

He stirred his coffee and we sat with the question. I looked at my watch. "I need to go. I have an appointment at the office in ten minutes." We left the restaurant in our separate cars.

I MADE IT TO THE church for my appointment with Jen and Pablo who were to be married in the summer. They came in arm in arm, looking happy with each other. "Welcome. You two look wonderful."

"Marcia, we are," Pablo grinned and leaned in close to Jen. "The wedding plans are about complete so the pressure is off."

They snuggled on the sofa. I pulled up a side chair and faced them. "The last detail is working Spanish into the service. I've given this much thought and suggest that we translate the entire liturgy into Spanish. Then have your friend Nancy read a section in Spanish followed by me reading the same words in English so that Pablo's parents and relatives will feel included and connected to it all. Here is a complete copy of the service."

Jen reached out for the folder and thumbed through the pages. "We'll get to work on the translation. Pablo can include local idioms that his parents will appreciate."

I opened the file with the details of their wedding and looked down my check sheet. "It looks like we have all the other details crossed off. Now it's time to enjoy the time before the wedding."

"Tell my mother that." Jen and Pablo stood.

"I know your mother is obsessed with details. I will try to keep her from bugging you."

"Thanks. She listens to you." Jen fingered the books on the table next to my desk as Pablo pulled her toward the door. "Humor books? What's that about?"

"I've created a course on the humor of God and Jesus as Jester and Clown."

"Do you think the folks will get it?" she asked.

"I'm not sure but I think the healing power of humor will intrigue them," I explained.

"I've never thought of church people as humorous. Good luck." I watched Jen and Pablo walk to their car. Then gathered my things and locked the door to my office and headed home.

BEFORE DINNER I NAPPED on the sofa and awakened wet with perspiration. In my dream I was stuffed in a large soda bottle in the busiest aisle of the grocery store. I was pressed against the glass calling for help. No one heard my calls. Parades of people walked by. I saw their eyes but no one sees me. I felt unwanted, invisible and crazy. I desperately wanted to be seen but the people avoided my pleas. Awakening from the dream, I heard Ken yelling at the back door, "I'm home."

"I'm on the sofa." He hung his coat on the newel post and looked at me.

"What happened? You are white and your eyes look strange." He sat beside me.

I grabbed his hands.

"I had a terrible dream." He held me as I talked. Later I wandered into the kitchen and warmed up some dinner for us. The dream bothered me all night — I tossed and turned, afraid to sleep, afraid to face the isolation and aloneness.

When I met with Carol, she listened to my terror while sitting on the edge of her chair. She asked, "Is that how you feel when you are panicked?"

"Yes. I'm locked in my own prison. I'm locked into pleasing others and meeting their expectations. Nobody wants to see the real me. They just want chunks out of me."

Carol leaned back in her chair. "Tell me more about that."

"I've never met my mother's notions of who she expected me to be. In fact she refers to me as 'the rebel'. Sometimes it's funny and sometimes it's not. She's harped on and on over the years about how I don't sort the laundry, or have dozens of cream of mushroom soup recipes or how I play with the kids instead of wiping out the refrigerator. When I work too much she wants me to slow down, when I am relaxing she wonders if I ever work." I took a breath. "I want to take the continuous tired soundtrack, those old tapes, and break them, shred them and yell, can't you accept me for who I am, not who you'd like me to be?" Sweat poured out onto my palms. "I don't want to hurt my mother, but…"

"You are not hurting your mother; you are claiming yourself. Talking about it — taking it out of your hidden places over time will allow you greater freedom. You are so busy performing for others and doing it well but in the more personal area of your life you have lost your voice. You need to claim it. Take time for yourself. Practice self care."

As we turned to the third leg of the stool, the stress in my life, I rambled on and on about the pressures, triangles and jealousies within the church and church staff. "I am not good with confrontation, so I get boxed in and want to jump ship, get another church." It felt good to be in a safe place to release my anger and frustration.

Thanks to Carol's listening, with practice I learned to tune out, ignore and focus on the one issue at hand. I led groups through a process of conflict resolution aiming for reconciliation. A reconciliation that sought deeper and stronger relationships, that believed people can change, that affirms that our future together is far more important than the conflict that has come between us. Through planning and facilitating these discussions, I found that reconciliation is not placating those with whom I disagreed, or hoping for hurt feelings and resentments to simply go away, but using what has happened as an occasion for reaching out as soon as possible before a wall of anger, fear, or resentment grew higher and thicker. My anxiety diminished.

All through the months of my work with Carol, her book became my bible. I made flash cards to look at and recite when my mind raced ahead and elevated my anxiety. "This feeling does not mean I am going to die." "This feeling has come over me before and nothing dreadful happened." "Anxiety sensations are normal physical reactions and not harmful." "Focus on the Rational You. Don't allow the Frightened You to take over." I kept them with me everywhere I went.

It was not easy to catch the sly and slippery anxious thoughts that drove me on to panic, but eventually I began to interrupt the panic cycle, access the situation and lower my anticipatory anxiety.

By summer of 1996 I felt I understood the three legs of the stool enough to attend my silent retreat and travel to see old friends and my daughter. As the date came closer, my anxiety level rose. I tried to push it down, to dismiss it. I pounded around the house shouting, "I should have this figured out by now." I tried to relax on our screened porch, but the bizarre thoughts and feelings roared in.

I called Rosemary and she came to the house. I sat in a beach chair and she sat in another across from me. She listened as I talked of demons that sat on my shoulder and pecked at me and hovered and pulled me into the darkness. As my intensity and fear grew, our dog Ebony, all sixty pounds of her, climbed in my lap.

Rosemary threw her head back. "Jesus, Mary and Joseph. What a sight!" Laughter erupted. The absurdity of Ebony settled on my lap quieted my anxiety.

Rosemary put her hand on my shoulder. "You need to call and cancel your trip."

"How can I disappoint my friends and especially Maureen?"

"You need to."

I made the calls. I'll never forget my daughter's words. "Mom, your health is more important than a visit. Disappointing others does not mean you lose their love."

I hated to disappoint. I'd rather use all my energy to the last than disappoint. Disappointing meant failure to me and I hated to fail. So my disappointment was twofold: one, that I had to cancel my trip and two, that, "it" had come back again.

I made an emergency appointment with Carol. She assured me. "You are being too hard on yourself. Progress is gradual and recovery takes time. Be patient with yourself. Trust your body. You are learning to trust a relaxed body. You are too hard on yourself. Can you take some time off?"

A Month of Self-Care

WITH THE SUPPORT OF the church and staff, I took a month off. Our screened porch became my sanctuary. I pulled my great aunt's oriental rug to a place that captured the sun almost all day. I set my boom box on the picnic table bench along with tapes, CD's and books.

I plunked five zinnias in a vase and placed it on the oak table in the corner of the porch. I focused on them daily and photographed the light coming through the petals, their shadows on the table as the sun moved across the sky. I studied the layers deep within each flower. I tried counting the petals, but became confused with what were petals and what were stamens and pistils, the seed producing part of the flower. I laughed at myself — so easily I had returned to my years of teaching science.

Each day I sat in my striped beach chair with a high back. I began each day by listening to *Come As You Are* by Paul Gurr. I wanted to brand the words on my heart.

> Come, as you are, that's how I want you.
> Come, as you are, feel quite at home;
> Close to my heart loved and forgiven.
> Come, as you are, why stand alone.
>
> No need to fear; love sets no limits.
> No need to fear; love never ends.
> Don't run away shamed and disheartened,
> Bask in my love, trust me again.
>
> I came to call sinners not just the virtuous.
> I came to bring peace not to condemn.
> Each time you fail to live by my promise,
> Why do you think I'd love you the less?
>
> Don't run away ashamed and disheartened,
> Come as you are why stand alone.
> Come as you are that's how I love you,
> Come as you are trust me again.[15]

Daily, the words dug deep in my soul where I felt as though I'd disappointed God, where shame about my anxiety and fears and failures lurked. "Gentle Spirit, sustain me on this journey of soul mending and healing."

I turned to the Psalms. I read and re-read their organic and earthy translations in *The New Jerusalem Bible*.

> My eyes, too, are worn out waiting for your
> promise, when will you have pity on me?
> For I am like a smoked wineskin....
> *Ps. 119:82*

> Listen to my pleading; an enemy is in deadly
> pursuit, crushing me into the ground,
> forcing me to live in darkness, like those
> long dead.

> Answer me quickly, Yahweh, my spirit is
> worn out; do not turn your face from me, or
> I shall be like those who sink into oblivion.

> Yahweh, for the sake of your name, in your
> saving justice, give me life, rescue me from
> distress. *Psalm 143.*

The Psalmist's emotional outbursts opened the blocked emotions. Their honesty pushed me to look within, to see the darkness and the shadows, to name them and bring them to light where God would nourish them and set my shadow side free.

I filled two small blue-lined notepads with words; thoughts I needed to see. I devoured Carol Goldman's *Calm Down* tape as I tightened and released muscles, trying to become familiar with a relaxed body. I practiced being and not doing. I memorized mantras. "Help me to be compassionate with myself. I will not let others' expectations of me run my life." I made a tape from "The Guide" meditation at the end of Joyce Rupp's *Dear Heart, Come Home* with Wynton Marsalis's Skylark from Standard Time Vol. 1 playing gently in the background. Hearing my own voice instructing me, led me deeper into a state of relaxation and trust.

Ebony, my black Labrador, kept me company through the days. She watched me move from one activity to another; from listening to writing to just sitting, to making tapes, to reading and reciting mantras as she moved her old body with the sun around the porch. She sat on my feet when emotion weighed me down.

At the end of each day's work, I sat back in my chair and listened to J. M. Talbot's *The Quiet* and studied the zinnias. On most days as the CD ended, Ken pulled into the driveway and we shared supper. I listened to his day, and he, to mine.

THE LAST WEEK OF THE month I stepped out of my sanctuary and went to the Fruit Center Grocery Store. The anxiety went with me, but I didn't run away from it even as I stood in a very long line. At the post office, I distracted the need to escape by practicing my breathing. At home I had a congratulations party with Ebony. She got an extra bone and I had a small glass of wine. I felt energized and returned to work.

As life would have it, the first call I received when I returned to the office announced the death of Melba Kemp, a woman who understood that God answered prayer in a variety of ways. I met with her son and we walked in Melba's Zen Japanese Garden.

Mark led me along the rock pathways through moss and sand and miniature evergreen plants. "For my mother the garden was not meant to be decorative, but a place of calm and peace, a place that captures the essence of things. She told visitors the path draws one in and asks for our participation. The twists and turns and the contorted branches reflect our life journeys. The moss endures all weather and shows us tenacity. The rocks are catalysts for thought. The plants, like us, are slow growers and gradually harmonize with the garden over the years."

"A writer I know wrote that making a garden is not a gentle hobby, to be picked up and laid down like a game of solitaire. It is a passion and seizes the whole person."

"This garden seized my mother and reflects her very spirit—tenacious, peace-filled and looking for harmony." Mark stood against a stone lantern that marked the end of the path. "Mother is being cremated. She knew I was afraid to look at her body, even look at death."

"I understand." I put my hand on his shoulder and we

stood in the quiet. I understand more than you know.

"Marcia, thanks for coming. I needed to walk the garden and talk." He hunched his shoulders. "Now back to details," he looked at his watch, "it's time for me to meet with the funeral director."

"Mark, do you mind if I stay for a while and walk in the garden?"

"Mother would love it." I heard Mark's car start as I entered the garden. I walked and contemplated, memories surfaced as I lingered on each stepping stone. I drove home, turned on my computer and reflected on a time in 1977 when I felt like Mark not wanting to look at the body.

November 1977
You Mean I Have to Look at the Body.

BASKETS OF CLEAN FOLDED laundry sat on the kitchen table. I picked up one basket to walk down the hall to the bedrooms when the phone rang. Ken reached for it. I watched his face tighten as he listened to the voice at the other end of the receiver. Hanging up, he turned to me. "It was my Dad letting us know that Grandpa Cham died."

An immigrant from Poland. A Lucky Strike smoker. Grandpa Cham. Frank. Dead. I pulled out a chair, set the laundry basket down, slumped over the kitchen table.

Cold and clammy, fear struck. I needed to do something. "I'm going to make a pot of coffee, do you want a cup?" Ken nodded as I moved across the kitchen to the coffee maker.

Ken took my hand. "Marcia, this time you are going to have to look at the body. I know looking at the body is going to upset you, but it's the Polish way that I learned as a boy. When we went to funerals, we lined up and passed by the casket, knelt and touched the body."

I filled our mugs, brought them to the table. My hands cupped around the mug absorbing the heat. As I took a sip, the coffee warmed and calmed me. Ken looked into my eyes.

"It's out of respect that we have to pass by the body. It's out of respect and tradition that we will kneel at the casket. We will then sit with Grandma Cham during a short service at the funeral home before they close the casket and we proceed to the church."

A feeling of dread came over me. I was going to have to look death in the face, close up. My thoughts raced. Is there no way out of this?

"Ken, the kids are too young. They'll be frightened and have nightmares. The whole body thing is archaic. I want to remember him as he was." I clung to the now-cold mug. "Out of respect and tradition." Ken's words repeated in my head. My fear rose. I was not going to be able to stand in the back of the funeral parlor. I was going to see death in the face of Frank Cham, whom I loved.

I ironed the kids' good clothes, packed our suitcases, and Ken loaded the car. We traveled from Hickory, North Carolina to Cleveland, Ohio to Grandpa Cham's funeral. When we arrived the funeral home was quiet. Some forty metal chairs stood in rows facing the casket surrounded by gladiolas, Frank's favorite flower.

Eleanora, Ken's strong and sturdy grandmother, who had orchestrated her family's life for years, sat alone in the front, looking frail as she fiddled with a handkerchief and dabbed her eyes.

Ken guided our family, Mike, Maureen, David and me to the casket. David turned his face up to mine. "He looks waxy."

"You can touch him if you like," Ken whispered to the children as he reached out and touched his grandpa.

Mike reached into the casket and touched Grandpa Cham's hand. "He's really waxy." His lips turned into a silly grin.

Maureen studied his face and touched the shoulder of his jacket. "He looks like he's sleeping."

A satisfied curiosity showed on their faces. Ken gave me a knowing nod. I touched Frank's face and admired his rough-aged hands.

We filed into a row of metal chairs and took our seats behind Eleanora, out of respect. The children eager with curiosity, the gentle look on Frank's face, and Ken's arms around me allowed my body to relax a little. I touched Frank's face and I'm okay. I'm still alive. The kids are fine.

We watched as others filed by the casket and found their seats. After a while the priest came in, greeted Eleanora, and stood by the casket. He shared words from the Psalms and a prayer of thanksgiving for Frank's life. Beginning from the back row of chairs, all the guests rose, walked to the front, and passed by the casket. Some knelt. Some stood. Some greeted Eleanora.

The funeral workers directed us to our car and told us to turn on our lights. A funeral flag had been attached to the car radio antenna. The hearse led the slow procession that wound its way from the funeral home to the Polish Catholic Church. Silence filled our car.

The procession slowed to the curb. The funeral home staff signaled for us to leave our cars. As we walked by the hearse Ken, along with the other pallbearers reverently pulled the casket from the hearse, passing the weight of it from one man to the next. With great care, they carried it inside and placed it on a rolling frame. Ken joined us as we squeezed beside it and walked down the aisle to our seats near the front of the church.

Twisting my head back, I watched while the priest circled the casket with smoke and incense, and then two of the pall bearers guided the casket to the front of the church. Before they marched to the back of the church, each one bent over and kissed the casket.

I felt cocooned in the dark, yet warm, ornamentation of the sanctuary. The Polish priest vested in gold robes of old world traditions spoke fondly of Ken's grandfather.

"Mr. Cham came to America with his brother. He found work as a machinist and upon retirement he farmed. During his only return visit to Poland in 1962 to see his sisters, he left them ten dollars. The ten dollars allowed them to have a well dug for the family to enjoy running water. Frank's warm and generous ways will be missed."

The candles flickered, the organ played and a mystical presence filled me as a soloist sang, "Be not afraid. I go before you always." The palatable presence calmed me and assured me of God's hand on mine in spite of my fears. The presence held me with a love that made me feel safe, a sense that I was not alone.

When the service ended, we filed out and followed the long black hearse to the Polish cemetery in North Royalton. Inflated balloon toys and plastic flowers of all shapes and colors decorated the graves. Ken grinned at me.

"It's a Polish thing. Pretty wild, isn't it?"

"Talk about a sight to make me forget why we are here."

The burial was short and solemn. I cried at the finality of Frank's death, until out of the corner of my eye I saw the bright balloons and inflated toys bobbing in the breeze saying, "This grave is not the end, this is a new beginning for Frank's spirit."

Out of tradition we returned to the funeral home, but this time we descended to the basement where we celebrated the release of Frank's spirit with highballs, loud voices and a meal of hot kielbasa, stuffed cabbage, sweet pierogi, and butter-baked koloches. Eleanora huddled with her sisters and watched the great-grandchildren toast with kiddy highballs.

I SAT BACK IN MY chair, read over my writing and turned on my printer. A copy of my words came pouring out. I straightened the pages and stretched out of my chair and stood looking down into the yard. Ken by my side grounded me. The well-defined cultural expectations provided a framework, comfort. The processions, the personal comments from the priest, the inflated toys, and the highballs…all seeped into my well-guarded wall of protection from death and dying and began to loosen my fear of death.

I folded my story and slid it under a pile of books. I began to plan Melba's service. I hope that something in the service will ground Mark and provide him a speck of comfort with death.

A Transition

B Y WINTER I DISCERNED it was time to begin the search for a pastor position at another United Church of Christ. I knocked on the senior pastor's door.

"Ned, do you have time to talk?"

"Yes, come on in." Ned rose from the chair behind his desk and moved to the chair opposite me.

"I am going to activate my papers to search for a church."

Ned looked down at his hands. "I knew this was coming. I know you are ready and there is a church somewhere that needs you and your enthusiasm and your warmth. I wish I could say that I'm retiring and you could apply to this church, but I'm not ready."

"I don't think it would be wise for me to take this church even if you were retiring soon. I would have to give up what I do now for what you do. I don't think that the church would accept that change. I think they'd want me to do it all, what I'm doing now and all you do." Ned nodded in agreement.

"I'll be sad to see you go. Anyway I can help, let me know."

We talked for a long time about the strengths both of us brought to the church and how we had learned to work together.

A new excitement grew in my body. Now I knew the excitement could bring on tension which could bring on anxiety. I enrolled in a yoga class that I'd always intended to take. The class met in Mia's basement that she had transformed into a place of beauty and simplicity. A Buddhist gong stood in the center with red hangings surrounding it. Mirrors covered the walls and the carpeting felt soft on my bare feet. Mia's gentle voice and deep 'Om' began each session.

The yoga exercises opened my chest and hip areas and relaxed the bowling ball of weight I held in my shoulders. At the end of each session, she instructed us to lie down on the mats. She covered us with a warm sheet blanket and we lay there for ten minutes as she asked us to repeat mantra, "I am miracle enough." I left each day feeling proud for giving myself the gift of self-care.

I CLIMBED THE STAIRS to the office on the second floor of Union Congregational Church of East Bridgewater. My eyes focused on the table in the center of the room decorated with a vase of strange artificial flowers and a box of tissues. I heard chairs pushed back and saw five hands coming toward me. Each member of the Search Committee introduced themselves and shook hands. The interview began. The committee was impressive with their initial questions and their follow-up questions. They had been well prepared. I left the interview at Union Congregational Church of East Bridgewater elated.

During the drive home, I felt an inner stirring, "they need my gifts." After two more interviews, I trusted that I was being called to Union Church. Some asked me how I knew the call was real. Knowing they wouldn't understand the spiritual stirrings to the new church, I said, "Three things solidified the call for me. First, Skinner's Ice Cream and Candy Store is within walking distance; second, Ken's company made the electric meter on the side of the church, and third, the parsonage garage has electric door openers." They church issued a call; I accepted.

IN THE HEAT OF THE summer, we moved from our own home to the parsonage. I managed the excitement and the transition with visits to Carol Goldman, allowed frequent times for spiritual direction and practiced yoga. I wore out the tape of Chuck Girard's, *Slow Down*, trying to keep centered and balanced through the meeting of new folks. And I prepared for our daughter's wedding.

One day I had bridal magazines strewn all over the coffee table. I threw one down and grabbed another. I thumbed through it looking for a mother-of-the-bride dress that did not look like a mother-of-the-bride. My frustration point had reached its peak when the phone rang.

"Hello, Mom." I heard Maureen say. "What are you doing?"

"I'm searching for that perfect dress for the wedding." I dropped the magazine on the table.

"Mom, you don't have to look for a mother-of-the-bride dress, I want you to be my matron of honor and wear a simple black dress like my other attendants." The honor stopped me in my tracks.

I caught my breath. "Are you sure?"

"Yes, I'm sure."

As she answered I heard another call coming in. "Maureen, let me take this call. I'll talk with you later."

"Hello. Marcia Cham speaking."

"My name is Daphne. I'd like to have my daughter Cheryl baptized. She is nine months old."

"Daphne, thanks for calling. We'd be happy to baptize your daughter. But let me explain. During the summer because of the heat, we meet in the vestry and worship is very casual, so we have few, if any, baptisms. You may want to wait for fall."

"We need to have Cheryl baptized as soon as possible." I felt alarm in her voice. "Will you come to our home so we can talk?"

THE NEXT DAY I DROVE to Daphne's home. Daphne and her husband Joe greeted me warmly and guided me to a chair while they squeezed together on the sofa pushing books and toys aside. Cheryl sat reclined in her baby chair. Her warm eyes and pink cheeks drew me into her heart and her into mine. I held Cheryl as we talked.

"We worked for seven years to conceive a child." Joe talked wringing his hands.

"The pregnancy was great news for us. After eleven years of marriage, Cheryl was born nine weeks early." Daphne looked happy and joy filled her face. "We brought Cheryl home to her nursery and toys and books on her three month birthday."

Joe motioned for me to hand Cheryl to him. She settled in his arms and he stroked her face. "Since she was early we had to monitor her development. Each day she lagged more and more behind." His shoulders heaved. "Is God punishing us?"

Daphne reached for Joe's arm and picked up where he left off. "It has been frustrating with test after test, and watching Cheryl being poked again and again. Being told we'd know something tomorrow and tomorrow would come and more promises while Cheryl's health declined." Daphne paused and took in a deep breath.

"Two days ago they told us that Cheryl has a neuromuscular disease…Spinal Muscular Atrophy, Type 1. The life expectancy of a child born with this particular form of the disease is less than one and a half years." While tears flowed and bodies shivered, Cheryl looked up at Joe then across to Daphne.

"Why would God do this to Cheryl…to us?" Joe stared at me and handed Cheryl to Daphne, opened the door, and walked out on the porch.

Daphne cleared her throat and hugged Cheryl close to her.

"We don't know how long we will have her, so that is why we want her baptized now."

"I see," was all I could mumble as I sat with my own thoughts while Jan caressed Cheryl. Why, this beautiful child? I didn't know what to say to Cheryl and Joe. I could say, "God is as sad and crushed as you are that this disease struck Cheryl." But at this moment that line sounded trite. Joe's anger, frustration and questions hit hard.

"We have not told our families. We want to get through the baptism first. I want to know she will be with God through all eternity."

"She will, Daphne, she will."

Joe joined us. He collapsed on the sofa next to Daphne and Cheryl. They held each other. Exhaustion poured out from sharing this news with an outsider…a stranger.

I DRAGGED MYSELF HOME. I felt run over by life. I contacted the deacons and we met to discuss this baptism. "Baptisms are always a celebration. This one will be different knowing what we know. I can't imagine knowing your child will die within a few months."

"Marcia, this is going to be tough for you, too. How can we help?"

"We need to protect the parents so that we do not give any indication of Cheryl's diagnosis. And as you pray for them, pray for me." We sat in silence receiving comfort from each other.

Daphne and Joe and Cheryl arrived early at the church. Cheryl dressed in pink and her parents all dressed up for the sacrament of baptism and the celebration after. They proudly carried Cheryl to the front and held her so that all could see and admire. Oohs and ahhs traveled through the congregation.

"Cheryl, you know it not, but Jesus Christ died for you, so you would have life…have abundant life." I paused and tightened my hold on her. She looked at me with a love that entered the depths of my soul.

"I baptize you in the name of God, the Creator, Jesus Christ, the redeemer and the Holy Spirit that will sustain you through life."

Daphne and Joe beamed. The congregation nodded their blessings toward the proud parents. Deacon Pat carried her around the church as we all sang, "Child of Blessing, Child of Promise."

I KEPT IN TOUCH with Daphne and Joe through the fall months. They made runs to the emergency room when Cheryl's breathing ran shallow. When necessary, they spent the night in chairs at the ICU in Children's Hospital. As the nurses tended to Cheryl, Daphne read to her.

"The nurses are like angels hovering over Cheryl. They give us comfort and strength," Daphne stood holding Cheryl in the early hours one morning in the hospital.

Joe walked back and forth with heavy footsteps through the corridors in despair — all was out of his hands. Nothing he could do.

Cheryl died in December before her first birthday. Daphne called and said with her voice filled with sorrow, "We will have a private wake at the funeral home before the service. We want you to be there and to join the procession to the church with us. After the burial, we want you to come back to the house. Our friends are preparing food for an army." A hint of light slipped into her voice.

AT THE FUNERAL HOME, all sat in tear-filled agony. Before the casket was closed to travel to the church, Daphne and Joe picked Cheryl up from the tiny coffin and held her. They kissed her good bye and gently put her back and placed special stuffed animals around her.

"Daphne, I need some air." Joe kissed Daphne and he walked toward the door. She knelt at the casket and pinned a tiny cross on Cheryl's pink dress. Friends helped Daphne to her feet and she leaned on them as she exited the funeral home.

I stayed with Cheryl until the casket was closed and the flowers were gathered and placed in the hearse. John, the funeral director, led me to the hearse and I took my place in the front seat. Then the procession made its way to the church.

JOE, DAPHNE AND I gathered with their parents and close relatives in the parlor while the funeral workers placed the casket in the front of the church and surrounded it with flowers. Nervous chatter and apprehensive looks were scattered through the room.

"It's time," I said with gentleness as my arms encircled Daphne and Joe and invited everyone to join us in a circle. I prayed.

> God, this is a hard day for all here in this
> room. Hearts are crushed by the death of
> Cheryl. Give us courage and strength to
> hear your words and receive comfort from
> friends, family and co-workers. Bless this
> time as we celebrate Cheryl's life and with
> sad hearts give thanks. Amen.

The church overflowed with guests. Three of our church angels showed up, unannounced, and directed traffic so that all ran smoothly for the family and the hundreds gathered in pain and grief.

I began the service with a lament—a crying out to God, 'Why?' Then at the request of the parents, I continued with words of celebration.

> Cheryl's life was short and filled with trauma,
> but it was not all tragedy. She gave Daphne
> and Joe countless moments of joy, laughter
> and love. They treasured her infectious
> smile, her love of books and the sounds of
> delight she made when tickled. She loved her
> Pooh video, and they watched it over and
> over enjoying all that much more because of
> her joy.
>
> When they were outdoors, they listened to
> her high-pitched giggle as the wind tickled
> her face. Her eyes followed the sun as it
> streamed in the windows on cooler days.
> Daphne and Joe began to take time to enjoy
> the beams of sunlight, too.
>
> Betsy gave them the gift of being aware each
> moment of every day, a gift they would like
> to pass onto us.

I offered a prayer.

> God danced the day you were born, Cheryl.
> You brought a profound joy, a joy only found
> at those thin places where love and sorrow
> meet. Our faith knows that you are with
> God, continuing to delight and share the
> gifts given to you at birth.
>
> Your parents learned to be truly present with
> you…finding joy in every small movement,
> in every look. They cared for all your needs
> in a gentle and loving manner even though
> their hearts ached. They tucked you into
> their hearts and made life safe for you. You
> have made footprints in their hearts. You will
> never be forgotten.
>
> Through your life and your baptism, you
> are part of the great cloud of witnesses…an
> ongoing spirit throughout all time. We thank
> God for the gift of your presence. Amen.

The crowd filed out and the police escorted miles of cars to the gravesite. Sadness, questions, and the cold wind of approaching winter gathered around the burial. Clinging hugs supported the crowd and carried them to Daphne and Joe's house for food and conversation. I waited at the gravesite for all the hundreds to leave and stood in silence as they covered Cheryl's casket with dirt. Despair and sorrow hung onto my clothes. I couldn't make myself go to the house for the food and visiting. I'd practiced my breathing and recited my one-liners to keep the fear at bay.

A call from a clergy friend waited for me on my return to the church after Cheryl's funeral and burial. "Take a week off. It's the only way we can get through the death of a child." I followed that advice. I was exhausted. I'd had a funeral for a church member the morning of Cheryl's service. I arranged for some days at the retreat center where each year I lived for eight days during my silent directed retreat.

BACK IN MY PLACE of solitude, in dark of my room overlooking the ocean I listened to the steady rhythm of the waves as I wrote,

> *The death of a child. The tiny casket. The*
> *mother holding the dead child. The milestones*
> *that will not be lived…the first word and*
> *steps…the first day of school and birthday*
> *parties and dates and graduations. None of*
> *it will be realized. How does one cope with*
> *dreams broken, hope put on hold, and faith*
> *jarred?*

THE NEXT DAY I WALKED, kicked sand, rested on the rocks and let the spray of the waves fall on my face. Visions of Cheryl and her parents consumed my restless sleep. A gray day followed. Sleep and meals prepared by the staff filled my hours.

God greeted me the next morning. That night I wrote,

> *In the pre-dawn I dressed and stood on the*
> *cold frosty rocks looking over the Atlantic*
> *Ocean. I ate yogurt as the sun rose. Its rays*
> *struck the water and bathed me in a focused*
> *light. I received the light. I settled in my chair*
> *and found a comfort in Carolyn McDade's*
> *words and music, As We So-Love—This*
> *Ancient Love.*
>
> *The instruments, the minor sounds of the*
> *oboe, the deep vibrating strings of the cello,*
> *and the sounds of the flute reached deep into*
> *the depths of my being. The recorded sound*
> *of the birds from the salt marshes mournfully*
> *interrupted and spoke, 'For I so love this*
> *world, I walk with you.' The interludes of the*
> *flute and oboe cut deeper into my heart and I*
> *yearned for more.*
>
> *"Stay with me now," sang the tape, "so that I*
> *may feel the shadow of your wings on mine."*[16]

*The ocean came alive as the sun rose higher
and wispy clouds gathered and became a
whimsical angel dancing in the sky, a sign to
me that Cheryl was dancing with the angels.*

I took one last walk on the rocks and studied the tide washing into the shore. My time away has refreshed me and connected me to God and the Spirit with these profound moments in the predawn light. I've felt God's shadow on me. Grief for Cheryl and her parents will come and go like the tide as I return to the church. I want to be okay. All I need is time to get these experiences behind me.

Ebony greeted me at home with her tennis ball, gooey from munching on it all day. She nudged me back outside where we played catch until Ken arrived. "Do you feel like going to the Lobster Hut tonight?"

"Sure." I put Ebony in the house and we drove to dinner where I shared a little of my time away with Ken. Then we turned to talk of Maureen's wedding; coming up in two weeks.

THE WEDDING, WHAT A crazy time. The Chicken Shower, with all the women dressed in chicken visors and Barb, demonstrating how to prepare and cook a chicken, about exhausted us from laughter. At the wedding reception we applauded with joy, when Maureen and Pete, introduced as the newly married, entered the reception with lab coats over their formal wedding gear. Surprises continued as Pete held Maureen as she showed off her new white hiking boots under her gown. Italian music pulled everyone to the dance floor. Dave and Mike embarrassed themselves with their rendition of "YMCA" and Pete's brother brought down the roof with "New York, New York."

Ken and I recovered with a few days in Maine.

HOURS AFTER OUR RETURN, a call came to inform me that Ruth Wilson, a neighbor and church member had died. The loss of her warmth and generosity weighed me down as I listened to the family and prepared her service. I slept soundly but before the alarm sounded on Sunday morning, the phone woke me out of a deep sleep. "Marcia? Helen Hoyt's neighbor. Her son's wife, Jenny, woke up this morning to Duncan's cold body. Her only son is dead. Can you come over?"

Catching my breath I said, "I'll be right over." I dressed, walked to my desk and pushed my sermon aside and picked up a clean yellow-lined pad, grabbed my coat and drove to Helen's.

Helen melted in my arms. "Duncan." Shock set in and a neighbor made tea and we sat in the emptiness. "Oh, Ian, my grandson…he loved his dad." She heaved with grief. "And Jenny, imagine finding your husband cold next to you in bed." Cold waves of pain for Helen traveled through me. A forty-eight year old father and husband, dead in his bed. God, why? Helen warmed her hands against her tea cup. "You need to get to church. I'll be all right." At the door I held her and asked God for strength.

At church the announcement that Helen's only child was taken during the night, silenced the church; some remembered Helen and Duncan and his family, others remembered their own experiences of sudden death. I changed the closing hymn to "The Lord is My Shepherd." I needed to know God would lead Helen and all of us through this death.

The church reached out with casseroles, cards, and prayers to both families. Monday we celebrated Ruth's life in the sanctuary and days later the funeral home filled with Duncan's family and friends. I read Jenny's ten-page eulogy for the love of her life. Heartbroken for Helen, I visited her each day for weeks. I knew she was coping when she announced, "I'm going to line dancing tomorrow."

THE EMOTIONS SURROUNDING THE tragic deaths and heavy funerals, even the joy and celebration of our daughter's wedding mounted up. Anxious thoughts crept in. I called Carol Goldman. She suggested I contact the Panic and Anxiety Clinic at Boston University where they researched and practiced the latest therapies for the disorder. I filled out countless inventories and sat through several telephone interviews to be accepted into the program as part of their studies.

They worked with me to understand the chemical and physical reality of the disorder. I'd heard it before but, finally, it sunk in that I was not going crazy. I was experiencing a chemical imbalance. My family history made me more susceptible to a chemical imbalance. They too believed the drug helped my body chemistry.

As part of the program at the clinic, I agreed to participate in written exercises. I worked hard. I charted situations or events or thoughts that raised my anxiety. On an exercise sheet "Countering Anxious Thoughts" I wrote, *I have a wedding this afternoon. What if I have to leave the service? What if the out-of-body sensation consumes my thoughts and I can't go on? What if I need to sit down?*

I recorded evidence—self-talk for or against this happening. *I've experienced anxiety before weddings and nothing has ever happened. I've never had to stop or sit down. I've informed the organist that I might have to leave and she'd have to take over, but that has never happened.*

So what is the realistic probability of anything drastic happening? *Zero to ten percent. I have a choice. I can let the thoughts and sensations control my life or I can not let them interfere. They are only sensations. Nothing bad has ever happened. I am not going to let them ruin my life. I can challenge my thoughts. Bodily anxiety is normal. It does not mean anything worse is going to happen. I am in charge of a special day for the couple. It is normal to feel some anxiety.*

What is the worst thing that could happen? *I might have to pause and collect myself. I might need to recognize my breath and use it to calm myself.*

Through the weeks of challenging my thoughts and charting my responses and predicting the realistic probability of anything drastic happening, I began to believe that nothing drastic was going to happen. I recognized that some amount of bodily anxiety is normal.

At the Institute's direction, I intentionally exposed myself to anxiety-producing situations. I rode escalators and sat in chairs shaking my head and spinning around as fast as I could to simulate the anxiety and chart the elevation of anxiety and the deceleration. I learned how quickly the feelings would subside if I didn't tighten and hold them.

At my eight-day directed silent retreat, I continued the spinning; Rosemary timed the sessions. I hated it. I pleaded with Jesus and God in my journal.

*I am tired of spinning in chairs and having
my reactions recorded. I need your help with
the shadow, the ugliness that comes out and
onto my shoulder. The darkness. The suicidal
thoughts. I thirst for your support, assurance,
closeness. Make this go away.*

*Trust my body…you must be kidding. God,
you say, 'Fear not.' Do you know how hard
that is?*

And at the same retreat, I ran headlong into evil. For two nights my room was a battle ground. In my sleep, I ripped sheets and blankets off the bed. I threw the mattress cover over the rocker. I sat on my mattress that was askew on it frame feeling locked in the arms of evil shouting inside, "What do you have against me, Jesus?"

Feeling slimy, unsteady, and embarrassed, I searched for Rosemary in her room.

I squirmed in the chair opposite Rosemary. "Evil is lurking in my room. I can taste it, feel it. It wants to consume me."

Rosemary reached across for my hand. "As a child I had fears. My grandmother came into my room with a piece of tall grass and brushed it over all the walls and corners and under the bed. It cleansed my room of the darkness, of the evil."

Rosemary understood. I wasn't crazy. Evil is real. From Rosemary's room I walked downstairs and outside to a stand of grasses. I listened to the wind rustle through them. I repeated a phrase from my favorite childhood hymn, 'in the rustling grass I hear God pass.' I cut two stems of grass and carried them to my room. I brushed them over the walls and in the corners and swished them over the curtains and the bedclothes. I lodged the stems of grass behind a crucifix that hung in my room. Each night I lay in the bed worried that evil would pounce again. It didn't.

At the end of retreat, I took the stems of grass home and tucked them behind a painting in the bedroom. The phone rang as I stood back to look at the grass lodged behind the picture of an old worn mountain man. "Reverend Cham, Sage Ford. I have an unusual request. My grandfather died and I need the family to gather for a kind of service for him." She stopped as if there, I've said it.

"Sage, I am sure we can work that out."

"With horse shows most weekends, the rest of my family doesn't do church. They've agreed to gather for a fifteen-minute service one evening around 6 p.m., can you do that?"

"Sure. What day is good for you?"

"Wednesday if that is okay with you." She paused. "Marcia, since horses were my grandfather's life, can we sing 'Happy Trails to You'...the Roy Rogers theme song?"

I swallowed my surprise. "I'll contact our organist, Jean Brooks and we will have the song ready for the service."

"Thanks Reverend Cham." I called Jean.

"Jean, Marcia. We have an unusual request for a fifteen-minute memorial service Wednesday night, are you available?"

I waited as Jean gathered her thoughts. "Yes. I can do that. Fifteen minutes, what are you going to do?"

"I'll do words of comfort and something about horses." I bated Jean.

"Horses. Yes. The service is for Sage Ford's grandfather, the local horseman. Sage wants us to sing 'Happy Trails to You.'"

"The Roy Rogers song? And you said yes?"

"Right. Can you find an arrangement?"

"I'll get to work on it." I heard her musing to herself as we ended the call.

Wednesday at 6 p.m., two rows of family filed into the front pews. I opened with prayer and readings about the beauty and strength and companionship of horses. Then Jean began to play. The family looked to the organ in shock and then smiles spread over their faces. They stood and we sang and as we sang their spirits lifted and Sage nodded and winked at me.

After the family left, Jean said, "I felt strange playing it but it was right for them, wasn't it?" I walked home feeling full, this is what I do best, meeting the needs of the people, no matter how strange.

I continued to work with the Panic and Anxiety Clinic to understand the disorder. Deaths and crisis situations, weddings and celebrations continued to surround my work and me. I knew I must learn to live with them.

Ken and I took a cruise to Europe for twenty-eight days. On deck enjoying the freedom, I studied three lines in my journal.

> *Mark 5:36, "Fear is useless. What is needed is trust." Henri Nouwen's words, "Hope means to keep living amid desperation and to keep humming in the darkness." And Macrina Weiderker's, "Walk gently with your frailty, allow it to bless you. It will not cripple you unless you run from it."*

I prayed these daily.

More anxiety surfaced after our European trip so I enrolled in a ten-week session at the Stress Reduction Clinic at South Shore Hospital. I worked hard with tapes and stress reduction exercises. I felt free. I set aside flash cards. I no longer carried Ativan with me. I understood my fears of death. I'd accepted normal body anxiety. I thought I was all done.

The Valley of the Shadow of Death

WITH THE TABLE SET, the standing rib roast ready for the oven, the gifts under the tree, I disappeared into my office to review the details for each of the Christmas Eve Services. I looked over the 7 p.m. Family Service. I hoped it would be engaging enough for the excited and wiggly children. I leaned back and pictured the kids dressed up, eyes bright with expectation and remembered the seriousness with which each year they held their lighted candles as we sang "Silent Night." As I glanced down the order of worship for the 11 p.m. service, nostalgia surrounded me at the familiar texts and carols. I rose and stretched. When I returned to the kitchen, I caught Ken munching on the frosted Christmas cookies. "I couldn't resist," he said. "Are you all set for tonight?"

"Yes. You'll be here to greet the Scotts, the Martins and the Hannans and Amy for dinner if I am tied up in conversation after the early service?"

"Sure, I'll be getting them loosened up with some wine."

"I can't wait to see Amy and hear, first hand, the story of our David asking her to marry him and see more pictures of their Halloween costumes as he presented her ring."

"Since you can't drink until the services are over, I'll have the champagne ready to celebrate their engagement after the late service."

I PULLED ON MY COAT and walked the four hundred feet to the church. I greeted the young and old alike as they came out of the cold wearing expectation on their faces. When it was time for the impromptu pageant, the children ran down the aisle; shepherds wrestled over staffs, angels sorted through wings and pulled them over their heads, some of them upside down, Mary and Joseph came in from the back with a live baby Jesus, and the Magi with an array of gold colored packages raised high above their heads marched in from the east. I read the traditional Christmas reading Luke 2:1-20, 'And it came to pass…'" Then the candle lighting, the quiet and a rousing "Joy to the World."

My steps were light and my heart bursting with joy as I walked back to the parsonage to greet our dinner guests. They were enjoying hor d'oeuvres. I hugged each guest, admired Amy's ring and responded to their questions.

"How was the service? Was the church full?"

"Wonderful. A crowd full of energy and anticipation. The children sparkled."

"Marcia, here's your half-glass of wine." Ken handed me the glass and turned to his task of carving the rib roast. Over dinner Amy told the engagement story and caught us up on the wedding details that were already in place. I helped Ken clear the table.

WHILE TENDING TO THE DISHES the world darkened... fear jumped on my back. I slumped onto the sofa. My heart raced. My palms sweated. I, the pastor, couldn't break through the ugly fear sitting on my shoulder. I had to sit down and share my problem. Some stayed around the table and others crowded around me on the sofa. Amy's Dad, Dave leaned down and put his arm on my shoulder. "Do you want me to take you to the hospital? I can get you help right away." Dave was CEO of the local hospital.

"Let me just sit. I don't want to give in to the fear. I need to practice my breathing." I tried to breathe and relax. Ken breathed with me. "What about the late service?" They all wondered.

Ken pressed next to me. "We'll take care of that. Where are your notes?"

"They are on the corner of my desk." Amy found the notes and the guests gathered around the dining room table and divided the service, each taking a part. I went to bed feeling defeated.

Amy reported to Ken "The service went well even though I mispronounced many words in the Christmas Story."

The next morning Ken asked, "Are you sure you want to go to Pete and Maureen's? I can cancel our flights. They will understand."

"Yes, I want to go. I'll be okay."

KEN AND I FLEW to Florida to celebrate Christmas with our daughter and her husband. Instead of practicing breathing and relaxation exercises and rationally predicting the peril of each situation, I grasped towel bars in bathrooms and bargained with God to get me through the holidays. The anxiety escalated. Night after night, deaths of four women in their early forties,

Karen, Judy, Barbara, and another Judy marched through my mind. Their ravaged bodies paraded before my eyes, their devastated families hung onto my legs, their deafening shouts of being struck down in their prime filled my ears. "Cancer stole my life." "Life cheated me." "God abandoned me."

I put up a good front. Even on our return home from Florida, I fooled myself into thinking I could spend the New Year's holiday with our son's family in Connecticut. As we started the drive, a cold fear forced me to tell Ken to drive me to my doctor's office for an emergency visit.

Kate, my nurse practitioner, set her eyes on me. "Marcia, I am going to prescribe Celexa — a new anti-anxiety and anti-depressant to raise your level of serotonin."

"Kate, I don't want to be dependent on a drug."

She laid her hand on mine. "Marcia, you know that Ken has taken medication for many years to control his blood pressure. I know your fear of addiction, but your body needs medication to raise your chemical level of serotonin. You may need it for many years to come." I cried and Kate sat in silence giving me the gift of her calm presence. Ken and I made the trip.

FIFTEEN DAYS AFTER THE Christmas Eve attack, I scribbled in large letters in my journal,

GOD, HOW CAN I BEFRIEND MY FEARS AND MY FEAR OF DEATH?

I contacted a grief specialist, Sherry. I worked with her weekly for four months in her warm office with soft draped furniture. I needed some answers and some freedom. I needed to be able to trust my body.

Sherry knew each of the women who had marched through my life. I talked about their ravaged bodies, their deaths, their families, the dissolution of their hopes and dreams. As with the old wringer washers, I squeezed their stories through my heart over and over until I sobbed. I shouted at God. "God you cut them down. You ravaged their bodies. You gave them no time. You robbed their families. Where was your mercy? You squeeze my body in a vice."

I acknowledged the expectations that created tight muscles in my body...old family tapes, the friction between me, the irreverent Reverend and the more traditional understanding of Reverends, the challenge of preaching Jesus — or of preaching the 'feel good' stuff the church wanted to hear.

At the end of a session Sherry quipped. "You've been framed." Her comment startled me.

"What do you mean?"

"Think of a picture of your family. Describe it." I leaned forward with my elbows on my knees, hands rubbing my face.

"Dad is dressed in a shirt and tie, Mother in a blue dress that matches the blue in her eyes, Barb, Marge and I are in white blouses and taffeta skirts and patent leather shoes. I am sandwiched in the middle."

"Talk about image."

"It's a tight frame. My parents put up with our shenanigans but we knew we had to get back in step. I think they had little understanding of what to do when I stepped outside their picture of what family meant to them. Issues or arguments were silenced or swept under the rug. I buried my questions and rebellious nature and played the game. Framed...I guess that's what we were...framed in the expectations of my parents."

The line, 'You've been framed,' became a working phrase as I dug up and overturned my life with Sherry.

I investigated the places and situations of illness and death where I had been left to feel vulnerable and yet expected to be okay. Snapshots of the past flashed through my head. I saw the family Desoto coming to a stop on the street beside a funeral home. My parents opened the car doors. They twisted around to my sisters and me in the back seat. "Crack the windows. We will be back in a few minutes." We waited in the car, fiddling with the window handles and door locks.

A few minutes later Mother and Dad returned. "All set." There was no mention of the dead person inside that building, no visible sign of emotion.

I wanted to ask, "Who died? Was it a friend? Did I know them, too?" But something in the air said, "Don't talk about it, it will go away."

Another memory found me huddled to the left of the front door of the funeral home near a stack of folding chairs in a dark heavy room. From my position the body of my aunt lay silhouetted by the pale yellow light from the floor lamps. I felt as pale as that light. I pinched myself to be sure that I was alive.

On the drive home, my mother questioned Dad. "Was it suicide?" Dad shrugged in annoyance with her speculation.

"Suicide," I whispered. A sharp chill passed through me like the winter wind whipping through a door before it is firmly latched.

In my mind I tried to form questions to ask about death and dying, but fear of being dismissed — not being heard — kept them locked in a deep place under my façade that said, 'Everything's okay.'

Like Mother and Dad, I'd locked my feelings inside.

I shared these snapshots with Sherry. "Was there anyone in your life comfortable with death?"

"My Grandmother Mitchell, 'Mom.' Her comfort with Pop's death astounded me. I haven't thought about that in years."

Sherry put her notepad on the table next to her and settled back in her chair. "Tell me Mom's story."

After Pop's viewing, Mom rode with my Mother, Dad, my sister Marge and me to our house. Dad helped Mom out of the car. She took his arm as they climbed the stairs to the back door. I followed behind with Mom's overnight bag. Inside she shrugged out of her winter coat. Dad draped it on a wire hanger and hung it in the guest closet. Dad leaned close to her. "You will stay in Marcia's room." She smiled and tugged on my sleeve.

"Marcia, follow me up the stairs. I may need a push. I'm exhausted." Carrying her bag, I followed.

I set her bag on the extra bed in my room. She opened it, pulled out her night gown and headed for the bathroom. I changed into my pajamas and crawled into bed. It felt good to be back in my own bed after the months of occupying the top bunk at college.

Mom came in, set her glasses on the dresser, leaned over and gave me a kiss. She pulled back the blankets on her bed and stretched out. I turned off the table lamp next to my bed.

With the lights out, I whispered into the darkness. "Mom, I thought Pop would always be here. I dread the funeral tomorrow."

"I know." The love in her voice lent me peace and I slept.

Mom rose early the next morning. I watched as she put on her glasses and made her way to the bathroom. When she returned, she noticed me awake. She sat on my bed for a few moments, silent. I touched her hand. She slumped into me. Shivers traveled from her body into mine.

She patted my hand, stood up, slipped out of her night gown, and stepped into her white cotton petticoat. She glanced at me and sighed. "I feel lost."

I didn't know what to say. Staring into the mirror over my dresser, she hummed, "What a Friend We Have in Jesus," as she powdered her face and pulled her lace- trimmed print dress over her head. Mom decorated her dress with two necklaces, one pearl-like and the other pink and blue crystals, one brooch shaped like a rose, another like a musical note. Then she picked up her timepiece that dangled from a ribbon of gold, and with a determined look and louder humming pinned it to her collar. After one last look in the mirror, she headed downstairs.

I washed and dressed. I walked down the stairs, peeked around the corner into the living room. Mom stood near the front window, gazing off. I tiptoed to the kitchen and nibbled on toast with jam. Mom's in the living room by herself, I need to be with her.

When I returned to the living room, Mom was seated on the sofa. She reached for my hand and pulled me down close beside her.

"Last Sunday Pop and I took the phone off the hook, fixed a tray of root beer and saltines, and nestled together on our sofa. I felt his head for a fever. He drew my hand away, laughed, and whispered. 'I was thinking of your sisters. They thought we were crazy for enjoying the cold of Upper Michigan. I can see us now, bundled up and traveling the snow-covered roads in our horse-drawn sleigh and skiing through carved tunnels to visit our friends.'"

I started to ask more about the tunnels, but Mom didn't pause.

"I squeezed Pop's hand as a memory floated past my eyes. 'Will, remember we wanted to be the first to bring in the fragrant arbutus. As we jolted off the less-traveled roads over fallen twigs and brush, we came upon a patch that looked likely to have the sought-after flowers. We brushed off the cold crust of snow and found the treasures we came to find. I held the arbutus to your nose and you hugged me.'

"Pop and I huddled even closer with the mention of cold. We laid the photos albums across our laps and enjoyed the pictures of the picnics, the Easter egg hunts, tractor rides, and Christmas dinners on the farm. Each picture brought back memories and, even more treasured moments."

Mom's eyes drifted away. I waited for her to continue.

"On Friday night, with the saltines and root beer about gone, Pop unfolded from our nesting place and stood. 'It's time for me to bathe.' He bent down, kissed me, and touched my hair. 'I'll be back in a few minutes.'"

Mom took a deep breath. My hands began to sweat and my heart pounded faster. She went on. "I heard a deep gurgling sound and headed for the door. Before I opened it, I knew he had slipped away." She took my hand in hers. "Now, I have my own guardian angel."

"A guardian angel," I stammered

We lingered on the sofa for a while, then, Mom looked at her watch.

"It's time to go to church." She walked to the hall mirror and with her fingers fluffed the curls around her face and re-arranged her jewelry.

I stayed glued to the sofa. I watched Mom until she was out of sight. Mom made Pop's death seem a normal part of life with the saltines, root beer, memories, a kiss, and a touch. And then her faith — he is not dead as in dead but her guardian angel. Her strength hung in the air and I tried to absorb it.

Sherry stood and come over to me. She reached down and gave me a warm hug. "Hang onto Mom."

"I will."

AT HOME THAT NIGHT, I surrounded myself with photos of Mom and Pop. I ran my hands over their oak table and chairs that are now in my kitchen. I found the carvings on the front of Mom's dressing table and followed the design with my fingers. I felt a warm touch on my arm. "Marcia, I'm here with you as you dig into your life." A deep calm came over me; I held onto a feeling of being safe.

At my fall retreat, I watched storm waves dig into the shore re-sculpting the shore line. As the storm grew, I dug for and brought to the surface deep emotions, anger, guilt, jealousy, and indifference. Anguish and torment flowed over me. In the midst of the storm I wrote,

> There's a person inside me who's needy, but
> afraid to ask for care. She tries to control
> instead of dealing with feelings.

There's a person inside me who wants to know
herself — the positive and the negative — the
light and the shadow, so I can accept me, so I
don't continue the struggle for approval, the
struggle is tiring.

There's a person inside me who is a rebel —
yet feels guided by God — who is scared when
all goes well — yet is humbled by her sacred
story.

There's a person inside me who longs to love
and to be loved but struggles with intimacy,
who builds walls of confidence and efficiency.

There's a person inside me who has so many
rough places, who wonders why and how
others love and care for her.

It's lonely in this place.

Again with Sherry, I befriended dark words that had troubled me...evil, shame, and rebel. I slid out of the family frame on my taffeta skirt. I drew in courage to design a new frame for my life...a fluid frame with no corners in which to hide expectations and fears. The boundaries were my growing relationship with my inner self, God and those around me — boundaries always subject to change.

AT MY LAST SESSION with Sherry, I brought along the prayer "Teach me How to Die" by Ted Loder. "I want to read this prayer to you."

Teach me, please, how to die!
    not that I want to any time soon,
      or exactly need to know before doing it,
        or that I won't learn on my very human own,
          but that is why I pray, plead, now:
            Please, teach me how to die!
    Teach me to trust, at least a little more,

that your grace and providence
    extends even to your gift of death,
        so I will become a little less afraid,
            though I confess I still wish a gentle
            passing,
                a brief contraction or two,
                and the assurance that someone
                will be there to receive me

Teach me the ways of courage past bravado,
    that whether death come gently or harshly,
        be brief in coming, or lingering,
    I will be able to face it
        without flinching or complaining—
        except perhaps an excusable little.
Please, teach me how to die![17]

She listened from her chair across from me. At the end you could feel the celebration in the air, see it on our faces and hear 'the whoopee's' running around the room bouncing off the walls, windows and mirrors. I'd befriended death and by befriending death I befriended myself.

I found the courage to give myself the kind of attention I'd been giving others. I opened my heart to all aspects of me that I'd been running from without even knowing that was what I'd been doing.

Freedom came with shoveling it all out and bringing it all to the light. Putting names to my fears and feelings took away their powerful hold. I remembered the phrases in a journal from my sabbatical.

Freedom and independence can't be wrested
from others but only can be developed
painstakingly from within.
                      Colette Dowling

The other side of every fear is a freedom…
we must take charge of the journey urging
ourselves past our own reluctance and
misgivings and confusions to new freedom.
                      M. Ferguson

And I remembered standing in front of the Korean War Memorial in Washington, D.C. and noticing in the background a standing slab of black granite with the words "Freedom is not free" in silver in the upper left hand corner. So true. Freedom comes with a struggle and a price.

OVER THE YEARS SINCE the first anxiety attack after Karen's funeral, experts have guided me. My family and friends have supported me and I've learned to challenge my fears. As I've shared episodes of my life story over and over again, pieces of light have broken through with each telling. I've gradually begun to understand my body's reactions to life. I've learned to accept that at times my body is tight, my breathing shallow, and my anxiety present. I've learned to befriend and respect death. Will there be setbacks? Of course. Is there still more to experience and understand? Yes.

Intimacy
with Death

Be patient toward all that is unsolved in your heart
And try to love the questions themselves...
The point is, to live everything.
Live the questions now.
Perhaps you will then gradually, without noticing it,
Live along some distant day into the answer.
Rainer Maria Rilke[18]

Are We Ever Ready for Death?

AN IMAGE OF BERT, my four-year-old grandson, popped into my mind as I walked through the hospital parking lot after a visit with Bessie. He was tugging at the blankets on my bed. "Grandma, the telephone's for you. Grandpa thinks you'll have to be going home." Awake I looked at Bert; the disappointment in his eyes crushed me. I struggled out of bed and we walked hand-in-hand downstairs to the kitchen. Ken handed me the phone and whispered,

"It's Deacon Dick about Donna." I listened and hung up. I looked around at Mike, Maggie, Bert, and Harrison and the pile of buns, chips and paper plates on the counter waiting for the Fourth of July cookout.

"We have to go home. I need to be at the hospital. Donna Dixon is near death. I'm sorry to miss the Fourth of July celebration."

"We're sorry too," Maggie said as she hugged me. "We know she needs you. Be safe."

Now, AS I TURNED the corner out of the hospital parking lot after a number of hospital visits, I sighed. It never ends. It never gets easier. Since our visit with the grandchildren, I've been with two families and conducted two funerals. One for Donna where we played Helen Reddy's, "I am Woman Hear me Roar" to honor her determined spirit, and the other, for a twenty-four year-old troubled youth where despair stifled the air.

At the last stoplight before reaching home, my cell phone rang. I fumbled in my purse. I tried not to let my voice show my exhaustion so I chirped.

"Hello."

"It's Ken. Where are you? I've been trying your cell phone."

"I had it turned off while visiting Bessie at Brockton Hospital. What's wrong?"

"Beverly called. She's in the emergency room. Bunky died. She needs you there."

"But he was doing so well. If she calls again, tell her I'm on my way." I turned around at Dunkin Donuts. I wasn't ready for Bunky to die.

Bunky lay on a sterile table in one of the emergency rooms. Beverly, his wife of forty-eight years, stood at the side of the stretcher-like table rubbing his head. Steve and Debbie stood behind Beverly with their hands on their mother's shoulders. Daughter Cindy, drawn and pale, sat on a chair on the other side of Bunky.

Beverly started, "Our day had been normal. We took the car in for a check-up, worked out, and called a realtor to look at our house. Then, while I was changing the bed," she hesitated, "he fell on the stairs. I ran to him, and he died in my arms."

I swallowed hard and rubbed Bunky's shoulder.

Beverly grabbed my other hand and pulled me close to her. "The emergency attendants pounded on his chest and brought him back to life in the ambulance. I wanted you here so you could say good bye with us."

I reached down and hugged Beverly. "I'm sorry. I wish I'd been here. I loved Bunky."

Cindy stood up, walked around the table. "Marcia, we're glad you are here now. We need a prayer." We held onto each other, and I prayed.

"God, our creator and friend, we sit here with Bunky's physical body. We loved this man as he loved us. He lived many years with his breathing troubles and we find it hard to believe that he's gone today. We just weren't ready. Be with Beverly, Cindy, Steve and Debbie. Hold them and catch their tears. Help us to accept the shock. Amen."

Beverly bent down near Bunky's ear. "As much as I hated lugging your oxygen in and out of the car, I'm..." Grief caught in her words.

Cindy reached for her dad's lifeless arm. "With our many runs to the emergency room, Dad, I thought we'd be prepared for this, but the reality is so silent and final."

As I drove home, I pictured Bunky and Beverly each Sunday sitting two-thirds of the way down the aisle, always on the right side of the worship room. They came in from the front of the church, so Bunky would not have to walk as far to his seat. When the organist played the hymns too slowly, being former Methodists, they motioned with their hymnals to crank up the tempo. I smiled at the image.

THE DAY BEFORE BUNKY'S service I walked across the driveway of the parsonage to the cemetery fence. I watched the cemetery superintendent, a tall thin man in his seventies digging Bunky's grave. Sweat poured off his body as he squared the corners.

"Dick, how would you like a beer?"

"Pastor, I'll have one if you'll join me." As we shared a beer, Dick talked and shoveled. "The grass needs trimming but I can't do it today." He stopped for a long drink. "Yep, Grandma Leland might appear out of that grave over there." Dick pointed to a marker three rows over. "She had strict rules — no cutting grass on Sunday."

"This is Sunday, what about digging?"

"She didn't like it, but sometimes with death's timing she excused the digging." He grinned and continued to work his artistry.

I leaned against the fence and watched. Dick paused a moment, stood back and looked at his work. "There. It's the last thing I can do for Bunky."

I felt Bunky's presence. He nodded in appreciation of the time-honored tradition of hand-dug graves.

THE MEMORIAL SERVICE CELEBRATED Bunky's full life with thanksgiving. The pallbearers walked the casket down the uneven pavement to the gravesite. The rest of us followed. Again I pictured Bunky, pleased that we had resurrected another old practice for his burial. Quiet filled the air as a veteran presented Beverly with a flag in honor of Bunky's years of service to his country.

At the end of the graveside service, I watched Dick shovel the dirt over the casket. Bunky's grandson, Jake, 11, came and stood by me. "Marcia, since you live right next to the cemetery, will you put on the light and go out on the porch each night and say good night to Papa?" I rubbed his head and said, "You bet, I will."

I JOINED THE FAMILY for pizza at Beverly's house after the reception at the church. Teenagers and adults alike carried pizza on paper plates to any comfortable place in the house, kicked off their shoes and settled back. The phrase,

"Gosh, I should have been ready, but I wasn't." circulated among the adults.

Everyone gathered around the kitchen table strewn with leftovers from the reception, Beverly asked, "Marcia, is any one ever ready for death?"

I put down my cookie which was overloaded with chocolate bits and paused for a moment. "Yes, my friend Ernie was. He even called it an adventure. Then there's Karen — she and her family were ready to let go because the cancer had destroyed her being. But I wasn't ready for Ken's mother's death, even though we'd had many scares and knew it was coming, just like you and Bunky."

Beverly probed more. "Are you ready to die?"

"No, I'm not ready. I have too much living to do."

Beverly touched my arm. "What about your mother, she's going to be 90 next year, is she ready to die?"

"Today she played cards and drove to have her hair done. Tomorrow she'll be glued to the last day of the Firestone golf tournament and soon professional basketball starts. Is she ready? No. She told my sister last week after visiting a friend, 'I don't want to linger in a nursing home with my head bobbing against my chest. I think I'll just pop off, but right now, I'm having too much fun to die.'"

"That sounds like your mother. She's such a character," Beverly said after she stopped laughing.

Beverly and I washed up the few dishes. "Does your mother speak of her death?"

"She doesn't talk about it, except for those little quips, but I believe she thinks about it. A year ago Mother hugged Maureen as she prepared to leave our house after Thanksgiving. Then she sobbed. I hugged her. 'The good-byes are harder and harder, aren't they? You wonder if you will see us again, don't you?' She sobbed. 'Yes.'"

After we recovered from a good cry, I stood back and grinned at Mother. "Mother, I have to tell you, I'm apprehensive about your spirit when it's set loose. When your spirit's flying around here and advising us of this and that, you will be unstoppable. We won't be able to turn you off. That's what I am afraid of."

Beverly leaned against the counter. "Are you ready for her to die?"

"No, not yet, but when the time comes, I hope she'll pop off watching Tiger Woods sink an impossible putt or, Lebron James of the Cleveland Cavaliers sink a three-pointer at the ending buzzer."

"No lingering illness." Beverly hugged me.

"Right, no lingering illness. She's been too active for that."

Small talk continued for hours. Hugs warmed my departure. I drove home. I parked, walked in, and immediately switched on the light to the back porch. I stepped out and looked over at Bunky's grave. "I love you, Bunky. Good night."

T-shirts and Bumper Stickers

Several months after Bunky's death, Beverly gathered the energy to go on a senior citizen bus trip for the day. Late that afternoon, I saw her pounding her way down the driveway to the parsonage. She knocked sharply on the door. She charged through the family room to the kitchen. "As I got on the bus, a jerk stopped me and said, 'You're smiling. You must be over Bunky's death.' Of all the nerve." She made a fist and pumped her arms as she paced around the kitchen. "What did he think? Over Bunky's death!! I smiled so I could cope. I wanted to belt him."

I stood with my anger rising along with hers.

"How many insensitive remarks am I going to hear?" She threw up her arms in anger and frustration. I shrugged and suggested we sit. My dog leaned against Beverly's legs and she reached down and scratched her ears. Her anger cooled. I moved the morning paper from the wingback chair that faced Beverly and sat. I debated what to say next — a little humor maybe.

"Ken once said, 'Congratulations' as he greeted a widow at the wake."

"You're kidding."

"No, I'm not. And if you think that is insensitive, a friend at the same wake said, 'So glad to be here.'" We laughed until we were silly.

Catching my breath I said, "Beverly, maybe you need a t-shirt with 'I'm smiling so I can cope.' across the front."

Beverly stood and demonstrated. "How about this one, 'Am I still grieving? on the front and 'Is the grass still growing?' on the back." We were on a roll.

"When my dad died, I wish I had one that read, 'if you say, you've grieved long enough, I'm going to belt you!'"

Beverly joined me for supper and we laughed over marketing plans for the t-shirts and even weighed the idea that the sayings might be suitable for bumper-stickers.

Weeks later Beverly stopped in my office. "I've been to my hospice grief group and I told them about our t-shirt and bumper sticker ideas. They laughed and came up with more slogans."

"Come sit. I'd love to hear them." Beverly sat on the love seat, and I took the rocker.

"Joan, who sits next to me in the group, said she's tired of people asking her how she's doing and then walking away as she begins to speak. The group came up with, 'Don't ask to be nice, ask when you really want to know AND ARE WILLING TO LISTEN.'" Beverly rolled on.

"Sally's husband died three years ago. Her daughter came over to have a 'talk' and tell her that it was time to move on. 'Move on,' we said in unison and came up with another bumper sticker. We don't move on, we integrate."

I nodded in agreement.

"Marcia, you know how I say, if I do this it will bring closure, if I do that it will bring closure?"

"Yes, for some reason I have trouble with the word closure," I added.

"Me, too, I've decided. Another saying could be, 'Closure? Hell! It's Adjustment.'" Beverly clapped her hands against her knees.

"I like it." We played with more marketing ideas and then a time of quiet slipped between us. I rocked and my thoughts turned more serious.

"Beverly, you know the hard part is that most of us have little practice with grief and death."

"Yeah, you're right." Beverly shrugged.

"So what can people say to the grieving?"

Beverly's face looked thoughtful and sad as she looked from me to her hands and turned her wedding ring around and around. "A simple 'I'm sorry' and a hug is all that's needed. A thinking of you card once in a while. It's the gift of their presence and their remembering that says more than any rehearsed or practiced words."

We let a silence fall between us. Then Beverly looked serious. "Maybe you should make a list of what to say and do and what not to say and do for to the grieving."

"A good idea. I'll work on that."

We hugged. Beverly opened my office door and stood in the doorway. "One more thing. Last night I heard a hornet buzzing on the ceiling. I jumped up, snapped on the light, got a broom and climbed up on the bed. I swatted the hornet. It landed on the sheet. I pounded it killing it over and over again yelling,

'Bunky, the killing of hornets was your job! How dare you leave me?"' A mischievous grin covered her face and a tear chased down one cheek. She punctuated the air with a wave. "How's that for good grieving?" She pulled the door shut.

Can you believe it? I Really Died!

THE LILLY FOUNDATION SABBATICAL Grant materials consumed my office. Maps and guide books, train schedules and lists lay spread out over the top of my sermon preparations. Historical books on Poland and Prague, Rick Steve's *Europe 101*, Berlitz cassettes and phrase books in Italian and French wobbled in a stack on the corner of my desk. On a yellow-lined pad I had written in bold letters, "The Religious Imagination." I had outlined each day of my upcoming five weeks in Europe in columns noting where art, architecture and cultural diversity might stir my imagination. I had just written "Auschwitz" when the phone rang.

The young male voice choked out. "My name is Chris, and my brother's Jeff. Our mother Carol Coffey's dead…suddenly dead." He took a breath. "I think she attended your church."

"Chris, I'm sorry. How can I help?"

"We need someone to do a service Thursday at 2:00 p.m. Will you do it?"

I glanced at my calendar. "Chris, Thursday is fine." I heard a sigh of relief as Chris turned to someone else and whispered, "She can do it." Then he returned to me.

"We can't believe she died — we needed her." After a deep breath and a change in his voice, Chris continued. "When can we come to meet you?"

"How about tomorrow morning at 10?" I gave them directions to the church and added, "Chris, my dad died the same way, suddenly, so I have some idea of your pain and confusion. You and Jeff, go gently."

CHRIS AND JEFF, TWO LANKY twenty-somethings, arrived the next morning. We walked across the vestry to the meeting room. Antique tables and stiff side chairs gave the appearance of a parlor. Each boy dragged a padded chair away from the conference table and sat with their long jean-covered legs stretching far under it. Their short-sleeved T-shirts revealed an array of tattoos on their arms.

Jeff leaned back in the chair, his finger tips balancing him on the edge of the table. "Reverend Cham, I don't get it. Mother played with her granddaughter, Kara, all day until 5 p.m., and then by 8 p.m., she was dead. Dead in her chair watching TV." He leveled his chair, put his elbows on the table, leaned his face into his hands, and tears dripped between his fingers. "She died alone."

Chris touched his brother's shoulder and looked at me. "Did she know she was going to die? For some reason, did God need her?" His eyes pleaded with me for an answer.

"Chris, I asked the same thing when my Dad died. Your mother's body..."

"It's a dirty trick. She'd been working on her life; she could see the light at the end of the tunnel." Jeff wiped his eyes on his sleeve.

"We know she wasn't ready, with another grandchild on the way and all." Chris added. We sat in the silence of the room listening to the tick of the antique wall clock.

Jeff traced his left index finger across the tattoo of a conch shell on his right arm. "Mom loved life. Simple things...," he hesitated, choking back tears. "When we needed to straighten-up, she sounded harsh, but we knew she loved us." He stopped and looked into the shell on his arm. A brief smile came over his face. "She loved seashells. She created stories for the kids at school about the critters that lived in those shells. The kids called her Maw." Jeff sat back and folded his arms across his chest and closed his eyes.

Chris stretched his arms over his head. He studied his fingers as he drummed them on the edge of the table. "Reverend Cham, at times, when Mom was sick and not feeling good, Jeff and I talked, not to be morbid, but just because, I guess." He shrugged his shoulders. "We talked about how we were going to feel when Mom died. Is that strange to think about?" Chris relaxed into his chair.

"No, Chris, it's..."

"Strange or not, now we know. We feel crappy, just crappy." Jeff slammed his hand on the table. Then folded his shoulders down and mumbled. "And it's so final."

I listened hard as their emotions and questions continued flooding the room. Their passion, their honesty stirred me. At their ages I'd never thought about death, nor questioned God. And if I'd had questions to ask, I wouldn't have known whom to trust with them or who might not dismiss them as trivial. Here they were, two twenty-somethings trusting me. Chills ran deep into my heart.

I decided the boys neither wanted nor expected answers, especially any theological ramblings or pat responses. They needed someone to listen without judgment to their pain, sorrow, and frustration.

We talked for a few more minutes ironing out the details, including the directions to the funeral home they'd chosen. They stood and scooted the chairs back under the table and with slow steps we walked arm in arm to the door. They reached down and hugged me, and I watched as they climbed into their red pick-up truck and drove off.

I WALKED TO THE PARSONAGE, grabbed my walking shoes, threw them in the backseat of the car, and drove to the beach. The loamy, dank smells of low tide filled the air. The gulls stood with their backs against the wind, feathers ruffling. I walked with that wind at my back. I remembered asking my mother at the time of Dad's death, "Did you think Dad knew he was going to die?" I felt again Mother struggling for words. "Before we left for Florida, in your Dad's off-handed way, he said, 'I think Mayhew's Funeral Home needs business.' I started to say something, but I knew he had turned his ears off."

As I walked further down the beach, I remembered the letter I wrote to Dad a year after his death. I'd asked the same question knowing I'd never receive a response. I still didn't know the answer to the questions. Did Dad know he was going to die? Did Carol Coffey know she was going to die? I've heard people say they could see signs after the death, maybe inklings but no real evidence of knowing before. "So Chris and Jeff, I don't know."

I stopped to watch and listen to two gulls squabbling over a clam shell that had been washed up by the incoming tide. I looked around and walking behind me was a couple, arm-in-arm. My mind shifted to Cathy and Steve, their wedding and, then Steve's death from the moped-bike accident. I asked of the wind, "Why, when life blessed them with love and a new start, why this accident? Why now?" No rational reasons surfaced as I kicked sand trying to cover up the memories of Steve's tragic death. The words "ACCIDENTS HAPPEN" flashed like a brilliant neon sign through my mind, a reminder of the reality of life.

I reversed direction and walked into the wind; waves crashed into the rocks. My niece's explanation to her daughters after the accidental death of their daddy came into my mind. "Jesus needed him."

I shouted to the wind and pounded my feet on the sand. "No, God did not need your daddy. God does not willy-nilly zap someone dead for God's need. I do not believe the time-worn statements, 'Our days are numbered. It was just his or her time.'" I stopped, walked a little further and almost screamed, "I don't believe in a God whose computer board pops up and says, 'Joe's time is up.'"

"Chris and Jeff, God didn't need your mother. Her heart gave out. God feels sorrow along with you."

At the end of the beach, I sat on the rocks and watched the waves bring the tide in. Chris's words rumbled through my head. "Jeff and I wondered how we were going to feel when our mother dies. Is that a strange question?" My mother is 90 years of age. Is it time for me to ask this question?

I looked into the depths of the tidal pool caught in the rocks at my feet. "How am I going to feel when my mother dies?" Words came from the pool as though from the bottom of my heart. I will miss her phone calls, the click of her receiver on the answering machine because she doesn't want to waste her money listening to the message. I will miss her visits and everyone commenting on her spirit and life. I know her spirit will be alive in my life, the lives of my children — her grandchildren and great-grandchildren. I know that if we mess around too much at her funeral, her spirit will tell us to shape up and practice some decorum.

I caught myself and realized these words of knowing dodged the real question: how am I going to FEEL? I readjusted my position and looked into the bottom of the tidal pool and waited. An answer slowly emerged: empty. When my mother dies, I am going to feel empty with a huge hole in my life.

I stretched and watched the incoming tide. I thanked God for the words and revelations. I breathed in deeply as I walked to my car and returned to the office to prepare for Carol's funeral.

AT THE FUNERAL HOME, kneeling in front of the casket, I knew at first glance that Carol Coffey had attended worship occasionally. Sadness filled me as I leaned forward and whispered in her ear, "You've met my dad, haven't you? He is one special guy, don't you agree?" I wiped tears from my eyes before I stood up.

Jeff, standing behind me, whispered. "What did you say to her?" I turned to meet his eyes.

"Since my dad's death, rightly or wrongly, I believe that Dad greets the people whose lives I am invited to celebrate and remember. I asked her if she'd met Dad yet."

"Hmm?" Jeff narrowed his eyes and fixed his gaze on me. I saw curiosity flash over his face, something new to contemplate.

As family members and friends arrived, knelt at the casket and greeted the boys, country music played in the background and casual conversation circulated around the room.

The funeral director introduced me. I stood at the lectern. My eyes scanned over the guests and landed on Chris and Jeff.

"We are here to celebrate the life of Carol Coffey, loving mother to Chris and Jeff."

I read scripture and offered prayers as the guests' tears and sniffles packed the room. I said the eulogy and invited others to share memories and stories about Carol. Carol's brother approached the casket. He stood between the casket and the rows of guests. He looked at them, then at Carol and back at them and gestured toward Carol.

"Carol, if you could speak, I'll bet you'd be shouting," he paused for effect, "can you ...can you believe it? I died. Can you believe it? I really died."

Some, drained from tears, broke into belly-laughter. Others looked paralyzed by the question.

"CAN YOU BELIEVE IT? I died. I really died." Carol's funeral marked the first time I'd heard that question. That afternoon I called three clergy friends and related the question and asked, "Have you heard that question voiced?" No one had.

The question made me think of the opening scene of the movie *Defending Your Life*, where the lead character is struck by a bus. In the next scene he finds himself in a golf cart being squired around a Disney-designed heaven. The look on his face asks, "What happened? Did I really die?"

That evening I leaned back in the chair in my home study and imagined me, in a flash of time, turning around and saying, "What happened? Did I really die?" As I sat, my imagination embraced the questions and a spirit tapped me on the shoulder and brought its right arm around my neck and gave me an elbow hug and said, "Welcome, Marsh." I recognized Dad's voice, and behind him stood Carol, Gertie, Ernie, Helen, Pop and Mom, the Judy's, Ruth, and a parade of others. At the end of the line Matt waited with two cold drafts. My questions disappeared in the warmth of the welcome. I squeezed Dad's hand and my imagination returned to the reality of my calendar in front of me and tomorrow's day full of more mysteries to integrate.

Intimate Moments

M Y BULGING BAGS WITH flight tags hanging from them, stood in the family room. A canvas tote filled with photos and souvenirs leaned against the legs of the wing-back chair. Ken and I breathed in the smells of home after our three-month sabbatical. The phone rang.

"Hey, Marcia, it's Bill." His voice sounded exhausted and without emotion. "Linda fell into a coma. The nurses say it won't be long. Can you come to the ICU?"

"Oh, Bill, I'm sorry. Of course I'll be there."

"Her lungs failed more during the last few days. The doctors are finding it more and more difficult to keep her comfortable."

"Bill, I'll be right along." I grabbed for my purse. I stopped and flipped through a book, *Out of the Ordinary* by Joyce Rupp, and ran my finger over the heading, "Blessing for One Who Draws Near to Death." Is this a time to use this blessing? Is it appropriate for Linda? I marked the blessing with a small piece of yellow-lined paper, stuffed the book in my purse, and headed for the hospital.

LINDA HAD COME TO church eight months earlier in July. She sat on the right side, four pews from the front. With her broad face shining, she leaned forward a bit as she listened. Her height made it easy for me to see her inviting smile. I watched as she absorbed the words and the music and the love of the congregation. We met over coffee.

"I've worked with the Brockton Housing Authority for years setting up after-school programs and crime-watch centers. I'm depleted, empty of things of the spirit, I guess you'd say. I come to worship seeking peace after my first and I hope only bout with lung cancer." She reached out and touched my hand. "I feel like your preaching is meant just for me."

"Thanks." I paused and sipped my coffee. "Linda, sometimes churches are the last place to find peace, so I'm pleased that you're finding something here to help you."

"I want to help out. What can I do?" We talked about some volunteer opportunities: the church fair and teaching Sunday school. Then an idea struck me.

"Linda, we are having a women's retreat in January at the Sisters of St. Joseph Retreat Center on the ocean in Cohasset. It's the place where I find peace. It's a place I go when I'm empty to fill my spiritual tank. Think about coming."

Six months later on a cold Saturday in January, the retreat began. Twelve women gathered around the fireplace. I asked each person, "What is it that you hope to find during this time away?" Linda spoke last. The radiance of her face and smile lit up the circle as she looked at each person. "I am in remission from lung cancer. I've come to find peace."

I played a piece of music, and we sat in silence for a few moments. "Now, I invite each of you to find a quiet place and let the living water of God's love run over you and within you. Let it shower you with blessings." I watched the group scatter. Over the years the group was accustomed to the routine of a few words and then invited to go off and listen to the silence.

I bundled up and sat on the porch. I watched Linda walking the rocks. I hoped she was drawing in life from the rhythm of the sea.

Late that night, the group gathered around the fire and listened to it crackle. Some knitted; others read books, some talked quietly. One by one the others made their way to bed, leaving Linda and me in our robes sitting on white wicker rockers. We pulled our rockers closer to the fire and stared at the glowing embers, each with our own thoughts. Linda broke the silence.

"What a place and the group...they've taken me in. I love all the hugs and the smiles." Her face beamed.

"I treasure this time each year. The prayer and sharing refreshes us and connects us at levels we could never reach in a coffee hour or church meetings." I stood and poked the coals, returned to my chair turning it a little more toward Linda.

She turned her face toward me. "This afternoon while sitting on the rocks, the smell of the sea air, and the rhythm of the tide settled in me. It's like I can feel peace is making its way into my soul." We touched hands. Linda stood and reached down and gave me a hug...I watched her walk up the stairs.

I lingered for a while longer and prayed. Then pulled myself out of my chair, reached for the poker, and separated the coals. I climbed the stairs to my room with gratitude in my heart at God's presence in this place.

During our closing worship, Linda thanked the women for their prayers and support. She made it to worship the next two weeks, but then, her place on the right, four pews from the front, sat empty for two weeks. I called Bill.

"Linda's lung cancer has returned with a vengeance. She's at Mass General. I'll keep you posted."

Now, an hour after Bill's call asking me to come to the hospital, I was pulling into a multi-story parking lot of the hospital. I grabbed my purse, walked to the elevator and pushed the button for the ICU unit. I checked in at the desk. They directed me to Linda's room. Bill met me in the hall with a lingering hug. "I'm glad you're here. Linda's parents...they need to lean on you."

"That's fine."

I opened the door. I reached up to hug Linda's father, Bud, and down to hug her mother, Helen. They drew me in and introduced me to family and friends who surrounded Linda's bed. I looked on Linda's face as sorrow for her pending death and thanksgiving for having known this woman traveled through my body at the same time.

Several friends encircled the bed and did Reiki, a natural act of 'laying on of hands' to promote peace and harmony, to ease the departure of her soul. As they worked, an aura of peace enveloped Linda. Her parents rubbed her hands and her feet. Staff of the critical care unit worked efficiently monitoring the drugs to keep her pain free. The hours clicked on as visitors stopped by to say good bye. Linda's dad took me aside.

"I'm worried about Helen and Bill. They're exhausted."

"How about you, Bud?"

"Me, too."

I took a break and traveled down the elevator and ordered soup at Au Bon Pan on the first floor. I reached into my purse and pulled out the book *Out of the Ordinary*. I found the yellow-lined paper and opened the book and read through the blessing as I sipped my soup. Yes, it's right. I tucked it under my arm and returned to Linda's room where I found Bill staring out the window. "Bill, you and Linda's folks are exhausted. I have a blessing for one who draws near death that might help us. What do you think?"

For a long time Bill stared and bit his lip. He turned and gave me a hug. "Linda trusted you. Let's give it a try."

I touched each person — Linda's parents, her three friends and a cousin — and issued each an invitation. "Will you join Bill and me around Linda's bed? Stand where you can easily touch Linda's body." The sound of shuffling feet disturbed the silence.

When all were in place, I said, "I'm going to lead you through a blessing to send Linda forth on wings of love. When I name each part of her body, please touch that part while I read the blessing. At the end of each blessing, we will share in the response. 'Linda, you will always be a part of our hearts. Go in peace.'"

I opened my book to the yellow-lined paper. My hands shook and my voice wavered. "Linda, we are going to bless your body. It has housed a wonderful spirit for many years and been a gift both to you and to us. Thank you for the privilege of blessing you." I blessed her head and the group responded. "Linda, you will always be a part of our hearts. Go in peace." A felt presence calmed me. The blessing of her head, eyes, ears, mouth, hands, feet, womb, and heart, drew us deeper into Linda and letting go. After the benediction, "May the angels of eternal life draw you into the Divine Presence. May the angels of mercy comfort you and bring you peace as you depart from us. May the angels of hope take you by the hand and lead you home,"[19] hands lingered on Linda's comatose body and tears rolled down cheeks and left pools of moisture on the sheets.

Helen touched my arm, "Thanks. I needed that. I felt energy coming from Linda into me."

As the evening went on and more friends and family arrived to say good-bye, Bill asked that we participate in the blessing again. By the end of the night, we'd repeated the blessing three times, each time finding more strength and courage to let Linda go.

Far into the night deli sandwiches arrived. Conversation lightened and funny stories passed from one person to the other. In fact, the group was so absorbed in Linda stories that the nurse had to interrupt us. "If you want to witness the passing, you need to pay attention to Linda's breathing."

Silence filled the room. One shallow breath. A long wait. Then another. And an even longer wait. Then the last. Linda's last breath — quiet and gentle as Linda had lived.

Exhausted and filled with sorrow, I made my way home. The next day I met with Bill at their house to discuss the funeral and to try to connect with their son, Sam. Sam, age 14, could not make himself come to the hospital, and Bill understood.

I said, "Hi."

Sam looked down at his shoes, his body stiff. He mumbled, "Hi." Then he laughed as I jumped back. He leaned down and picked up a reptile-like creature. "It's my mother's iguana, Liz." The iguana whined in front of the refrigerator. Sam gave her a stalk of celery, and she scampered to the top of the TV and munched.

"Sam, I didn't know about the iguana." He smiled, accepted a quick hug and disappeared into the basement listening to music with his friends. My heart broke for him.

Sitting in my study after the celebration of Linda's life and the burial, I remembered Sam and his buried grief. Then the image of those deli sandwiches and the blessing and the iguana and Sam's smile came into my mind. I mused about the connection between the profane and the sacred in this dance called life. Funny isn't it, as creatures in your realm O God, we, and even iguanas, are conduits for the sacred. God works through us and our stories and even our deli sandwiches and iguanas to reveal moments of the holy.

My body relaxed into the chair and I smiled to myself. An image of Linda breathing freely passed through my heart. Her smile burned into me. A spark of energy moved me to think of the blessing as a new intimacy with death. I found tears cascading down my face. A prayer formed in my heart.

> Intimate Creator, you've been with me
> through my growth — my gradual journey
> to find an intimacy with death. You've
> held me through the necessary levels of
> travel. You've been with me through my
> questions, my information gathering, and
> my experiences where the dying became my
> teachers. You've stayed by my side through
> my anxiety, my periods of gestation, even

the refining fires of my fear of death to an
almost unedited acceptance. I desire to
grow even more, to greater acceptance and
more freedom. The blessing with Linda was
another step where I reached another level. I
am grateful.

God's Power Working in Us

"I GUESS PASTORS NEVER completely retire." Becki said as she squeezed my hand. I opened the door and stepped out of her car to depart for my early morning flight from Chicago to Charlotte.

I paused a moment before closing the door. "Especially, when a friend of twenty-some years calls and needs me."

In the late afternoon, my flight from Chicago arrived in Charlotte. I drove up the mountain to Blowing Rock. Ken greeted me with a kiss and poured a glass of wine for each of us. We sat on the deck overlooking the gorge and studied the infinite numbers of ridges in the distance. After I heard his story of helping our daughter and son-in-law move to their new house, Ken refilled my glass. "I'm sorry I was away when Becki called. Tell me about it?"

I sipped my wine and began. "At first, Becki asked about us and the family, then she her voice changed. She broke the news that a friend had found Tony dead in his apartment. She was caught off guard because he'd been doing so well. She thought maybe this time he was on the right road and off drugs. She lamented that he was just thirty-seven. Then she asked 'will you come and do the service for us?' Of course I said I'd be honored.

"I tried to sleep, but images of walking the beach with Becki, hearing about her hopes and dreams for him raised and then shattered, consumed my mind. I roamed the house trying to absorb the news and Becki's trust in me to do the service for them.

"During the early hours of the morning, I found myself sitting on the floor of the family room surrounded by a pile of photo albums — the albums from our days in Burlington, Iowa, where we first met Becki and her family. I was searching for a picture of Tony, at age 14, with his infectious smile enjoying life in his quiet way."

Ken cleared his throat. "Did you find it?"

"No, but what I did find were the pictures of the going away party that Becki and Bob threw for us when we left Burlington for Boston. I laughed at the picture of Becki and me dressed like old ladies for a back-to-school lunch. And to my surprise, there was a picture of the Thanksgiving we spent with her family when they moved to Connecticut.

Ken touched my arm. "Refresh me. Debbie is Tony's oldest sister, isn't she?"

"Yes. She was a life guard at the Burlington Golf Club pool. I had more than a few intense religious conversations with her around the pool." I smiled remembering Debbie's questioning spirit. "Sara, of course, is the youngest and we didn't know her as well.

"Anyhow, it was almost morning by the time I put the albums away. I ate breakfast and over the next few days, I read through scriptures, readings and prayers trying to find the right tone and the right words for the service. No judgment. No platitudes. Just love. And the affirmation that Tony was free now living in the loving presence of God.

"During my flight to Chicago, I relaxed for the first time in days. Becki and Debbie picked me up and Debbie drove us to her condo. I listened to her stories. 'Tony had been doing well. Two weeks ago he looked great. He was following an exercise program and taking his good medications. He died alone.'"

I looked over at Ken; tears glistened in his eyes. I sipped my wine and continued. "After our conversation we drove to the church where Debbie had arranged for the service to be held. The minister welcomed us. He suggested that we might find the chapel more intimate for the size of the group we were expecting for Tony's service. We stood in the chapel. He knew our needs. He knew we'd be swallowed up by the immensity of the sanctuary. He cared." I paused. "Ken, do you want to hear all of this?"

"Yes, go on." He turned his chair more toward mine.

"Thursday, the day of the service, I woke early. I turned on the light next to my bed and reached for my binder. I read through the service. I still needed an image. The first image that surfaced was a roller coaster. Tony's addicted life certainly took on the characteristics of a roller coaster ride: the dips and climbs, the risks and the straight away, but it didn't feel right. I struggled. Then from the depths my soul an image emerged that I hadn't thought of for twenty years. There, in front of me, was a twelve-foot wall with no foot holds or pegs…just a flat wall. The wall was the next obstacle in a ropes course on Thompson's Island in Boston Harbor. I was with a group of eight high school students and the object was to get all of us over the wall."

Ken stretched his legs under the table and shifted his position to be more comfortable. "As I remember you had one young man, skinny as a rail and 6'6"and another at 5'8" and over 200 lbs."

"Right." I took a sip of my wine. "I remembered being flat against the wall with kids pushing up on my feet with the tips of their fingers and Tom, the tall one, reaching over the top of the wall trying to grasp my fingers. They pushed and reached and hollered for me to let go and trust them to get me over the wall.

"Remembering that moment made me think of Tony's life — trapped against a wall of addiction — with his family and friends supporting him and reaching for him. Tony stuck, yet not alone. Help within reach, but he just couldn't make it. His physically addicted body kept him pinned, even creating an impression in the wall.

"The image was a gift. I'd waited six days for the image to emerge and it finally did." Ken and I lingered in the silence of the evening watching the shadows from the setting sun playing on the ridges.

As darkness set in Ken gathered the wine glasses and I followed him inside. After washing and putting the glasses away, he reached for a hug. "I'm glad you could be with Becki."

THE NEXT MORNING I sat on the deck watching the morning sun glaze the ridges and wrote in my journal.

> For Tony's service, I needed to wait patiently
> for you, O God. I had to trust the image
> would come. On my flight home my
> paraphrase of Ephesians 3:20 came to mind.
> "Glory to God, because of your power working
> in me, I can do infinitely more than I can ask
> or ever imagine." Thanks.

I CLOSED MY JOURNAL and lingered on the deck with my well-worn, spine-torn *New Jerusalem Bible*. I unfolded the bulletin for Tony's service and read the words we'd printed on the front, 'God has raised you up on eagles' wings, and raised you up on the breath of dawn.' I paused and looked into the rising sun. A hawk soared and then glided on the wind.

Note to Myself

YEARS AFTER THE DEATHS of my grandfather and grandmother, Pop and Mom, in papers given to me at my uncle's funeral, I found an article that Mom had had written sometime after Pop's death. As I read it, I felt Mom's presence travel through me.

Arbutus Hunting

By Elizabeth G. Mitchell

It felt just like one taking part in a play as my
sweetheart helped me into the buggy. The
heavy winter coat and galoshes weighted me
down, but kept me warm. It was sunshiny,
but snappy cold, on this first day of May in
northernmost Michigan. To be the first to
bring in the fragrant arbutus was our goal.

The horse responded to the "giddy yap,"
and jerked us back in our seats and on our
way. Through the slushy roads, half-thawed
and half-frozen, we rode along toward
Lake Superior. The road kept open by the
lumberjacks was pitty and joggy, made many
an excuse to hang onto each other. As we
jolted off on a less-traveled road over fallen
twigs and brush, we came upon a patch that
looked likely to have the sought-after flowers.

The wind was stronger as we got near the
lake, and we wondered how flowers could
grow in such a freezing climate .I climbed
gingerly out with Bill's help as he yelled to
the horse to "Whoa!" I stepped in the slush,
crunching through the snow, and felt glad
I had worn my winter togs as I fastened
my muffler closer around my neck. A few
feet away we started kicking away clumps
of snow, and sure enough, there were the

hidden treasures we came to find. First the
large leaves and underneath the fragrant
pink and white star-like arbutus clusters.

There were many exclamations as we
rejoiced over each patch we uncovered.
We sniffed and admired the large bunch
that soon formed in our cold hands. We
breathed in the beginning of spring. The
more we picked the more we wanted of the
sweet-smelling beauties. They transmitted to
our souls God's wonderful work of nature.
How could such a fragile bit of beauty grow
underneath the snow and ice of winter, and
be ready so early in May?

Although we repeated this for several years
in May, we always remembered the first
time best. Just the recollection brings back
pleasant memories of odors and beauty, and
refreshes our beings. God works in many
ways His wonders to perform.

The bumpy ride in the horse and buggy, the
sloshing and kicking away the clumps of
snow in each patch, paid off in many ways.
The effort took winter out of our beings and
made us ready for spring.

If there is a lesson in this personal
experience, it could be this: Let us seek
and find life's deep treasures underneath its
cold crusty surface, and pass them along to
increase the enjoyment of everyday living.[20]

Through working with the individuals and families in this
book, I've kicked away clumps of fear and anxiety. I found not
just the cold reality of death, the hard crusts of life, the questions
with no answers and the depths of grief, but also treasures.

Silence and the soul-shaping of the sea. The human
cries of the Psalms. Ernie's adventure with death. Beverly's

bumper stickers. Helen's letters. The chutzpa of Gus. The honesty of Maude. The earthy palette of Lily. Freshly baked cookies. Barbara's black humor. Gladys's crocus. Daddy's quilt. My letter to Dad. Judy's full-length mink. Another Judy's creative imagination. Margaret's great-grandchildren. The blare of a car horn. My anger. Beer with Matt. Jeff and Chris's questions. Charlotte's song. Gertie's parade. Ruth's solid cherry casket. Karen's video. The power of fear. Becki's trust. Mom and Pop. And the professionals: Rosemary, Lisa, Gini, Carol, Sherry. And the personal: Ken's gentle touch.

I continue to respect the anxiety in my body, monitor my stress and breathe from my gut. Each breath reminds me that life is precious. Each breath connects me with God who reminds me, "Fear is useless; trust." I find that in trusting life, I trust death as a passage to another life...even an adventure, right Ernie and Helen?

Now, retired and working as an on-call chaplain in a local hospital, death remains a constant... the death of the elderly, of babies and children, sudden death and prolonged death. I take the strength of the lives in these stories with me to the hospital. They are a cloud of witnesses when I am with young parents, spouses, and strangers. They press against me and give me courage and words of wisdom. Their teaching continues as I live among the mysteries of death and life.

Appendix

What to do and say and not do and say for the Grieving.

- A simple "I'm sorry" and a hug is all that's necessary

- Never say, "I know how you feel."

- Do not say, "Call me if you need anything." Just call.

- If they do not answer, leave a few simple words on their voice mail.

- If you are calling to drop something off, call ahead and tell them what you want to do and that you will be in and out in five minutes. Gain their permission.

- If you want to visit, call and say you are on your way somewhere and have a few minutes, would it be okay to stop in for fifteen minutes? The grieving have only so much energy and they appreciate knowing you are not coming to camp for the day.

- If you call and they answer and say they are not ready for a visit, simply say "Take care." Do not negotiate to see them out of your need. Contact them in a day or two to see if they are ready for a visit, a walk, lunch or…

- Have someone in charge of food. Organize a list of the family favorites and the quantities needed. Make a schedule so that the family does not have lasagna or pasta at every meal. Make sure all food is taken in disposable containers. The grieving do not need a table full of unmarked Tupperware and casserole dishes to return.

- When someone from your regular dinner group dies, do not sit the widow or widower across from the empty chair when going out to eat. Seek out a round table. That empty chair does them in.

- Send a card and continue to send cards especially after the first couple weeks. Remember the year anniversary.

- You forgot to send a card or note? Send one even several months later. It feels wonderful to know everyone has not forgotten. The grieving value the note that can be read countless times.

- Encourage your friends and loved ones to grieve and let them know that grief comes and goes as the tides. Let them know there is help from their local hospice groups. Find a book about grief and give it to them. Be the friend who listens without judgment.

- Listen to their stories as often as they need to tell them. Why? Isak Dinesen, author of *Out of Africa*, wrote, "All sorrows can be borne if you put them in a story or tell a story about them."[21] Sue Monk Kidd in "The Story-Shaped Life" affirms that "Creating a story is an act of healing. To fashion an inner story of our pain carries us into the heart of it, which is where rebirth inevitably occurs. Telling our story puts us in an inner room with our suffering and allows us to dialogue with it in God's presence, to reinterpret it in the light of God's participation."[22]

- Know that the road to travel is an unfamiliar one for the grief-stricken, an uneven road that takes twists and turns; a road that needs patience and humor and the gift of time. A road not to be missed. Remember the words from the Twenty-third Psalm, "Even though I walk through the valley of the shadow of death." Notice the word "through." The psalmist did not say around, over, under, or avoid the valley of the shadow of death; but the psalmist said through it. Grief rains on everyone with all its questions, depression, anger and pain. Encourage them to walk through the valley for good physical and emotional health.

Letter One. For a Good Death

Dear Ken and Family,

I hope that I'll be ready for a good death. I hope my enthusiasm for living continues to the final moments. After the much publicized Terri Schiavo Case of 2005 and its confusion over whose wants and desires should be honored, I need to keep the practical details current. I need to keep my will up to date and make sure you, along with our attorney, have copies. I need at least one of you to know the combination to the home safe and have access to my online financial records.

I need to complete a Living Will and review it periodically so that it meets the legal requirements of the state where I am living. A copy of the Do Not Resuscitate (DNR) order needs to be in a visual place in my home and on the door to any hospital room and registered with my primary physician.

I need to assign a Health Care Proxy, make sure my driver's license reads Organ Donor and keep a current list of names and numbers of doctors and other health care providers.

I want one of you to meet my doctors and their office managers so that you've established a relationship with them before my health deteriorates. From my experience I know the professionals will answer your calls and questions in a more responsive manner if they have established a relationship with you.

My Christmas card list will be tucked in the same folder as my will. I want you to send a note to each person with the news of my death. After years of Christmas connection, I think it is only fair to inform them so they are not left wondering.

As my health deteriorates and the quality of my life diminishes, I want to know all the facts about my condition. I don't want any pussy footing around bad news. If the doctor thinks it is his or her duty to do more life saving measures than I requested, and I cannot communicate, I trust you will listen with an ear to my wishes. If there are difficult decisions to make, I know you will make them with care and love. After the decision is made, do not second guess yourselves.

And please let the hospital chaplains or local clergy help us. Request them to pray for courage and strength and for my peaceful passing when the time comes. Periodically, we need to review my plans so that we all are clear about my wishes. I don't want us to hide from death.

Love and Hugs,

Marcia — Mom, Grandma and Great-Grandma

Letter Two. For the Celebration of My Life

Dear Ken and Family,

Today there are a plethora of options surrounding the celebrations of life. Body, no body. Viewing or no viewing. Calling hours or no calling hours. Burial or cremation. Funeral or memorial service. Spreading the ashes or dividing the ashes. And who knows what others will be created by the time I die.

So for now, I want to be cremated with my *New Jerusalem Bible*. It has the difficult passages underlined with questions in the margins that I want to put to God. Family members who need to see the body before cremation may do so, but no general viewing. Plant my ashes in a memorial garden at a church in a biodegradable container. List my name on a plaque inside the church or on the wall of the garden or whatever the church offers.

I want my memorial service to be a testament to my life. I want what journalist Liz Carpenter who served as Lady Bird Johnson's press secretary described in her book *Getting Better All the Time*.

"I want the church full, and I want open sobbing, not just a few wet eyes. I want good press and glorious obituaries with some irreverent anecdotes about my life. And I want laughter along with tears. I want friend and foe alike to know I had a whale of a time walking about God's earth."[23]

At the service, praise God through the reading of Psalm 150, recall God's steadfast love and constant presence with Psalm 139, hire a New Orleans style band. Play and sing, "Here I am Lord," "Just a Closer Walk with Thee" and "When the Saints Go Marching In." If you can't sing, hire a soloist to lead you. Share stories and more stories. Add any readings that have meaning for you. Play Louis Armstrong's "It's a Wonderful World." Find a copy of the St. Francis Prayer, "Lord, Make us Instruments of Your Peace" and read it together. Put the following on the cover of the bulletin and take it home and use some tasteless magnet to attach it to your refrigerator.

EPITAPH

When I die
give what's left of me to children
and old men that wait to die.
And if you need to cry
cry for your brother and sister walking the street
beside you.
When you need me,
put your arms around anyone
and give them what you need to give to me.
I want to leave you something
something better than words or sounds:
look for me in the people I've known
and loved.
And if you cannot give me away,
at least let me live in your eyes
and not on your mind.
You can love me most
by letting hands touch hands,
by letting bodies touch bodies,
and by letting go of children
that need to be free.
Love doesn't die, people do.
So that when all that's left of me is love,
Give me away.
I'll see you at home in the earth.[24]

Follow the New Orleans Band to a hall. Enjoy eating, drinking and sharing stories. Then return to life. Share your grief and your mutual loss. Recognize your pain and your sorrow; find support among family and friends. Remember my spirit will be alive and well in you, whom I've loved.

Love,
Marcia — Mom, Grandma, and Great-Grandma

Books on My Shelf

Bahior, Shirley and Carol Goldman. *Overcoming Panic, Anxiety, and Phobias: New Strategies to Free Yourself from Worry and Fear.* Whole Person Associates. Jan. 1996.

Bloomfield, Harold H., Melba Colgrove and Peter McWilliams. *How to Survive the Loss of a Love.* Mary Boods/Prelude Press. Allen Park Michigan. 2000.

Brown, Laurie and Marc Brown. *When Dinosaurs Die. A Guide to Understanding Death.* Little Brown Young Readers. 1998.

D'Arcy, Paula. *When Your Friend is Grieving.* Harold Shaw Publishers. Wheaton, Illinois.1990.

deMello, Anthony. **Awareness.** *The Perils and Opportunities of Reality.* Image Books. Doubleday. New York. 1990.

Droege, Thomas A. *Guided Grief Imagery. A Resource for Grief Ministry and Death Education.* Paulist Press. New York. 1987.

Hanh, Thich Naht. *Peace is Every Step. The Path of Mindfulness in Everyday Life.* Bantam Books. New York. 1991.

Heegaard, Marge. *When Someone VERY Special Dies. Children Can Learn to Cope with Grief.* Woodland Press. Minneapolis, MN. 1988.

LeShan, Eda. *Learning to Say Good-By. When a Parent Dies.* MacMillan Publishing Company. New York. 1976.

McCue, Kathleen. *How to Help Children through a Parent's Serious Illness.* St. Martin's Press. New York. 1994.

Mitsch, Raymond R. and Lynn Brookside. *Grieving the Loss of Someone You Love. Daily Meditations to Help You through the Grieving Process.* Servant Publications. Ann Arbor, Michigan. 1993.

Nouwen, Henri J. M. *The Wounded Healer. Ministry in Contemporary Society.* Image Books. Garden City, New York. 1979.

Nouwen, Henri J. M. *In Memoriam.* Ave Maria Press. Notre Dame, Indiana. 1984.

Rupp, Joyce. *Praying Our Goodbyes.* Ave Maria Press. Notre Dame, Indiana. 1995.

Rupp, Joyce. *Out of the Ordinary. Prayers, poems and reflections for every season.* Ave Maria Press. Notre Dame, Indiana. 2000.

Scrivani, Mark. *I Heard Your Daddy Died.* Centering Corporation. Omaha NE. 1996.

Sherman, James R. *The Magic of Humor in Caregiving. The Caregiver Survival Series.* Pathway Books. Golden Valley Minnesota. 1995.

Weems, Ann. *Psalms of Lament.* Westminster John Knox Press. Louisville, KY. 1995.

Endnotes

1 Author Unknown.

2 Paraphrased from Frederick Buechner. *Telling the Truth: The Gospel as Tragedy, Comedy and Fairy Tale.* (New York: Harper Row Publishers. New York 1977), P. 56.

3 Reprinted from *Book of Worship* © 2006 by United Church of Christ, Local Church Ministries, Worship and Education Ministry Team, Cleveland, Ohio. All rights reserved.

4 Public Domain.

5 Author Unknown

6 Public Domain.

7 Author Unknown

8 Excerpted from *Reaching for Rainbows* by Ann Weems. (Westminster John Knox Press, 1980) 22. Used by permission of the publisher.

9 Author Unknown

10 Folk tune

11 Family heirloom

12 Author Unknown

13 Used by permission of Colette Dowling.

14 Excerpted from *Voices: A Woman's Journal of Self-Expression with Quotes and Space for Notes.* (Philadelphia: Running Press., 1993).

15 Used by permission of Paul Gurr.

16 Used by permission of Carolyn McDade.

17 Excerpted from *My Heart in My Mouth* by Ted Loder. Used by permission of Augsburg Fortress, 2000.

18 From Wikiquote.

19 Excerpted from *Out of the Ordinary: Prayers, Poems, and Reflections for Every Season* by Joyce Rupp, OSM. Copyright 2000 by Ave Maria Press, Inc. Used by permission of the publisher. Copies available at 1-800-282-1865 or avemariapress. com.

20 *"Arbutus Hunting"* by Elizabeth G. Mitchell. Publisher unknown. Date unknown.

21 From an interview with Karen Blixen. New York Times Book Review. Bent Mohn. November3, 1957.

22 Sue Monk Kidd. *"The Story-Shaped Life." Weavings Volume IV, Number I,* January/February. (Nashville,1989), 24.

23 Excerpted from *Getting Better All the Time*. Liz Carpenter. Doubleday 1986.

24 Used by permission of Merrit Malloy